The Skeleton Cupboard

The Skeleton Cupboard

THE MAKING OF A CLINICAL PSYCHOLOGIST

TANYA BYRON

FLATIRON
BOOKS
NEW YORK

www.flatironbooks.com

Designed by Steven Seighman

The Library of Congress Cataloging-in-Publication Data is available upon request.

ISBN 978-1-250-05265-0 (hardcover)
ISBN 978-1-250-05380-0 (e-book)

Flatiron books may be purchased for educational, business, or promotional use. For information on bulk purchases, please contact the Macmillan Corporate and Premium Sales Department at 1-800-221-7945 extension 5442 or write to specialmarkets@macmillan.com.

First U.S. Edition: April 2015

Originally published by Pan Macmillan in 2014

10 9 8 7 6 5 4 3 2 1

For Bruce and our children, Lily and Jack

CONTENTS

Introduction: My Grandmother's
Frontal Lobes   1

One   The Eyes Have It   7

Two   At the Bottom of the Deep Blue Sea   49

Three Practice Tales   85

Four   Harold and the Nazis   138

Five   The Skeleton Cupboard   184

Six   Dodging Stones   240

       Epilogue   297

       Acknowledgments   307

The
Skeleton
Cupboard

MY GRANDMOTHER'S FRONTAL LOBES

Frontal lobe *n.* (*pl.* **frontal lobes**) **1.** Each of the paired lobes of the brain lying immediately behind the forehead, including areas concerned with behavior, learning, personality and voluntary movement. **2.** A region of the brain that influences higher mental functions often associated with intelligence, such as the ability to foresee the consequences of actions, planning, comprehension and mood.

I first became fascinated by the frontal lobes of the human brain when I saw my grandmother's sprayed across the baseboards of her dark and cluttered house. I was fifteen.

Much later, I discovered that a young woman—eight months pregnant and a heroin addict—had battered my grandmother about the head with an iron fire poker. The woman had been a tenant of my grandmother's and she knew that her former landlady, a German Jewish refugee recently converted to Christianity, had treasures and cash galore stashed among the chaos of her large house, the top two floors of which she rented out.

A few blows to the head, a quick rifle through purses and drawers, and she was off, cash in her pocket to pay off her dealer and secure her next hit. My grandmother lay on the carpet of her front room, bleeding from a large head wound. I don't know whether she was conscious or not. I do know exactly how she died: by slowly asphyxiating, choking to death on her own blood.

Asphyxiation: That was the problem, of course. If only she'd died instantly from the head trauma, the crime would have been treated as murder. If only she hadn't been a stubborn, willful woman—a woman who had fled Nazi Germany pregnant with my father, a woman who had lost many of her family members in concentration camps, a woman who never took anything lying down, except when she was beaten with an iron fire poker.

There she lay, refusing to die, until she choked on her blood. The woman who had beaten her was sentenced to only three years for involuntary manslaughter with diminished responsibility. She had her baby in prison and was out within eighteen months.

Okay, to be honest, I am not entirely sure that my grandmother's brains *were* on the baseboards when I went into her house that day at the age of fifteen. Is that a direct memory or something I told myself later on? In fact, I'm not sure I remember much of that day at all except two things: a massive bloodstain on the carpet and my father making a noise like an animal caught in a trap.

In that moment I became the rational coper. As my darling father howled, I shut down and began to try to understand how and why.

Had she died in pain? Did she know she was dying before she died? What had compelled her murderer to smash her head in? Had the woman planned it? Did she want to kill my grandmother or merely maim her so she could plunder? I wanted to understand the mind of my grandmother's killer—what was she thinking as she struck my grandmother with the poker, as she heard the crack of her skull? How, indeed, could a human brain not stop its gruesome fantasy from becoming a horrific reality?

All these questions about the shit end of life, at a time when I should have been unthinkingly hedonistic. I was fifteen years old, and my frontal lobes were in a post-pubertal stage of reorganization, which meant I should have been taking my own risks and thinking bugger all about the consequences.

Beginning that March morning it was only and all about frontal lobes: my grandmother's on the base-boards, her murderer's—clearly underfunctioning—and mine, clicking into a precocious place of calm rationality that I now believe began my journey into the profession of a mental health practitioner.

This book tells the story of my clinical training. It takes place over the course of three years from 1989 to 1992, when I was in my early twenties, during which I underwent a series of placements in different mental health settings and worked with several distinct kinds of patients: troubled children; families in crisis; men and women dealing with the encroaching effects of dementia; those struggling with drug dependency, eating disorders, sexual dysfunction and terminal illness; and, in one case, a sociopath.

After completing my undergraduate degree in psychology at the University of York, in the north of England, I moved back to live in a flat in London, the city in which I grew up. My childhood had been busy, creative and exciting. My father was a successful TV, film and theater director—a brilliant, highly emotional, inspiring man. My mother was a senior operating-room nurse and occasional model. My sister, Katrina, only fifteen months my junior, and I grew up surrounded by art and culture—which I loved—and went to a highly academic all-girls school—which I hated. Life was full of interesting people coming through our house; dinner conversations were always lively and passionate; my mother was a calm, steady presence in the busy, sometimes manic, creative world of my father.

Although I had long been fascinated by mental health and the inner workings of the human mind, when I graduated from university I thought I wanted to work in film and TV, making documentaries about social issues. Quite unexpectedly, I managed to get into a postgraduate training program for clinical psychology and decided that a further three years would allow me to make authentic films and TV programs about mental illness. I wanted to demystify and destigmatize it, to stop the judgments of those with real difficulties who required care and compassion. Mostly, however, I wanted to explore the workings of the human mind and all its dark corners and perhaps, I now recognize many years later, I was still looking to answer the fundamental question that hit me full in the face at the age of fifteen: Why do some brains allow their host to kill?

Now, almost twenty-five years later, I still practice clinically. I also write regular columns for several newspapers and magazines, produce and host television documentaries and advise the British government on child and social policy.

While I recognize that rage and grief were underpinning my career choice—I wanted to understand how disturbed mental functioning can lead to destructive behaviors—I now realize that my three years of clinical training took me to a deeper place of understanding that enabled me to accept the complexities of who we are and how we function. Throughout my training I met people who were struggling with mental health difficulties—difficulties that were affecting their quality of life, their relationships with others, the choices they made. Some of these people frightened me, others left me emotionally drained and wanting to weep for them, yet none of them really helped me answer the question that began my journey into mental health: Why do we kill those whom others love?

This is the story of my training. I was a well-meaning but inexperienced young woman who had to learn on the job: I spent half the week at University College London, receiving lectures and attending courses in models and approaches in mental health. I wrote essays and case reports about the psychological models and theories I was studying, completed a dissertation and took exams. I spent the other half of each week on a series of six-month placements, attempting, with regular supervision, to apply what I was learning in the classroom.

These placements fell under the auspices of the British National Health Service, and I spent time in hospitals, clinics, mental health outpatient units and GP practices. I saw patients referred to me by many different specialists in health and mental health. These patients were struggling with acute, chronic and at times profoundly debilitating mental health difficulties. Some were mildly impaired, others were dealing with long-standing issues. Occasionally there were patients who presented such a degree of risk to themselves or others that they had been deemed extremely mentally unwell and so unable to function or were involuntarily committed by judges and law enforcement officers.

Over three years I completed six six-month placements, which were structured to provide a complete training experience across the age span and full spectrum of mental health issues by the time I qualified.

There is no other way to narrate the training of a clinical psychologist than to tell the stories of those I encountered. This book highlights the specific cases that helped to establish my thinking as a doctor and profiles the individuals whose stories I still think about today, nearly twenty-five years later. However, because confidentiality is a core principle of my profession, I have changed the names and circumstantial details of all the people I write about. The characters in this book are constructs drawn from real clinical practice and influenced by the many incredible people I had the privilege of meeting during my training.

I dedicate this book to them.

Tanya Byron
London, 2014

One

THE EYES HAVE IT

I sat in an uncomfortable chair in the first office I had ever had and took a deep breath. The word "office" might be an overstatement. George, the friendly elderly porter who had welcomed me to the outpatient psychiatric department—"Welcome to our happy home"—had pointed out that before my arrival the space had been a storage cupboard.

"Storage for what?" I asked, thinking about asbestos.

"Storage for everything: dressings, commodes, the old drug trolley. It was only when the department had to take on more fresh blood that we converted it—some kind of regulation, I think."

"What kind of regulation allows a windowless office?"

George smiled. "Fresh blood see the jumpers."

"Jumpers?"

"The ones that go straight for the windows."

Why on earth had I thought I could do this?

Alone in my office, I put my head in my hands—perhaps it wasn't too late to accept the researcher's job at that TV production company. Christ, I was twenty-two, in my own flat, living in arguably the best capital city in the world. I could have glamour, a better wage, less responsibility. What the hell was I trying to prove here?

The other people in my training course seemed much more competent. To begin with, I was the youngest out of our group of twenty. Most of them had come from research or other clinical backgrounds and I felt intimidated, even though I'd only just met them; they seemed to know stuff. I wasn't looking forward to our time together. I would obviously be the dunce of the class, just as I had been in high school.

Shit. I knew absolutely nothing.

Feeling sorry for myself, I looked around my cupboard; it smelled musty, a complete contrast to the glass, marble and chrome atrium I had walked through downstairs less than an hour earlier. This was a flagship hospital. It had been like entering another world—calm and clean. Even the signs advising against physically attacking the staff were printed in gentle sans serif, muted and almost apologetic for the crassness of their message.

The staff down in the reception area were friendly too—all smiles and uniforms and endless leaflets about patient rights and complaints procedures. It was not a hospital; it was a shiny, upmarket hotel lobby.

I had taken the elevator up to the eighth floor with several hassled-looking members of staff, none of whom had been even remotely interested in the fact that I had just joined the team. I looked at my new staff identity card and made sure it was facing outward. "Clinical psychologist in training." No one gave a damn. I felt like the new kid on the first day of school.

It had taken me five minutes of circling the four-sided eighth floor before I'd located the outpatient psychiatric department—I had dismissed it on circuits one to three because it looked like the entrance to some sort of supply room. Nothing here reflected the opulence of the hospital downstairs.

The grumpy, round-faced woman who greeted me when I finally got to the psychiatric outpatients' reception managed to thrust me my room key, point to the cupboard door and say, "You see them in there," all without once lifting her eyes from *Woman's Own* magazine.

"Is everything all right?"

Chris, my supervisor, the woman assigned to mentor me throughout my training, stood over me, jolting me back into the room.

"Oh yes. Hi. Gosh. Sorry." I'd been slumped over the desk, lost in thought.

I scrabbled to my feet.

Dr. Chris Moorhead was renowned for being a brilliant supervisor but one hard-core, fiercely intelligent, no-nonsense woman. In my interview for the clinical training course, she never cracked a smile. She didn't make small talk. And she asked the most difficult question: "Why do you deserve a place in this training course any more than all the other people who want it?" After I was accepted, when we were told who our supervisors were to be, more than a few of my fellow trainees sighed with relief when my name was matched with hers. A few second- and third-years laughed and patted me on the back. "Good luck," one said.

A tall, slim, angular woman who had the unnerving habit of maintaining unbroken eye contact, Chris gestured to the man standing just behind her.

"This is Professor Horace Winters, head of the outpatient psychiatric department. Professor Winters, this is my trainee. She'll be here two and a half days per week for the next six months."

The prof offered his hand, making zero eye contact. His words sounded as if they'd been worn smooth by repetition.

"Welcome to the department. I hope you enjoy your time here. I'm always at your disposal. I'm looking forward to the valuable contribution you will make to my team."

With a flourish, he turned and walked out. I wanted to giggle, but Chris clearly wanted further words.

"They very rarely take unqualifieds in this department, but I told them you'd do good."

"Chris, that's so great of you. Thanks."

"Don't thank me. Just don't let me down."

After Chris left, I found a way to wedge some old and slightly damp prescription pads under the tilt mechanism to keep my chair from tipping over. Welcome to the publicly funded great British National Health Service— the NHS.

As I was rearranging my cupboard office, I heard the sound of singing—a small voice growing in volume and then, just as the melody was decipherable, getting fainter again. I could have sworn it was a song from *The Sound of Music*.

Maybe I was hallucinating. No—it got louder again:

How do you solve a problem like Maria?
How do you catch a cloud and pin it down?
How do you find a word that means "Maria"?
A flibbertigibbet! A will-o'-the wisp! A clown!

It was extraordinary—a little voice, but one with such purity and clarity that it cut through the growing noise of the busy reception area outside my door.

Why was no one else hearing this?

I left my room and looked around. I had two hours before my first appointment, I was alone and I wanted to know who belonged to that voice. But when I stepped out into the waiting area, I was stunned by what I saw, and the song—although still lilting in the background—became peripheral.

If my mother had been there, she would have instructed me not to stare.

When George appeared with two mugs of tea, I was able to tear my gaze away.

"Gender Identity Clinic."

He sat down on a waiting-room chair and gestured to me, telling me to join him, which I did. The sugary orange brew calmed me and brought me back to a clinical state of mind. *I inhabit a nonjudgmental space*, I reminded myself.

"Gender Identity Clinic?" I asked.

"Yep. The boys come in because they want to be girls. Prof Winters is their man. They get assessed, and if they can live for five years as the gender of their choice, then they get the op, the deportment classes, the whole works."

"The works?"

"Adam's apple shaved, makeup tutorials, how to dress to suit your shape—you can cut off a penis, but you can't rebuild a brick shithouse."

I looked around and had to agree, as much as I hated the indelicacy of George's language. There were some who could only be described as pantomime dames. There were also some incredibly good-looking women here.

There was one mesmerizingly beautiful woman. Slight and delicate, she had the most incredible curtain of straight, shiny black hair hanging down to her waist. She certainly knew how to dress to suit her shape—"classy not brassy," as "my girls," my three best friends, would say. She even gestured in a manner that, despite the slight exaggeration of movement and eyelash flutter, was all believable, even if it was sort of hyperfeminized.

I felt challenged. My clothes—a charity shop man's suit with crisp white shirt, tight vintage Dior belt and Doc Marten shoes—made me feel frumpy.

How can a man look a better woman than me?

I was rescued from this thought by the appearance of two other people coming out of the women's toilets. The smaller of the two was startling. She was wearing the sort of dress that my late grandmother would put on for a family occasion: good material, generously cut, but staid in its blue navy, with a tight, thin red belt, plunging neckline and cheeky sailor-striped T-shirt subtly covering the décolletage. She wore a wig of the brightest yellow perm, held a tiny red clutch in her enormous hand and tottered on blue wedge heels made out of the material that allows room for bunions—the sort of shoe that can be purchased from a catalogue that also sells lawn-aerating sandals, ladies' turbans and slow cookers.

The taller of the two women, at well over six feet tall, was broad, with calves the size of tree trunks and well-defined arms to die for. She wore a tight black dress, lap-dancing shoes with Lucite platforms and vertigo-inducing stilettos, and sported a straight, brown, honey-highlighted Mary Quant bobbed wig with serious attitude.

She was the Adam/Felicia character in *Priscilla, Queen of the Desert*, or Tony Curtis as Josephine in *Some Like It Hot*. The smaller woman, however, only managed Terence Stamp and Jack Lemmon—Bernadette and Daphne.

I was mesmerized. "Josephine" caught my eye, winked her giant eyelashes, poked the end of her tongue out from between her red, shiny lips and smiled. I felt hot and looked away.

Someone flew past me singing and then disappeared behind the central lift shaft.

How do you solve a problem like Maria?
How do you catch a cloud and pin it down?

"That's Edith," George explained. "She's an RDP."
"A what?"
"A revolving-door patient."
"And that is?"
"She is admitted by court order and taken into the inpatient ward on the other side of this floor. She is stabilized. She takes her meds independently. She is discharged. Care in the community takes over. There is no

care in the community. She drops off her meds, frightens the neighbors, so she comes back in. Revolving door."

I looked thoughtfully at George. He was in his seventies, I reckoned, perhaps ex-military, with his white cuffs visible a precise and equal distance under a pristine black sweater.

"Hello, Edith," said George, looking up at the person whose beautiful voice I'd heard.

"Well, hello, George. And who might this pretty lady be?"

Edith had wandered into the outpatient department and I found myself taking the hand that had been offered by the sweetest-looking woman that I had ever seen.

"Edith Granville, please say hello to our fresh blood."

"Hello, my dear. How are you this blessed day?"

Edith was so small and so smiley and had eyes so sparkly that I was almost too enchanted to reply. This tiny and compact black woman had a crisp white pillowcase pinned to her head. The pillowcase, I soon realized, was an attempt at a nun's wimple. Edith was Mother Superior.

"I know what you thinking, girl, and you's wrong."

"What am I thinking, Edith?"

"You's thinking that I Julie Andrews!" Edith cackled. "Oh, Georgie Porgie! She think I Julie Andrews!"

George was wheezing, bent over double, and coughing up many years of Player's Navy Cut.

"Oh, Edith, no, I don't think you are Julie Andrews. No, not at all!"

"Well, good for you, girlie, because:

When I'm with her, I'm confused,
Out of focus and bemused.
And I never know exactly where I am.
Unpredictable as weather,
She's as flighty as a feather. She's a darling!
She's a demon—

"*She's a lamb!*" I sang out as hard as I could. Bugger clinical training—there was nothing that an entire childhood of Christmas showings of *The Sound of Music* couldn't prepare me for.

Edith clapped her hands together as George beamed and I bowed.

"This your first day here, girlie?"

"Yes, Edith, it is."

"So what you think?"

"I think I don't know what to think."

"George, you say she fresh blood?"

"Yes, Edith, that is what I would say she is."

Edith threw her arms around me and held me tight. "Oh, sweetheart, you just joined. So new. Let Edith help you in." Edith took me by the hand, linked arms with George and skipped us all into my cupboard.

"Ah, we called this 'the Shithole.' Commodes, medication—all the shit was here. Yes, indeed, I think it were better when it were a cupboard."

Over the next forty minutes, as I perched gingerly on my chair and George brought us all another brew, Edith initiated me into the realities of my training by telling me her life story.

Born in Tobago in a small village by the Caribbean Sea called Black Rock, Edith was the second-youngest child of nine children. Her father, a Baptist minister, was a man of compassion to his flock, but not, it seemed, to his children. Father—that was his name apparently—traveled far across the width of the island from Plymouth to the capital, Scarborough, and the length from Charlotteville to Sandy Point. He held Bible meetings in Roxborough and Parlatuvier on the beach, and performed miracles in Moriah and on Cinnamon Hill. Father saved lives, and when he was away, the family was also at peace.

But when he wasn't away ministering, he struggled to contain the sin in his home. Edith told of the "whoopin's" and "beltin's" and beatings that had been part and parcel of her childhood. Especially for a young girl prone to daydreaming—a sin, said Father, when in church—and to singing—a sin, said Father, when not a hymn.

Poor Edith—the youngest of the sisters and the favorite of her mother, she was the first to be sent to live with her father's sister, Aunt Charisma, in Shepherd's Bush. It was there that Edith was to really understand how undesirable she was. At this point in the story, Edith broke into song again:

> She'd out-pester any pest,
> Drive a hornet from its nest.
> She could throw a whirling dervish out of whirl.
> She is gentle!
> She is wild—
> She's a riddle,
> She's a child
> She's a headache—

Edith suddenly stopped singing, and as her head fell backward, her eyes simultaneously rolled up until I could only see the whites. This seemed serious; I tried not to panic.

"Who's a headache, Edith? Tell me."

Edith's eyes closed and screwed up, and tears trickled down her cheeks. Mouth open, she began a low moan, before singing again:

She is wild—
She's a riddle,
She's a child
She's a headache!
She is wild—
She's a riddle,
She's a child
She's a headache!
She is wild—
She's a riddle,
She's a child
She's a headache!

Between bouts of singing, Edith told scrambled stories. "Stinging" was a key word. "Stinging" and "down there." The "downstairs department." Aunt Charisma and scrub, scrub, scrubbing. No dreaming. Bad dreaming. No singing. Bad singing. Only scrub and sting and Lysol.

"You lie, you Lysol. You lie, you Lysol," Edith kept repeating.

In my mind, I tried to sing ahead, to remember the

words, as Edith kept repeating the lyrics, her needle stuck in the groove:

> *She is wild—*
> *She's a riddle,*
> *She's a child*
> *She's a headache!*
> *She is wild—*
> *She's a riddle,*
> *She's a child*
> *She's a headache!*
> *She is wild—*
> *She's a riddle,*
> *She's a child*
> *She's a headache!*

I got it and belted out:

> *She's an angel!*
> *She's a girl . . .*

Then there was a complete stop. Not a pause but a stop. Silence. No song. No moans. No lies or Lysol.

The small woman stood with dignity and straightened the pillowcase on her head. She looked me directly in the eyes, and despite the streams of tears still coursing down her cheeks, she extended a hand. "A pleasure speaking with you."

"And a pleasure meeting you, Edith."

"Please call me Maria."

And Maria walked out of the cupboard and across to the other side of the lift shaft, where the inpatient psy-

chiatric department welcomed her with its familiar revolving door.

Seeing her go, I felt really sad. I thought about some
of the recent lectures exploring diagnosis and ethnicity
we'd heard at school. It had shocked me to learn that
there were disproportionately high levels of psychiatric
diagnosis and hospital admissions among black and
ethnic minorities living in the UK. African or Caribbean
immigrants were up to five times more likely to be
diagnosed with schizophrenia, due to the cultural in-
sensitivity that was ingrained in our diagnostic procedures. Poverty, racism and culturally rigid definitions
of mental illness all contributed to these troubling sta-
tistics and I wondered whether Edith was herself a
victim. After many years cycling through the revolving
door, had her diagnosed illness become a self-fulfilled
prophecy?

"As I say," said George, breaking the moment, "welcome to our happy home."

Alone in my cupboard once more, I shut the door and applied myself to getting the space to look more like a con-
sulting room. As it was, I worried it might be slightly
insulting for anyone who came in to see me.

"Welcome to the outpatient psychiatric department.
We have designed your treatment environment to match
the way you feel about yourself," the office seemed to be
saying.

I tidied up: old prescription pads, patient leaflets about
fifteen years out-of-date, a guide to electroconvulsive
therapy. The thought sent shivers down my spine. I opened

a small cupboard next to my desk and shoved the whole lot in.

The chairs needed replacing, so I wandered across the department to see what I could find. In an empty lecture room, I discovered a couple of low chairs. They would do nicely: no disparity in height between my patient and me. I dragged them back past the reception desk without anyone looking up or asking me what I was doing; I probably could have stripped the place entirely and taken it home piece by piece, and no one would have noticed.

Chairs in, positioned at forty-five degrees, it looked better. A few damp hand towels removed some of the visible dust, and then I was on the hunt for a potted plant, which proved more tricky. While considering whether to steal one from a doctor's office more plush than my own, I eventually came upon a bunch of plastic flowers in a small vase in the ladies' toilet. After a rinse and buff with yet another hand towel, they looked rather sweet. I got a coffee table too, and then stood in the middle of my office, pleased with my work.

Nothing to do now but wait for my first patient.

After three years pursuing my undergraduate psychology degree, fierce competition to get into a clinical training course, all the stress of moving back to London, renting a flat in the north of the city and getting myself set up, this was the moment I'd been waiting for. But now that I was here, I felt like running away.

The placement at the hospital was two and a half days a week, with the rest of the week and the odd evening lecture at the university. Effectively, I was seeing patients without any real knowledge of what I was seeing them about: My lectures and the learning I'd need to treat those patients were happening concurrently. Is this what medical doctors in training also went through? Imagine being operated on by someone who has never before put a scalpel into living human flesh.

George brought in another brew, orange, strong and sweet—perfect. He also dumped a pile of notes on my desk.

"Here you go—your first sets of patient notes. Have a read-through."

I sat there looking at the notes; now everything began to feel real.

There had been a long debate among my clinical year group about whether "they" should be called "patients." The psychodynamic lot was against it, believing the term demeans the individual, reduces them to a medical stereotype, colludes with the limited but prevailing medical model of mental health. They believed it was better to use the term "clients." The behaviorists were very much for it: They held that the patients are here for us to treat; they require our intervention; they need the clarity of the well-defined parameters of the relationship between them and us. The psychoanalysts, as usual, were nowhere and everywhere: Why did we want to call them "patients"? What did it defend us against in terms of our own unowned pathology? And equally, what projection did the label "patient" represent in terms of our *over-identified* pathology?

Oh bloody hell, I had always thought. They are so not my clients—I'm not a solicitor or a prostitute. They are patients and may Sigmund strike me down with the full weight of my unowned fucked-upness. They are patients!

However, as I edged myself into training and grew more accustomed to my little cupboard in the outpatient clinic, over the next few weeks, I soon realized that they were neither patients nor clients; they were people, real people, with lives and stories—vulnerable, sometimes deeply unhappy, interesting people.

My first few clinical sessions had been alongside qualified staff running anxiety-management groups, which helped me deal with my own anxiety as much as anything else. I then started working with an emetophobic woman who was trying to get pregnant and was terrified of the prospect of vomiting with morning sickness; a young man who was struggling with depression after a serious accident; a woman who had begun to have panic attacks on the Tube and in confined spaces; and an elderly man recently bereaved after many years being his wife's sole caregiver. I loved it. I was meeting real people, each with their own challenging story, who trusted me. I felt I was helping.

A couple of months passed. I discharged my claustrophobic lady, who was now back riding on the Tube. One morning I was sitting in my cupboard, flicking through the notes for a man I was about to see for the first time. It seemed straightforward enough: anxiety and panic attacks. We had had quite a few lectures about those, so I didn't feel as though I was going in totally blind. But a few lectures, some rather self-conscious role plays with my cotrainees and my one discharged patient still didn't allow me to feel quite adequate somehow. What if I made a mistake, made him worse? What if I had a panic attack myself?

A knock at my door and there he was: Ray Robards.

"Good afternoon, Mr. Robards."

"I'm Ray."

We sat opposite each other in the low chairs. We shook hands and then settled into a good mirror position; I felt pleased.

"Here's the thing," said Ray. "I'm a bit freaked seeing you—a head doctor and all. Like, I'm not a nutter, OK. That's the first thing we need to get clear, OK. I'm not a mental case."

"Why would I think you were?"

"In the waiting room, not only was I sitting among a bunch of tranny freaks in wigs, but I also saw some black bird singing something from *The* bloody *Sound of Music*. She's fucking insane. I'm not. Let's get that clear."

"I make no judgment, Ray."

"That's not what I'm looking for."

"Mr. Robards—Ray. Sorry, Ray. I am clear that you are not insane."

One–nil to the patient.

"OK, if you're crystal on that, then we're fine. So what do you want me to tell you?"

"What do you want to tell me, Ray?"

He looked blank.

OK. This is going nowhere. Too much to and fro—get a clinical grip. Get going.

"Well, Ray, why don't we start from the beginning? Why don't I tell you what I know and we can take it from there?"

"Sounds good to me. By the way, did anyone ever tell you you've got beautiful blue eyes?"

Two—nil to the patient. Don't blush. Shit, too late. Focus. Carry on. Maintain eye contact.

As I felt the familiar feeling of heat and color spread upward from my neck, I turned away to pick up Ray's patient file from my desk. I turned back. Ray was leaning back in his chair, arms spread behind his head, smiling at me.

"You had a series of unexplained dizzy spells at work. Quite worrying by the sounds of it. Can we start from there?"

"Whatever you say, Doc."

Ray sat forward, his gaze never once leaving me. "I used to collect rubbish. I worked the trucks and emptied bins. That's what I did—did it for years with the same team."

I smiled and nodded. Ray wasn't smiling anymore.

"Due to circumstances outside my control, however, I had to change jobs. I was gutted. But a man's gotta work and so I started doing security, working the doors, that kinda stuff."

"You're a bouncer?"

"Spot on, Doc. Clever girl."

"Do you miss doing the dustbins?"

"Doing the dustbins?" Ray laughed, mimicking my accent as if I were the Queen. "Yeah, but as I say, circumstances outside my control."

I was curious, but something stopped me from asking for further information.

"Anyway, Doc, it was"—Ray was counting on his fingers—"about eight months ago, when I first got pains in my chest. Freaked the fuck outta me—excuse my French."

"So you thought you were having a heart attack?"

"No, love, I thought I was coming."

Where were we now? Four–nil to the patient?

"Of course—sorry."

"Apology accepted, my beautiful blue-eyed girl."

This time I had no excuse to turn away and so I decided to front it out. I felt uncomfortable—this wasn't going well.

"To cut to the chase, my old man dropped dead of a heart attack when he was fifty-seven. He did the bins like me. He was an arsehole but didn't deserve to die at fifty-seven. He smoked, drank, the usual, but nothing more than the next bloke. Apparently he had a faulty valve or something."

"So this is when you went to see the cardiologist?"

"Right. They wired me up, got me running on one of them treadmill things. I had a what-d'you-call-them?"

"ECG?"

"ECG and every bloody test, but apparently"—Ray thumped his chest hard with his fist—"strong as a bloody ox."

"That must have reassured you."

"No, sweetheart, it didn't. Not at all. 'Cos I kept having these bloody attacks, as I call them, and they were coming more often and lasting longer, and like a bloody nancy boy I started fucking fainting. On the job."

"How did the frequency of the attacks change?"

"In English, please."

"Sorry. How many more were you experiencing? Did they become daily?"

"Yeah, but I could cope with those. The boys would see them coming and take me off the door until they passed. Problem was, also I'd get them sometimes in my sleep."

"That must have been really frightening."

"Bloody terrifying." Ray rubbed his face with his hands. The mask was slipping, the bravado disappearing. "I can only explain it like you're drowning. You wake up and you can't breathe—like you are trying to get to the surface but know your chest will explode before you do. I'd get to the window and open it and try to breathe, but nothing would go in—it was like my lungs had just packed up."

Ray stopped abruptly. Beads of sweat appeared on his forehead. I could see his breaths becoming faster and shallower. His large hands gripped the arms of the chair. He was beginning to panic.

Thank God for my few weeks sitting in on the anxiety-management group. I began to feel in control. Perversely, that felt good, despite the obvious discomfort of the man sitting opposite me.

"Ray, I want you to breathe slowly."

"I fucking can't breathe."

Ray was rasping, his pupils dilating. I leaned forward and took his hands in mine.

"Ray, look at me. Look at me. OK, now listen to me. I am going to count and you are going to count with me. OK? Here we go. One . . . two . . . Count with me, Ray. Three . . . four . . . That's it. Good. Five . . . six. Slow it down."

Ray was squeezing so hard I thought he was going to break my fingers.

"OK, Ray, now I'm holding a candle in front of you and I want you to blow it out in three breaths. Good. Now a little farther away—stronger breaths. Good. OK, Ray, keep blowing as I pull the candle closer to me. That's it."

A few minutes later Ray was sitting more calmly in his chair, drinking a cup of water. I sat back and felt good—really good. I'd brought his panic down.

I started taking a detailed history. The poor guy, I thought. No wonder he doesn't want to be here in the outpatient psychiatric department—he'd been through every other department in the hospital. Every part of him had been checked—heart, lungs, bloods, brain.

Classic. The medics sell the patient on the idea that their diagnosis will make it all better, and then when they draw a blank, they throw them over to the mental health services. "Sorry, mate—thought you were ill, but actually, as it turns out, you're not, so you must be bonkers."

I began to chide myself for being so easily intimidated by an obviously frightened and vulnerable man. I looked him in the eye.

"I can see that you have had the real runaround in this hospital. In fact, you probably know the inner workings of each department better than most of the managers!"

Ray smiled. "Yeah, this place could do with a quality-control audit!" His smile faded.

"OK. So now you're here, in this department. What we need to think about is what these panic attacks mean."

"Mean?"

"Yes—why are you getting them? What do they represent?"

"Represent? Look, Doc, sorry, but I just want whatever pills or whatnot I can take to control these bastards."

"It's not quite as simple as that."

"Why not?"

"OK, the thing is, yes, you are getting panic attacks. Severe ones. Yes, they affect your body and so theoretically it should just be possible to prescribe medication to calm everything down, but that isn't going to solve the problem. In fact, aren't you taking some meds already?"

"Yeah. Those little pink pills. And something at night—begins with 'D.'"

"Diazepam? How do you find them?"

"The pink pills are OK. They calm me down a bit. But I hate the night stuff 'cos I feel like shit next morning."

"Groggy?"

"Like I been on a major bender the night before."

"OK, so the medication needs to be reviewed, but—"

"But nothing, Doc. Give me my new pills and I'm on my way." Ray was beginning to get agitated.

"Ray . . ." I leaned forward and touched his beginning-to-clench fist. He grabbed my hand and my heart leaped into my mouth. "Listen, Ray. There are many things that we can do. Pills are part of it, but I am not the one to do the pill side of things for you. My role . . . my role is to help us understand why you are having the panic attacks, because—"

"Doc, look—"

"Because, Ray," I continued with a note of firmness

to my voice, "because . . . Think of it this way. You've got a wound that is infected, right? And that infection is treated by pills and creams, which temporarily relieve the soreness but do nothing to get rid of the underlying infection itself. We need to investigate what is causing the infection, and why it is preventing the wound from healing."

I shrugged. "Panic attacks can happen for a variety of reasons, most usually stress and anxiety. Something has happened or is happening in your life that leaves you feeling anxious. That makes you increasingly vulnerable to panic attacks." I sat back.

Ray looked evenly at me. "So, my dad was an arsehole. Is that what you wanna hear from me? Dad was an arsehole, useless. Mum was my life but died when I was nine. Is this right? Dad left us to our own devices, and my devices ended up getting me thrown into jail for a few short and one longish stretch. Am I getting anywhere, Doc?"

"Ray, I—"

"No, listen. My childhood was shit. Nothing like yours was, I expect. Total shit. But so were the fucking childhoods of most blokes I grew up with. So what? It was hard. We were poor. I had no mum—poor Ray. Bullshit."

Ray wasn't breathing too quickly this time. In fact, he was very still and very focused. I tensed in my seat. Something about the dynamic between us had shifted, like a change of air pressure. I scanned the room quickly. I realized I was looking for the panic button—there should be one in every room. I just wanted to know it was there. Where the hell was it? There. Other end of the desk. I hadn't given this any thought when I was first positioning the chairs for the session, and now I couldn't reach it from where I was sitting. My mouth was suddenly dry.

"Tell me about your life now, Ray." I wanted to keep him talking, to calm him down.

Ray took off his jacket and revealed his muscular torso, covered only by a Gold's Gym undershirt. Both arms were adorned in tattoos, and, as far as I could tell, so were his neck and chest.

"Here's my life, Doc."

I looked at the ink on Ray's skin. There were dragons and what looked to be a large cobra coiled around one arm. There was a nude woman on his other forearm and under that a list of names.

"Who are Brittany, Bethany and Brandon?"

"My kids."

I forced a smile, nodded. "Tell me about them."

"I love them."

"I'm sure you do."

"No, you don't 'I'm sure you do.' I would kill for them."

I believed him and that frightened me.

"They are all I have."

There was a long pause. I itched to say something, but instinct and a recent lecture on the importance of the "therapeutic silence" stopped me.

"Brit is seventeen. She's at beauty college—nails, hair, that kinda stuff. Beth is a bit wild. She's fifteen and has a kid, another on the way. Brandon is . . . He's my lad, my boy, my little mate."

Ray stopped and began to hug himself with his powerful tattooed arms. As his hug tightened, he bent farther forward, as if he were trying to curl up into himself.

"Ray, what's going on? Your chest . . . ?"

What came next shocked me.

It started with a groan, like Ray was in pain—not anxious, panic pain but a pain so physical, so visceral, that it shook me to my core. The first groan was guttural, seeming to push out from the depths of the big man and go on for ages. Ray was bent over double, his fists clenched into his sides. The groan continued for so long that I began involuntarily gulping for air—as if I could breathe on his behalf.

Then, like a diver reaching the surface, he pushed his head back and gasped—loud gulps that had the effect of releasing one small tear from the edge of his left eye, which traveled slowly down his check, meandering around the deep wrinkles in his face and finally dripping into his open mouth.

And then, suddenly, Ray punched at where he felt the tear tickle his top lip; the punch had such force that his nose started to bleed.

I felt both afraid and awestruck by the ferocity of the emotion from a man who had seemed so locked in, so unyielding. With a little stab of shame, I also realized how exhilarated I felt—I had done this. I had enabled this unhappy man, a man who, I assumed, would not normally allow himself to cry, to access his pain. We were now getting to the root and I felt myself relax.

Oh my God, you can actually do it. You can actually do this job.

It was extraordinary; it was a privilege; it was a total high.

"When I first held him, I told him I would never leave him. He'd never lose me." Ray's voice was low and hoarse, his throat ripped by sobs. "He was the most beautiful boy—everyone said he looked like an angel. He did. The girls were cute, but he was in another league. He was in the Champions League."

Ray began to uncurl his body and with a sigh rubbed his hands over his face, smearing the blood from his nose into a red mustache. He took a drink, sat back and looked at me.

"I can see that this is painful for you."

But Ray didn't seem to hear me. In fact, he didn't even seem to be looking at me. He was somewhere else.

"I couldn't bear to be away from him. I did every-thing for him—fed him, changed him. I even slept with him. When I went to the gym, I took a photo in a frame so I could look at him the whole time. We were mates; he was my best mate—my best little mate. He was my life. Oh fuck." Ray began to sob again, this time quietly.

"I fucked it up with the girls. Well, I didn't—their bitch of a mother did. She was bad, proper bad—got her girls, didn't want to know me anymore. She'd start pick-ing at me and I'd spend more time out of the house than in it—I had to, because I knew if I didn't, I'd have fuck-ing lamped her. She wanted that—she wanted to be the victim, so she could take my girls away from me and get me out of her life.

"She called me useless and a failure, a fucking waste of space. She told me I wasn't worth nothing to no one. That even if my mum had been alive, she'd have said the same and thought the same. She said that if Mum were around, she'd have been ashamed of me."

Ray paused, sniffing loudly before taking a tissue

from the box that I offered him. He blew his nose noisily and looked into the tissue. "Christ."

"Only a small bleed. It's stopped now. It looks OK."

Ray looked up at me as if he was, for the first time, suddenly becoming aware of my presence in the room. He looked dazed, a rabbit in headlights.

"Hearing those words about your mother must have been very tough for you, Ray."

"Yeah, tough." Ray gave a small smile. "Tougher for the bitch who said them, though. I put her in the hospital." Ray chuckled to himself.

"And yourself inside?"

"Yeah. It was one of the smaller stretches. Assault but diminished responsibility 'cos of her goading and my steroid use."

"Right. How is she now?"

"How the fuck do I know how she is now? Apparently she can feed herself again. More's the shame. I did her a favor, all those days on a liquid diet she'd have lost that big fat arse of hers. I reckon she'll have larded it on again." Another laugh.

"And the girls?"

"No. Nothing. Nix. Nada. Tried to contact them via relatives. The little one doesn't want to know me—she's an old slag like her mother. Two kids already . . ." Ray shook his head and tutted. "Brit sends the occasional message, but she doesn't want to meet up. Don't blame her."

Ray picked up the plastic cup, which was empty. I pushed my untouched water toward him. He took long, slow gulps.

"You really do have beautiful eyes."

"Tell me about Brandon, Ray."

He winced. "Oooh. Nasty doc. Nasty girl with the beautiful eyes. Like a shark, aren't you, sweetheart—sniff blood, circle a bit and then in for the kill."

"I'm sorry. I just—" I stopped as Ray put up his hand.

"Shush, sweetheart. I was joking. No problems, babe. You're just doing your job."

He leaned right back in his chair, pulling his arms upward and lengthening his legs forward as he stretched out his body with a grunt. He clicked his fingers at each joint. He was huge.

"Brandon. Yeah, my boy. The little lad I had with the other one, the cruelest cunt of cunts. My boy. My little mate. We did everything together. He was perfect. Beautiful. Clever. Funny. He loved me and I . . ."

"Where is Brandon now, Ray?"

I was expecting the worst.

"He's everywhere. That's the fucking problem—he's everywhere. He's in every song they play on the fucking radio. He's in the fucking stuffed toys that my old boss keeps shoving into the radiator."

I looked confused.

"Of the truck."

Ray took another drink. "He's on my arm. He's in my heart." Ray thumped his chest again. Hard. "He's in every fucking buggy I see and every bloody advert for nappies."

Silence again. Ray leaned forward and hung his head down toward his lap. I felt my heart pounding and took a deep breath.

"Is Brandon dead, Ray?"

Ray looked up, startled. "What did you say?"

"Oh, Ray. I'm sorry. I didn't mean . . ."

"Is he dead? You ask, is he dead?"

And then, just as loudly as he had been sobbing, he started laughing with such ferocity that I couldn't be sure whether it was only laughter or coupled with the rawest of grief. Unable to think of anything else to do, I leaned forward, proffering the tissue box; Ray took one and held it over his face with both hands, his body convulsing with emotion.

The fear was back. I'd drifted into deep water and now, unable to feel any ground beneath my feet, I began to worry. Introduction to anxiety management was one thing, but grief? Our first bereavement workshop wasn't scheduled for another week and I just didn't have a clue.

A sudden movement and I was jolted by Ray grabbing my hands—his face coming near to mine. I was now not only out of my depth, I was bloody scared.

"Oh, you beautiful-eyed goddess. You sweet little angel. You."

Ray gazed into my eyes and held the pause just long enough for me to begin to fear that I was going to be sick. He was so close to me that I felt his slow, warm, nicotined breath on my cheek. I didn't know what to do. Was this a good therapeutic moment that I had to contain, be the strong maternal figure who doesn't desert him or goad him, or do I begin to listen more acutely to the alarm bells in my head and find a way to close this session down?

Shit, I didn't even know what the time was—had fifty minutes elapsed? There was no clock on the wall, and I was too afraid to insult Ray by looking down at my wrist. He dropped my hands, sat back and, as if reading my mind, looked at his watch.

"Fucking hell, Doc, you're good. Got me going there for over half an hour. Oh yes, you did. Think we might have got to . . . What's it called? The root? What do you reckon, sweetheart?"

I tried to swallow imperceptibly and made a mental and physical effort to steady my voice as I spoke.

"Ray, can I begin by saying that I admire you. You are a man of courage."

"I am?" Ray smirked and I doubted that he was used to compliments.

"Real emotional courage. We've never met before. You've had a real shock being referred to this department—"

"The nuthouse?"

"And, Ray, you have found the strength to talk openly about your children and the pain of their losses to you, especially your little boy."

"I didn't lose them, love. They were taken from me."

"Yes, I understand that you would think that, Ray. Totally I do. And yes—your first wife . . . partner . . . who you seemed to have a sadomasochistic relationship with—"

"I did?"

"It seems that way, Ray. She set you up to make her the victim and you the attacker."

I was feeling back in my stride.

"So it was her fault, then?"

"I guess it's more complicated than ascribing fault. It's about understanding the dynamics of a relationship."

"Oh, I see." Ray clearly didn't.

"Let's put it another way. In relationships we inhabit roles. Often these roles reflect pieces of previous relationships that we have had with significant others"—*bloody hell, speak English*—"with people we love and care about the most. And I wonder, Ray, whether both the women with whom you have had children and whom you clearly have very bad feelings about—well, I wonder whether these women were selected by you because they were easy not to attach to and would one day leave you—just like your mother did."

Ray looked blank.

"It's difficult making attachments when previous experience says that with a close relationship, loving attachment is followed by heartache." I paused and wished that I hadn't given Ray my water. "You choose a woman who you know ultimately you can't love and the relationship plays itself out to its bitter end, which is horrible and painful for all, but at least it's safe. Familiar."

"Right, Doc. I did all that. Yeah, 'course I did."

"Ray, I'm not saying you consciously made it happen. I just—"

"Nah. I see that. Yeah, clever."

Another silence and a chance to glance down quickly. There were only ten minutes of the session left—time to wrap up, set some homework tasks for Ray to practice to manage his anxiety and book in next week's appointment.

"So, Ray, I think we need to pull everything together."

"Fair enough, Doc."

"OK. Well, what have you got out of this session?"

Ray laughed—more lightly this time. I was encouraged.

"I got that the panic starts from my head. I got that even talking about the fucking attacks can bring them on. I got that it was crap between me and the cunts because I couldn't be—what was it, Doc, attached?"

"That's right, Ray."

"And I got that I miss my kids and that is why I get stressed and that is why I panic."

I wanted to cheer. I wanted to hug Ray and shout, "Bravo!" at the top of my voice. I'd taken him from zero insight to a man of several hypotheses in less than forty-five minutes. Instead of cheering, however, I decided to compose myself to say what had to be said.

"You are right, Ray. This is about loss. Losing a mother so young. Then you have to manage the loss of your girls. Most especially, I believe that all this is about the death of your little son. The death of Brandon haunts you, Ray. You are stuck in your grief, and every trigger that reminds you of him—what you see by day or dream about at night—sets off these horrible attacks."

I sat back. Ray sat forward.

"Sweetheart, he's not dead—I never said he was dead. I just don't have no contact with him."

What?

"He's not dead?"

"Nah, nah, nah, nah, nah. Nah. He lives in Basingstoke with his cunt of a mother, been there since I broke her face."

The next couple of minutes were a blur. I struggled to manage the shock at being wrong-footed by Ray, and my annoyance at making such a stupid mistake.

Assumption is the mother of all screw-ups.

Ray seemed in good spirits, though. I was able to run

smoothly through the diary that I wanted him to keep every day, logging each of his panic attacks and how they affected him in terms of his thoughts, his feelings and finally his behavior. I then went on to teach him a couple of techniques to distract himself when he knew he was about to be triggered, in order to stop his mind hurtling toward the anxious thoughts and the accompanying bodily sensations.

"Stop myself thinking and freaking out by counting backward in threes from a hundred? I can't even count forward that far," Ray joked, and I smiled, glancing at my watch—only five more minutes and then, I hoped, the appearance of George and another orange brew.

"OK." I stretched back to my desk to get my diary. "Shall we put in the same time for next week?"

"Whatever you say, my beautiful-eyed girl. But before I go, can I show you something?"

"Of course you can." I smiled, writing Ray's next appointment in my diary, and then looked up at what I assumed would be a photo of Brandon he'd taken from his wallet.

Except that it wasn't a photo of Brandon. Instead, I found myself looking straight down at a shining switchblade, its point about a millimeter away from the tip of my nose.

"Oh, sweetheart. My beautiful-eyed doc."

With the blade still in its position, Ray began to trace my eye sockets with his fingertip.

He will kill me.

I'm not sure what happened next. Images flooded into my brain: women sucking liquidized food into broken mouths pinned together with steel; women in wheelchairs;

little children screaming as their mothers are pummeled and beaten.

I closed my eyes and struggled to breathe.

"Open your fucking eyes. Open your eyes, my pretty doc."

Ray pushed his finger hard into my eyelids and, with a small squeal, I opened my eyes.

He smiled. "Good."

He stared at me and, in total panic, I stared back. His eyes were gray, the right flecked with brown. I saw David Bowie, Ziggy Stardust.

Oh Christ. Oh God. Please help me.

He eased the point of the blade away from the end of my nose and for a moment I could take a breath. Maybe that was it. Maybe he'd made his point, reasserted his dominance after his vulnerability in the session and was ready to go.

I was wrong.

Very gently, Ray placed the blade flat side against my skin, next to my left eye.

"I want these eyes."

I began to cry.

"Oh, sweetheart. My beautiful-eyed doc, please don't cry. No. Shush now. No tears now, baby." Ray caught the tears on his fingertips and then licked them off. "Oh yes. You taste good. Very good."

He stroked the flattened blade around my left eye. "These are deadly weapons, you know, sweetheart. Little blue laser traps. And, boy, do you know how to use them, baby. Oh yes. One look and you are straight into one side and then straight out the other. Those eyes. Blue and innocent, but used to finding out all the secrets—aren't they, sweetheart."

Without understanding why, I felt like I had to nod.

"Yes. You know what I'm talking about, my baby. Blue searchlights." Ray raised his arm in a mock Nazi salute. "I vill mek you speek!

"You thought you'd got me, sweetheart. I saw it in that pretty little butter-wouldn't-melt sweet little princess face of yours. Young girl like you—Little Miss Know-It-All—thinks she can get inside a bloke like me. Just some thick, useless nothing like me. He's rubbish and he collects rubbish. Shit living with shit. That's what you thought, sweetheart, wasn't it?

"You know, I've met loads like you. Little Miss Do-Gooders. The ones in prison are the fucking worst. Patronizing fucking dried-up old cunts who can't get a man, so they have to spend their time with those of us locked behind bars who can't get away from them and their ugly mugs and whining fucking voices. They think that we need them and that makes them feel good. Do you know, princess, I think it makes them hot. It makes them horny. They are more fucked up than we are. Pathetic. They are easy—just like you were, sweetheart. Easy bait, easy fodder—so fucking easy to fool.

"What got you first? The tears? Did you think you was doing well when you saw the tears? Did you think that the tears meant you was getting somewhere? Did you think, Oh, bless him. Look at all these tears that he's never shed for his poor dead mum and his arsehole of a dad and his kids? That's what you thought, was it, sweetheart? About them tears? Same tears as these?" Ray closed his eyes and then opened them suddenly. A tear trick-led obediently down his cheek, and he smiled.

"Trick I learned inside when I was fourteen. Gets you all every time. Every fucking time." The tears contin-ued. "Oh boohoo. Poor me. Poor Ray—no mum, bastard for a father. Shit life. Poor little Ray."

He started to laugh silently but with a violence that made his whole body shake. The end of the blade jabbed into the soft skin of my temple.

I yelped.

Ray looked alarmed. The tears stopped and he pulled away the blade.

"Oh, sweetheart. No way. Oh fuck, baby. No."

He grabbed the tissue box and offered it to me. Shak-ing, I dabbed the edge of my eye; a small speck of blood stained the tissue.

"Don't worry, sweetheart. Only a small bleed."

"Ray, I need to leave this room."

"I'm sorry, sweetheart, you can't, not yet. Not till I'm finished."

"Finished what, Ray?"

"Finished with you, my beautiful blue-eyed baby girl."

"We have finished, Ray. It's time to go."

"No, babe. We finish when I say, and I say we haven't finished."

Later on, when I was thinking this all through, I couldn't be sure what it was that had been said in that moment, but suddenly the situation shifted for me.

No fucking way, mate. This is my office, and this is my session. We finish when I say, and I say now.

Outwardly I remained passive, but inwardly I felt busy.

Confront him. No, he'll kill me. Talk him down. No, he'll kill me. What, then? What?

And it was then as if descending from the heavens that Sigmund appeared to me, and with blinding clarity, I knew exactly what to do.

"That's a big knife, Ray."

He said nothing.

"A beautiful knife. And such a big, long blade. It really is beautiful. Can I touch it?"

Still saying nothing, Ray slowly offered me his blade.

I gently cupped my hands around its shaft. "That is long. Long and hard. It's beautiful, Ray."

Still no sound except his breathing—quiet but getting faster. My mouth felt like it was stuffed with wool.

"Yes, Ray, you are right. I am a little princess, but make no mistake about it—I know a good blade when I see one. I'm not completely inexperienced, you know."

Ray looked at me and I worked hard to look right back. Everyone and everything was calm.

"Can I stroke it, Ray?"

Exhaling, Ray closed his eyes and nodded and then opened them again to watch his blue-eyed goddess gently place her fingertips on the broad, flat edges of his long blade and slowly stroke them up and down the cold steel shaft.

Ray's breathing quickened, and as I continued to stroke the knife, he closed his eyes. I knew that this was my moment.

"Ray, I'm done. Thank you. You can put it away now."

His eyes still closed, Ray flicked the blade's safety catch and the knife retracted into itself. Silence. Ray continued to exhale audibly.

OK, I told myself. *Six paces to the panic button. Ten to the door. Stay with me. We're going to count. One . . . two. That's it, keep it steady. Three . . . four. Take your time. Five . . . Reach out and . . .*

"You cunt!"

Huge hands encircled my neck as I launched myself at the panic button. A siren went off and Ray shook me like a rag doll, my feet lifted off the floor. I felt like I was drowning.

And then, as I was about to go under, I saw the most incredible sight. In an explosion of light, the door to my room flew open and two large women burst in. While one punched Ray right in the face, the other kicked him hard in his testicles with the full force of her Lucite stiletto.

As I fell to the ground, "Josephine" caught me in her strong arms and held me into her muscular body and enormous breasts. She smelled of sweat, musk and heavy foundation. I snuggled into her, feeling safe.

Next to me, Ray was now being held facedown on the floor by two security guards, his arms locked behind his back. Crouching down next to Ray with her knee pressing onto the back of his head, "Daphne" slipped open her little red clutch and pulled out a warrant card. As I was helped out of my office, Ray was being read his rights.

First placement, first critical incident debriefing. I was still shaking, and now I had to meet my clinical training supervisor to talk about what had gone wrong.

Chris came into the room and I stood up, like a child

when the teacher arrives. I suddenly felt stupid. Chris
didn't seem to notice. She threw her bag down and put
her large takeaway coffee cup on the table.

Dr. Chris Moorhead—she who was renowned for being a hard-core and brilliant clinical supervisor—sat opposite me, staring. And here I was, the trainee she'd asked
not to let her down only a few weeks earlier. I'd royally
screwed up.

Chris was the one who would decide after each of my
training placements, over the following three years,
whether I would pass to the next, whether I would one
day qualify.

"How are you doing?" she asked.

"I'm fine. You?"

Chris stared straight at me. "I'll start again, and this
time, please answer me honestly. How are you doing?"

"I'll survive!" I smiled.

"Final time. Think carefully before you answer. How
are you doing?"

To my horror, I burst into tears.

"I don't know."

Chris rummaged in her large bag, pulled out a packet
of tissues and handed me one. "You have had a pretty
big shock."

I couldn't stop crying. I wanted to apologize to her,
ask for another chance. I couldn't get the words out.

"This sort of thing happens. Generally not so early
on, though, so I'm sorry that it happened to you."

I smiled and shook my head.

"Tell me as much as you can remember about the session." She handed me a glass of water.

As I took it, I could see my hand shaking. I took a

deep breath and tried to describe as much as I could remember: estranged from three children; obsessional love for youngest child, only son; ability to cry at will; my eyes; his knife; Freud and the penis. Shock does odd things to memory and I'm not sure how much she'd have understood. It all sounded bizarre.

I took a deep breath. "I'm sorry."

She raised her eyebrows.

"I know I have messed up big-time. It won't happen again."

"How did you mess up?"

I took a deep breath. "I should have seen it coming. I know this looks bad." Chris opened her mouth to speak, but I had to keep talking: I just couldn't bear to hear what she was going to say. I kept saying sorry.

She handed me another tissue. "Your nose is running."

Embarrassed, I blew my nose.

"I am not clear why you are apologizing."

This was torture.

"For messing up with the patient, for causing a scene in the department, for potentially compromising your reputation and the reputation of the clinical course, for . . ."

She raised her hand to silence me. "Did you know he had sociopathic tendencies?"

"No. Sorry."

"Did you know he was armed with a knife?"

Again I shook my head. "No."

"What's with all the mea culpa? When I interviewed you, I thought you were more confident." Chris sat back in her chair, took a gulp of coffee. "Please don't do a Mother Teresa on me, and please, please don't next pull out your sword and fall on it. OK?"

I took a deep breath. "I just want you to see that I am worth another chance."

Chris pushed a critical incident form across the desk toward me and handed me a pen. "Let's start with you filling this out."

I did. My hand was shaking.

Chris leaned over to look. "You need to write that bit out again—you've joined the 'l' and 'i' together so they look like a 'u.' He didn't attack you with a 'fuck knife,' did he?"

I looked up at her and saw a deadpan face. Her mouth twitched and we both started laughing.

"OK, I don't expect you to speak, but just try to listen. Mistake number one: They don't have to cry in the first session for you to be doing your job well. Leave that to the social workers.

"Mistake number two: Think about where you put the chairs and where you sit. If you need to ask them to excuse you as you make your way past them to push the panic button, then you are screwed.

"Mistake number three: If you ever feel out of your depth, then find a reason to leave and leave. This is a job, not a calling. If you want to save with self-sacrifice, then find a nunnery.

"Mistake number four: If they want to show you something, do not take your eyes off them as they reach for it. We do telling in our profession, not showing. Leave that to the drama therapists.

"Mistake number five: This was mine. I should have made sure that the department had screened this sociopath before you got him.

"Mistake number six: Don't discount Sigmund, because it seems you pulled him out in your hour of need and he came through for you. You crudely emasculated your patient and then cleverly rejoiced in his switchblade penis.

"Overall, well done. You did better than I would have expected from someone so inexperienced. Take a long weekend off and I'll see you next Wednesday."

So she made one mistake and I made five, but still I did a good job. Sigmund helped me out, my eyes were still in their sockets and all was well with the world.

But what about Ray? I couldn't help but feel that I had totally and utterly let him down.

Two

AT THE BOTTOM OF
THE DEEP BLUE SEA

When a child is hanging by the neck, grabbing her legs to hold her up isn't easy. They wriggle and they kick. Imogen struggled in silence. Then she kneed me in the face, hard, and I tasted blood. The stillness of the room belied the horribleness of the task.

"Hold her up, up, up!"

Grunts of effort in unison as a nurse and I hoisted the little girl's legs higher to relieve the pressure on her neck. Her dressing-gown cord had been looped over a slim copper pipe in the ceiling. Victorian plumbing was not designed with the health and safety of suicidal children in mind.

I couldn't believe how heavy a small-framed anorexic child feels when you have to support her as a dead weight.

"C'mon, guys—push up and hold . . . and hold . . ."

A snap of steel through fabric, followed by a bizarre pause in motion—everything still for a beat before the child dropped into our arms. My frustration melted into relief. I just wanted to hold this little vulnerable person and rock her gently, make her feel safe. Imogen, though, was having none of it. She lashed out, biting, kicking and snarling.

"Imogen, be still—let's work together here. Ow!"

Negotiations over, she was quickly flipped onto her stomach, arms held behind her back. Lying prostrate over bucking legs, I had a sudden urge to bite back, to sink my teeth into this angry, ungrateful kid and shock her into submission.

And then it was finished. Child sedated, taken off to the "chill-down" room—chic and bijou, nicely padded, sparsely furnished—while staff dispersed to other duties. Voices in the corridor: "What did the librarian say to the kid who wanted to borrow a book on suicide? Fuck off—you won't bring it back."

Third week into placement number two and already I wanted to give up and go home.

I can't remember what I'd imagined it would be like. I'd reluctantly agreed with Chris to do my second six-month training placement in a medium-secure inpatient psychiatric unit for twelve- to sixteen-year-olds. I was spending my days with kids who wanted to do all manner of harm to themselves or to other people—to cut, to starve, to stab, to kill.

Once I'd had my few days off to recover from having Ray threaten to cut my eyes out of their sockets, the rest of my first placement had gone more smoothly. I hadn't yet worked out Chris, but she was proving to be a great clinical supervisor and I enjoyed our sessions. She was calm and brilliant, and I loved her ability to pull the strands of the complex stories told to me by my patients into a coherent narrative—a process I was learning to call "formulation."

University had found a rhythm, and I'd made some friends among my fellow trainees. The lectures were interesting, even when I struggled with their content. I had already worked out that even though he had saved me in my moment of need with Ray, I was not a big fan of Sigmund and psychoanalysis. Interpretations, the unconscious, projection, transference and countertransference—it all felt so abstract and judgmental. And where was the evidence base?

I'd worked with some wonderful people since Ray. Occasionally George and I would have a brew with Edith, whom I'd grown to love. She'd been discharged and readmitted during my placement, just as George had predicted. My transgender heroes, "Josephine" and "Daphne," would regularly knock on my cupboard door and check in with me—they made me feel safe. Leaving that placement had been difficult, and in the final week Chris had met with me to discuss placement number two.

"So, kids. Do you like them?"

I wasn't sure. I didn't know many. "Yeah, I love kids."

"Good."

She bit into a biscuit. I had begun to notice that Chris did a lot of eating and talking during our sessions, which I found pretty gross.

"And," she continued, crumbs scattered over her shirt, "adolescents—you know, teenagers. You like them?"

Thanks for the translation—I know what an adolescent is.

I wasn't sure how to respond to this either. "Yeah?"

Chris dunked her biscuit into her tea and then extended a long tongue to lick in the sloppy, mushy end. "Were you a nice teenager?"

"I think I was OK."

That was a massive lie—just ask my mother.

Chris smiled. "Shame. I had you pegged as a pain-in-the-arse teenager."

I smiled, then wondered if I was allowed to. "I had my moments."

"Thought so. Anyway, here's the thing. We've got a regional shortage of child placements and so I volunteered you to do yours in an inpatient unit for young teenagers."

I had no idea what that was.

"Right . . ."

"You'll be dealing with kids who are presenting in a high level of crisis and so are too vulnerable to be treated in the community."

"OK."

Chris offered me the packet of Rich Tea. I shook my head.

"So," she said, chomping into a fresh one, "you'll spend the next six months in a unit just outside of London working with a specialist multidisciplinary team assessing and treating kids and their families, who are often in crisis." Chris smiled brightly and raised her eyebrows at me.

I swallowed hard. "OK. If you think I can . . ."

"Why wouldn't I?"

I blushed. I hated blushing. My heart started racing as I thought of Ray.

"Well, you know, it's just that I was kind of attacked by I guess what you would call a 'patient in crisis' in my last placement, and that was in an outpatient department . . ."

Chris stared at me, unblinking. "And?"

My face felt red hot. I didn't want to tell her I was scared. "Well, based on my inability to manage Ray, perhaps I'm not ready to do this placement. You know, with kids and their families in crisis."

Chris folded over the torn flap of the biscuit wrapper and shoved the packet into her large, overstuffed bag.

"I disagree. I think you can and should do this placement. You'll be protected by a strong staff team, and you've got me with you every step of the way."

And so, reluctantly, I agreed. And it had started well. The staff team was strong. I liked the young people. I was really enjoying it until Imogen decided, that morning, to attempt to hang herself. Now I just wanted out.

Walking back to my office, I wondered why I had let Chris talk me into this. What was I trying to prove? I suppose there had been some fantasy about sailing in on a cloud of compassion and being the one—the only one—who really understood these kids and could save them.

Pretty arrogant.

I was training to do a job where I had license to ask anyone anything and get an answer, where I would be part of a decision-making process that could fundamentally alter someone else's life—it was important to remember that this didn't make me all-powerful. I smiled at this last thought: I wasn't the first person to imagine that she was the Almighty in this place.

Time to grab a coffee and go into the critical incident debriefing. How did the suicidal kid have a dressing-gown cord? Wasn't she on highest-level observation? Who had done the property search when she was admitted? A head was going to roll—thankfully, though, not mine.

The following afternoon, sitting opposite Imogen in our next session, I felt a hot ball of anger and frustration gather in my throat. What was wrong with this little girl? Why wouldn't she communicate with me? How could I possibly help her if she wouldn't talk?

I thought about transference and countertransference, tried hard to work out whose rage I was experiencing. The look on Imogen's face left me in no doubt that she was pissed off at being thwarted in her attempt to hang herself. She wanted to die, and we had stopped her. I got that.

But there was a lot of my rage sitting there with us.

I'd been seeing this twelve-year-old since she was admitted three weeks ago. As a clinical psychologist in my first year of training, and eager to prove myself to Chris after the last debacle with Ray, I had specifically requested that I be assigned to Imogen as her individual therapist and case manager. At first I was refused on the grounds of lack of experience—she was a tricky one, a complicated case. The social workers wanted her, the family therapist wanted her and the analyst wanted her.

But in the end I got her. No one else was receiving training in cognitive behavioral therapy. She came from a loving family, so no social work was needed, thanks. The soft-spoken, leather-moccasined, vegan family therapist had too many other cases, and anyway, the focus needed to be on the child this time around, not the family. And the analyst? I wouldn't let him near any child, especially not one like Imogen.

Instinctively, I leaned toward the here-and-now type of therapeutic intervention. I was suspicious of therapists who asked their patients to lie down and then took them back to their relationships with their mothers, spending most of the session out of their line of sight, in silence.

I didn't get analysis. I might have been much more open to the ideas if the analysts themselves weren't so bloody full of it. They were up their own rectums with self-importance; they seemed to believe that only they had read and understood the Holy Scripture of mental health.

For me, analysis had always been a bit too much like religion—purporting to possess the key to understanding the fundamental questions of life, but unable to provide any evidence to back up its case.

"I am so sorry that you don't feel any better about life after two years of thrice-weekly sessions. It pains me that you are still unable to form a meaningful relationship, and that on some days even washing your hair feels like an unattainable goal, but to question whether lying here on this couch while I silently write notes and say little is the right approach is—forgive me for pointing it out—a symptom of the difficulty you have in really connecting with this therapy, indicative of your difficulty in connecting with other people more broadly. It is clear that this rebellion is you acting out and sabotaging our relationship—as you so readily sabotage other relationships in your life. It suggests to me that you now need to see me five days a week instead of three, for an indeterminately long time—apart from every August, when I will be away on holiday."

As I understood it, Sigmund Freud was a coke addict who fabricated the father-rape-wish-fulfillment scenario of his abused female patients in order not to upset the conventions of the time. Fathers and uncles were busy raping their daughters and nieces, but this wasn't the moment to out them. So Sigmund snorted another line and created the most damningly misogynist theory of all time. As I had seen firsthand with Ray, there may be a time and place for Freud, but Imogen's case wasn't it.

That analyst was not going to treat Imogen. I didn't like him and I didn't like the way he worked. And he knew it.

As I was sitting there, staring at Imogen, the words were just not coming. I had to move past my own frustration and relax. But it is very hard to relax when you are looking into the eyes of a mute little girl who wants to be dead. You don't want to relax; you want to run at her and pull her into your arms, hold her and then shake her until she tells you why. You long to say, "Why do you want to die? You're twelve years old."

My other problem was that I couldn't shift my focus from the angry red welt around her neck—that welt rendered us both mute. And while I knew silence could be a therapeutic tool, it was clear to me that this time it reflected the powerlessness that both Imogen and I felt. I wasn't good enough for her. She wasn't good enough for life.

I could feel my anxiety rising—my frontal cortex was shutting down. Soon I would be limbic, running only on raw emotion, and this was not a good place to be. I had to think, be rational, reconnect with the practitioner in me.

I ought to have felt more prepared for Imogen. I had tried to plan my psychological therapy session with her earlier in the day, but my meetings with Chris had become increasingly shambolic. That morning I'd rushed into Central London, but she had arrived at her office at the university late, stinking of cigarettes and cursing the people who'd been at the meeting she just left. Throwing her bag onto a chair, she began to make a Pot Noodle.

"OK, speak. I'm listening."

"Well, to be honest, I'm not sure where to begin. I had prepared an agenda, but I'm not sure we can fit it all in. I mean, I was expecting an hour."

"How's it going with the silent, self-starving one?"

I wasn't sure what disgusted me most—the smell of synthetic chicken, the accompanying sounds of slurping, the neglected dribble down her chin or the lack of an apology for being so bloody late.

"I'm not sure there's time."

Chris continued to eat, pausing only to wipe her mouth with the back of her hand. I drew a deep breath.

"Imogen Trent-Evans, twelve-year-old daughter of Mary Trent and Jim Evans. Mary, magazine editor, lives in London; James is now in Los Angeles with his partner, Angus. Mary has remarried—Jake Robins, a male fashion model—and they have, sorry, *had* Maisie, who was five when she drowned in the family pool last August. Imogen, an obsessive skipper and self-harmer, has—"

An abrupt slurp. "Stop! For Christ's sake, you're not presenting at a sodding ward round."

"Sorry, not sure what you mean."

"Tell me Imogen's story. About the child. I want to see her and hear her."

Blushing had always pissed me off—a sign of weakness, unintended vulnerability. That day I could do nothing except glow a rosy pink, and, to my horror, feel tearful. Chris wasn't sympathetic.

"OK, you feel uncomfortable here. Get over it. You have talent, but you are way too self-consciously righteous for my taste. If I am late, I am late. If I want you to present to me in a different way, then present to me in a different way. If this all feels too much, there's the door."

Chris lit a cigarette. "So, how does this child make you feel?"

"She makes me feel protective. She makes me want to look after her."

"And behind these obvious rescue fantasies?"

"Would you mind not smoking?"

Chris walked to the window, opened it and, with her backside pushed toward me, leaned out and blew smoke at Tottenham Court Road.

She looked over her shoulder. "I think this girl frightens you."

"I am not frightened of her. I just feel so *sad* for her. She's only just twelve. She lost her sister eight months ago. Bloody hell, the poor kid found her baby sister floating facedown. She never sees her mum, never, because the woman runs her magazine with more care than she gives her kid. And her gay dad is . . . well, he's on the other side of the world. To add to the bleakness, there's the housekeeper, Miriam, who speaks very little English but was the girl's constant other until the mother fired her after Maisie drowned. And finally, to complete this happy home, there is a grief-stricken model of a stepfather, Maisie's dad, who spends his entire time sobbing whenever he comes into the unit."

"A model of grief, or an attractive grieving man?"

That was funny and we exchanged a smile. "Both."

The cigarette had burned down to its filter and Chris extinguished it in the dregs of the Pot Noodle. She sat back down, facing me.

"She is so small and pale and just a tiny, tiny victim," I continued. "She is powerful, but she is also just a little girl cuddling her rag doll."

"A doll?"

"Yes, a rag doll. Apparently her dead sister's doll."

"Transitional object?"

"Well, she never puts it down, and we can't touch it. It really smells, but she won't let us wash it. At night she sucks—well, sort of suckles on its face. In the daytime it's tucked under her arm, constantly."

Chris went still. Then she carefully lit another cigarette. "And people would think to want to wash this doll, why?"

"Because it smells."

A long smoke exhalation. "Listen. I wanted you to be my trainee because I thought you were bright and we could skip the obvious stuff. So, doll equals transitional object, as in link to dead sister. No one touches it. The doll *is* her sister. Smell and all. I thought Winnicott was first year, first week of training, basic lecture shtick?"

Christ, this woman made me feel like an idiot. Of

course I knew who Winnicott was—the influential English pediatrician and psychoanalyst who transformed our thinking about the mind with his writings on object relations theory. Of course I understood that the doll represented Imogen's sister!

"OK. No sulking. Carry on with the story."

Aren't you supposed to start by hating those you'll later credit as being your mentors? With Chris it was too early to call. I took a deep abdominal breath and continued.

"When she was first admitted as an inpatient to the unit, she would skip obsessively whenever she was given monitored access to her skipping rope. Every moment she could, she'd skip and count constantly—and even now that we've taken her rope away after her hanging attempt, we can see her legs twitch up and down and her wrists circling. It was exhausting to watch. She was totally impenetrable—no one could engage with her. She'd stop skipping when any of us tried to talk and then the second we left, giving up on the nonconversation, the total lack of engagement, she would start again."

"How does this affect the team?"

"She totally splits us. Completely."

"How?"

"Pretty much the way you'd expect, because you know all the differences and interdisciplinary rivalries—the doctors get biological and diagnostic, and ram the sodding drug charts down our throats, while we sit with the social workers and disappear up ourselves with compassion, understanding and behavior-management programs. And of course, the analysts hover above us all with interpretations that make the team argue and end up disliking them."

"What, 'she unconsciously wanted her sister to drown'—that sort of thing?" Chris grinned.

"Yep, the very one."

"But what's wrong with that thought?"

"What?"

"Maybe she did want her sister not to be around anymore. Maybe she is very anxious and needs to control it all with obsessive and ritualized behavior. Maybe she has got some neurobiological problems that need pharmacological management. Maybe she has a sad little life underpinned by a family in crisis. Perhaps every discipline is on the button. But that's all maybe, and for now what I suggest is that here you have one powerful little girl on your hands who can split the team and stir you up while saying nothing, eating nothing, and trying to die."

In that moment I didn't know what frightened me most—my supervisor, my patient, or the way I seemed to keep getting this stuff wrong.

Later that day, looking at Imogen in our session, I saw hollow and empty. This tiny girl, one pale arm decorated with neat parallel red cuts, stared at me with large blank eyes and counted under her breath. Thinking over what Chris had said, I struggled to make sense of the word "powerful" in relation to this kid. Yes, small could be powerful, fragile also, but how can bereaved, emaciated, mutilated, anxious, and suicidal be powerful?

Chris had asked me for the story, and maybe that was where I would find clues—the clues to the hidden code that led to the unlocking of the child, of Imogen.

So I began to tell Imogen her story—as much as I understood it.

"Once upon a time there was a girl who lived in a big house in a big city. She lived with her mother and father and a nice lady called Miriam who couldn't really speak English. One day, when the little girl was three years old, her father decided he wanted to live in America in an even bigger house and in another city far away, with his friend Angus. The little girl was sad but stayed at home with her mother, who soon brought home a man with a lovely face who became the little girl's stepfather . . ."

Imogen had stopped counting, and her eyes were now completely focused on me. I felt my heart leap, my throat tighten. Her brown eyes were huge, framed by her tiny white face.

"The family lived together in the big house, and soon the mother and stepfather got married, not long after the little girl had her fourth birthday. The little girl was a bridesmaid and wore a pink shimmery dress with . . ."

There was a croak from across the room, and while I couldn't be sure, I thought that the croak was the word "blue."

"A blue shimmery dress . . . Is that right, Imogen? A blue bridesmaid dress?"

She started counting again. Shit—how could I have been so stupid? I continued.

"After the wedding the family lived together, and while the mother was traveling and working, the little girl stayed at home with her stepfather and Miriam."

Feeling my throat constrict, I suddenly realized that I had been mouth-breathing for too long; my throat was dry, and without a glass of water, I knew that I would start coughing uncontrollably and lose the moment, the connection—whatever was going on here.

How to get to the water, however, was beginning to panic me—I felt pinned into my seat by Imogen's wide, staring eyes. And then I started coughing.

The fit came with such force that I was left doubled over. The more I tried to control it, the worse it got.

I was bent over, with my eyes streaming, when I suddenly became aware of someone close by. Sitting up slowly, I found Imogen standing an arm's length away from me and holding out a glass of water. The start shocked me into stopping. I took the water and gulped it gratefully.

Imogen sat back down, the stinky rag doll under one arm, wrists circling and counting under her breath. And then she stopped and said in the tiniest voice, "My dress was blue."

The next few sessions were uneventful. This was because I pushed her too hard. Buoyed up by the "conversation" about the blue dress, I pressed for more. But Imogen was giving me no more—and why should she? She sat silently with her dead sister's rag doll. Her wrists rotated through half-turns and back, and she counted under her breath. I was going about this all wrong.

Chris and I met for a coffee between her meetings.

"Try to understand Imogen's communication. Stop trying to get her to communicate on your terms."

"What she's communicating is that she has given up and she wants to hang herself—I understand that, and I think she knows it."

Chris was shaking her head. "Hanging is not a communication strategy. Hanging is about coping. She feels alone, afraid and misunderstood, so she wants to leave the party. That's all there is to it."

I think I was shocked by this idea. I'd never thought of suicide as a coping strategy. I could see it as a way out for a desperate adult who has given life a shot but found it unlivable. For someone like that, suicide might be an active choice, something they could control and finally get right after a miserable life of perceived failure. But could a child think like that?

"OK, look at this another way. Stop pathologizing Imogen's behaviors. Stop trying to 'stop' her when she behaves in ways that seem 'abnormal.' Join her, get in alongside her, listen to what she is trying to tell you via her behavior."

"Her behavior is suicidal, pathological—how can I get alongside that? The risks would be—"

"You are not listening to me. Suicide is merely an exit strategy. Look at what else she's doing."

I ran out of our meeting because I had to get to a lecture, but driving back to the unit the following day, I kept thinking about what Chris had said.

Pathology: a variation in normal or healthy functioning; abnormal, or not typical, behavior or thinking that is caused by mental or physical disease.

A grim concept, and a bleak word to apply to a child. Where was Imogen being pathologized? She had been admitted in a crisis; she was on the highest-level observation; she wasn't allowed to possess anything that she might use to kill herself—her skipping rope, even her shoelaces had been confiscated. All that stuff *had* to be pathologized if she was to be helped, right? So what else was there that I could apply Chris's theory to?

What were we missing?

The unit was located on the grounds of a large, mostly derelict asylum, which was once a Victorian manor house. Apart from the more modern health-care center where we worked, one other wing of the old complex still housed long-stay institutionalized residents who were unlikely ever to leave. I drove in torrential rain through the vast hospital grounds and the detached infirmary, which had been built away from the villas as lodging for those with infectious diseases or terminal illnesses and those con-sidered so insane they were locked away until they gave up and died. This building was in the rear of the asylum, north of the other buildings, so that the prevailing winds, which blow southwest, would not carry its influence down into the city; in those days, pathology was believed to be contagious, a belief dating back to the Victorian era.

The Victorians thought it was possible to "catch" im-morality and insanity. In Victorian London, the domi-nating wind was a westerly one, and so the slums, in the poor end of town, were in the east—spatial order dic-tated social order. The insane were housed even farther outside the east of the city, so no one—not even the most poor—would be exposed to their influence.

Driving up the central road of the asylum, I knew that on my left were those villas that once housed the women, on the right those for the men. Every building had been a microcommunity of individuals considered unfit to live in civilized society.

Morally defective women—usually those who had been "in service" or had been raped by the squire or his son and had given birth out of wedlock—would be dumped here after their children were taken away. They would cohabit with epileptics who were considered "degenerates, lunatics and idiots" and others with depression, anxiety, learning difficulties and psychosis.

The "defectives" had to be gender-segregated. God forbid they fornicate and produce a new generation. The large bushes lining the long track, however, told the real stories: tales of furtive couplings, a need for contact and connection. There were awful stories about those villas: of the rape and sexual exploitation of residents by the people charged to care for them.

Considering the history of the place I was working in, I began to resent the word "pathology." Taken from medicine, in the mental health setting it nailed a boundary between "normal" and "abnormal" as if such a division existed. The language itself seemed to suggest it was right to segregate those with mental health difficulties from the rest of the "healthy" world. So much for our believing we're so enlightened nowadays. We might not still think mental illness is contagious, but the environment in which we treated the mentally ill hadn't changed a bit. Here we were trying to help these kids on the grounds of an early-twentieth-century asylum.

I thought about Imogen's skipping, her counting and those deep, parallel cuts into the soft skin of her left arm and both thighs—behaviors that had been labeled as pathological anxiety-management strategies, maladaptive coping techniques. The "wrong" sort of coping.

Which of course they were—excessive obsessional and ritualized behaviors do not make for an effective way of managing anxiety in the long term. Anxious thoughts may be managed in the short term by elaborate counting and other behavioral rituals, but long term, that kind of compulsive behavior would not enable Imogen to get to the root of her anxiety, her need to control.

This kid, unbelievably controlling in the external world, was, I began to realize, internally in complete turmoil. She felt out of control and afraid. Skipping was a way to keep it all together.

By pathologizing those behaviors, all we had done was see them as symptoms of an underlying condition. We'd responded with anxiolytic medications and behavioral boundaries—no skipping, no counting out loud and definitely no cutting while in the unit—and by doing that, we had effectively removed Imogen's only way to manage herself. We had left her with no way of coping with her painful and overwhelming inner world. We couldn't bear what she was doing and what we were seeing and so we had taken it on ourselves to put a stop to it. No wonder the poor kid wanted to kill herself.

Imogen is anxious, I thought. Why? That was easy:

1. Emotionally uncontained by an absent mother.
2. No connection to an absent father.
3. Nurtured by a woman, Miriam, who could be kind in a task-oriented way but did not have the language skills to enable her charge to learn to verbalize feelings.
4. The loss of Miriam when she was fired after Maisie's drowning.
5. Nurtured by a stepfather who was so able to emote that he was too consumed in his own grief to attend to that of his stepdaughter.

6. Guilt at finding her little half sister, Maisie, drowned but not being able to save her.
7. Perhaps even frightened by her own unconscious desire to get rid of Maisie, who had come into her life and so taken away everything that was once only Imogen's.

I was out of new ideas. Imogen needed help and I needed to find a way to give it to her. Maybe I would have to talk to the analyst after all.

These were real anxieties, understandable and obviously overwhelming for one so young. Imogen had no emotional constant to help her make sense of it all. No ability to verbalize what she felt tormented by. No one to help her understand that this wasn't her fault; she wasn't to blame; she didn't cause or will her sister to die.

But that didn't answer Chris's suggestion about getting into Imogen's painful world. I still didn't know how to do that. She still wasn't speaking. If she can't do words, what can she do?

And then, just as I parked outside the unit and turned off the engine, I got it.

She can skip.

I scrambled to grab my bags and climb out of the car. I needed to find the analyst, get my head straight. Turning to open my door, I jumped out of my skin. The naked buttocks of one of the long-stay residents were pressed firmly against my window. I crawled across to the passenger door to get out.

———

The meeting with the analyst that followed was full of clichés. Woody Allen meets Almodóvar.

I entered a small, dark room with the requisite couch against one wall. Abstract prints alongside postcards from Anna Freud's house in Hampstead, all dominated by a huge reproduction of a self-portrait by Frida Kahlo, with her complicated and untended eyebrows. Endless books stacked up (very few with the spine broken) on a faded kilim on the floor. It smelled dusty.

I told him that I needed to skip with Imogen. I asked him how I could persuade the team, especially the nurses who ran the health and safety of the unit, to give Imogen back her skipping rope.

"Why would they? Won't she hang herself?"

"Not with the skipping rope. It means too much to her. It's her voice."

Then silence. Interminable silence.

Just talk to me, tell me what you think.

"Are you asking me for permission?" he asked.

Oh, so bloody, fucking frustrating.

"No. I am asking you for your opinion."

More silence. And then, finally: "My opinion is that you should begin to value yours."

Sod him. I left and marched to the nurses' office. To my amazement, they said yes and handed me Imogen's skipping rope, although I did wonder whether it was done with an "OK, then—put your money where your mouth is, girl" attitude. And so I did.

I found Imogen sitting on the window ledge in the rec room with half-closed eyes, silently counting and twirling her small wrists.

This was her regular place. She could look out the

window at the pond recently dug by the other inpatients and staff. It was a great activity, but one we couldn't encourage her to join in on. Water was way too dangerous for Imogen, and for us as her caregivers.

"Imogen, it's time for our session."

No response.

"Imogen, I've come for you. It's our time together."

Nothing.

"Imogen, I believe this is yours."

I placed the skipping rope on the window ledge next to her and after a beat she turned to look at it.

"C'mon, Imogen, let's go outside."

Jelly in the dish,
Jelly in the dish.
Wiggle, waggle, wiggle, waggle,
Jelly in the dish.

Imogen stared as I sang the next rhyme and continued skipping with her rope:

Lady, lady, touch the ground.
Lady, lady, turn around.
Turn to the east, and turn to the west,
And choose the one you like the best.

No response.

I'm a little Dutch girl dressed in blue.
Here are the things I like to do:
Salute to the captain,
Curtsy to the queen,

Turn my back on the submarine.
I can do the tap dance;
I can do the split;
I can do the holka polka just like this.

No response.

A sailor went to sea, sea, sea
To see what he could see, see, see,
And all that he could see, see, see
Was the bottom of the deep blue sea, sea, sea.

I had never skipped so hard in my life. In fact, I hadn't skipped since elementary school, more than a decade ago. Sweat was pouring off me, and my calves and arms ached.

"I'm sorry, Imogen. I have to stop."

"I was at the bottom of the sea, sea, sea."

That was the longest sentence I'd ever heard from this most serious little person with a fading red welt around her neck and her dead sister's stinky rag doll tightly clamped under her arm.

"Were you at the bottom of the sea, sea, sea, Imogen?"

"I was at the bottom of the sea, sea, sea. In my blue dress."

We looked at each other. My heart was racing.

"I didn't want to."

"You didn't want to do what, Imogen?"

"I'm hungry."

"OK, Imogen. Let's go and eat."

I told myself I was getting somewhere. I was sweating, building a picture of what had happened to Imogen in my mind. I was feeling good about myself. I thought I was on my way to understanding.

I would turn out to be very wrong.

Sitting behind the one-way mirror in the family therapy suite and watching the family session was, frankly, exciting. I could see them, but they couldn't see me.

It was also uncomfortable—who thought up this therapeutic strategy? The family knew they were being viewed but were expected to "act normal." I felt guilty.

Imogen sat still and pale-faced between her mother, Mary, and stepfather, Jake. Jake cried; Mary didn't. They were reliving the moment of discovering Maisie dead. My soft-moccasined colleague was with them in the room, steering the event.

"Tell me about that day."

It was a normal day, they said: The girls were playing outside. Mary was working in her office in the house, on a call to LA, speaking with a celebrity's assistant. Jake was conferencing with his agent, publicist and manager about an upcoming photo shoot for designer swimwear. Yep, an ordinary day in an ordinary household.

"Where were you, Imogen?"

She said that she was at the bottom of the sea, sea, sea. And then she asked for me to come into the room and pull her out.

I am ashamed when I think back. When I entered the therapy session from that room behind the one-way mirror, there was a *moment* with Jake. A look we exchanged. I had seen him on billboards around London and in the pages of glossy magazines. And now I was in the room with him, for real, joining a family meeting as Imogen's individual therapist, and his eyes were the same, his slight smile the same, as they were in all the ads I had seen. He saw me recognize him, take in his striking features, and he knew exactly what I was feeling; worse still, he realized I knew that he knew. It was a split second, but Imogen *saw* it—saw that "moment" between her stepfather and me. I had let her down by being pathetically and predictably human. I snapped back into the room just as Imogen jumped up, lifted her chair, threw it at the one-way mirror and, with her dead sister's stinky rag doll under her arm, ran out of the room.

In the chaos, I leaped up and chased after her. As I left the unit, I heard the alarms going off; my heart pounding in my chest, I told myself not to panic.

Outside, it was raining, the type of dense, light rain that drenches in seconds and leaves everything looking oily. I could feel myself slipping, so I kicked off my shoes, immediately regretting it as the loose gravel bit the soles of my feet. No time to stop. I had to keep running—besides, the pain was my punishment for being rubbish.

I could hear colleagues behind me shouting and dispersing in tag teams to try to close down our little quarry. My name was being called, but I didn't dare stop or slow down because I still had Imogen in my sights. I was responsible for her running, so I needed to catch her.

As I got to the end of the central road that divided the asylum and rounded the corner toward the exit, my heart skipped. I had forgotten that leaving this closed community, I would enter the real world and the busy road that met the highway. I looked frantically left and right, and spotted a tiny figure sprinting toward the overpass.

I was panting and feeling leaden-leg heavy. It occurred to me to wonder—not for the last time—why the fuck we were housing suicidal children so close to a major road. These were big roads, ribbed with overpasses—perfect platforms for the suicidal. Thinking this, still running, I started to cry.

We were heading toward the highway, toward civilization and the big city. She was slowing down; I wasn't.

I was wet and cold and, I assumed, running for Imogen's life. I kept her in my sights as I watched her climb up onto the barrier of the overpass; I didn't blink or look away. My magical thinking told me that if I didn't take my eyes off her, she wouldn't jump.

As I got nearer, I could hear the noise of car and truck horns. People had spotted this little girl and stopped to jump out and call up to her. I saw two men leap out of a van and begin running up the embankment, someone else on the hard shoulder was talking frantically into a mobile phone.

As I approached her, I instinctively slowed down: Run at a person ready to leap, then leap they will. My feet were sore, my muscles ached, and my lungs felt near to explosion, so I stopped and stood still.

Imogen, on the barrier, turned to look at me; all noise was gone. She was calm; she smiled at me. I was soaking wet from rain and sweat, and panting harder than I ever had. I wanted to bend forward, put my hands on my knees and recover after my marathon, but I couldn't look away.

Imogen broke our gaze. She and her dead sister's stinky

rag doll looked over the edge of the barrier and into the road below, gridlocked with vehicles. In the distance, a siren was wailing. I started to walk slowly toward her.

"Imogen, shall I pull you out of the bottom of the deep blue sea, sea, sea?"

I felt calm; I was back in my grandmother's front room staring at her bloodstained carpet.

She looked at me again, her mouth moving and her wrists circling. She was deciding what was about to happen. I willed her into my arms.

And she came.

I held Imogen, locking my arms around her and pulling her into my body as we both flopped onto the oily, wet tarmac. I felt light, as if I were floating. And then there was a thud on top of me as we both ended up under male bodies, sweating and panting from their sprint up the highway embankment, wrapping their arms around us.

Life continued. Young people came and went on the unit. Imogen and I carried on with therapy—I was the only person she would talk to. And talk she did.

Over time she joined the unit school and after using the "sliding-in technique"—where a teacher would sit in a room while Imogen talked to me, getting closer and closer over days and weeks until our little charge felt comfortable enough to let him join our conversation—I was able to leave her with others, chatting confidently and engaging in lessons; she was a bright little button.

The skipping and counting stopped almost completely, reappearing only occasionally to remind us that we had missed something she was still struggling with.

Self-harm became a thing of the past. Imogen put on weight. Eventually she was able to wear her sneakers done up with their laces, and a dressing gown secured by its cord. It was time to plan her discharge from the unit.

Coming into an inpatient psychiatric unit is hideous for anyone, but leaving it can be even worse. As a team, we would spend months talking to the kids about leaving, giving them weekend leave, introducing their outpatient team to them and beginning to integrate them back into mainstream school. We told them that this process needed to be lengthy because there was so much to organize, and we needed to give them the chance to disengage slowly, to say good-bye to us. The truth also was that we took so long because we were reluctant to let them go.

We expected all young people to act out a bit before they left us—they were anxious and wanted to find a way to stay because the outside world felt too scary. Institutionalized children are difficult to support because their anxiety triggers a sense of protectiveness in us and we had to work hard not to collude with their need to remain with us. We wanted to keep them with us—to keep them safe.

If you know you've turned a kid's life around and she wants to live, how hard would you find it to send her back to the shitty world that made her want to die in the first place?

Imogen was dealing well with the discharge planning; in fact, she was managing it *too* well, and it spooked me. My colleagues, however, were careful to help me challenge my own reluctance to let her go, and so the frequency of my individual sessions with Imogen decreased.

Soon I was just another member of the staff team preparing her to leave us.

But this pissed me off big-time.

At this point I got the news that Chris would be off work for an "indeterminate" time; the rumor was she was in rehab. It was bad timing: I needed guidance. I resented the fact that I didn't have a way of getting in touch with her.

When I told my colleagues that I instinctively felt there was something that Imogen hadn't told us, they were kindly patronizing in expressing the need for me to "distance" myself from her; I was being told that these were my issues, not hers.

Since the mirror incident, everything had felt too smooth. Meetings with Imogen and her family were calm: Imogen talked more, her mother listened, and her beautiful stepfather stopped sobbing. Everything, like the mirror, was getting fixed.

So why did I feel uneasy?

I decided to consult my girls, my three closest friends, in the pub. I could always rely on them for support. Since I started my training I needed them more than ever.

Ali, whom I'd known since university, was an HR manager and asked, "Why, when you have a good outcome, with all family communication intact, would you doubt what you see before you? Discharge the girl—let her get on with her life."

The brilliant Megan, a research scientist, said, "This little girl has been in your unit, supported mostly by you, for months. Her symptomatic behavior has decreased to virtually nothing, she now understands the links between her thoughts, feelings and behaviors, and is choosing to engage with life. What's not to celebrate? Move on to the next patient—you've done your job here."

My oldest friend from primary school, the lovely, kind Rosie, who was doing her second degree while waiting tables, said, "If this doesn't feel right, then get some bloody advice."

But where the hell was I supposed to go? I felt abandoned, and angry with Chris for suddenly disappearing. I had not seen anything coming—she was odd, but nothing had led me to believe that she needed rehab. God, just how shit was I at this job? I couldn't even spot my supervisor having a breakdown.

The university administrators were being very tight-lipped about where Chris was and, because it was coming to the end of this placement, they felt there wasn't time to get another supervisor set up for me. It was suggested that I look within the unit team for some one-to-one supervision.

And so I did.

The room still smelled dusty, the majority of book spines were still unbroken, but actually it felt good to stretch out on the couch underneath Frida Kahlo.

"She's not ready to go."

Silence.

"It's too easy."

More silence.

I picked at my nail varnish and then bit my cuticles. "Oh, come on. Please talk here. We both know that this sudden recovery is weirder than an angry kid leaving us and getting on with their life to prove our rejection wrong."

I tugged at my sleeves—I'd bitten my nails to the quick. "I need to find out why she has bounced back. She was so . . . broken. There has to be a bigger narrative."

I realized suddenly that the analyst's silence had helped me understand that we didn't know Imogen's backstory. She had been silent about everything before her sister's death. We'd examined and controlled her behavior, but we still didn't really know what caused that behavior in the first place. We didn't know the end of that story I'd tried to tell her on day one.

And then he spoke.

"I think her story is bigger than the grief of losing her sister."

No shit, Sigmund. That's what I was saying.

"What else have you experienced with this child?" he asked.

I knew what I had to say, but I couldn't—it felt too clichéd to say while lying on a couch with an analyst.

"There was a 'moment' with her stepfather in the meeting before she ran."

I felt beyond foolish. He said nothing.

"OK," I backpedaled. "That was too much information. Irrelevant. Just tell me, what do I do?"

And then the pale, self-contained, silent, God-like analyst shocked me.

"Just bloody find out what this is all about, before it's too late."

Imogen was leaving in a week's time and I was under pressure. I hated psychoanalysts, but suddenly this one was my best friend at work. My head was a mess. I met with him again, but he'd reverted to mostly silence; I felt stupid for having brought up the moment of frisson with Imogen's stepfather.

Imogen's mother, Mary, and her stepfather, Jake, were happy. Mary was pregnant again and life held hope for Imogen after the freak accident that took her half sister: Here's a replacement puppy! Everyone be happy!

And why wouldn't they be? I was being selfish: I couldn't let go of a happy, healthy girl ready to move on.

I decided to stop the self-pity and we all prepared for the unit's summer fete on the hospital grounds, which was when I found her staring into the pond.

"Hey," I said.

She didn't reply.

"Imogen, come get some cotton candy."

She crouched down.

Imogen and water. Oh God, should I be scared? No, get a grip—evidence-base this girl's progress. She knows how to handle herself. Be calm.

"Hey, Imogen. What's up? Come on, cotton candy is beckoning! Race you to the stall."

She pulled the rag doll from under her arm, then threw it into the pond. I reached in, lifted the smelly rag doll from the water and handed her back.

"C'mon, sweetheart. Are you angry about leaving the unit? Tell me about it. Don't take it out on Rag Doll!"

She threw the rag doll back into the pond at my feet. And then she said, quietly and clearly, "I am sorry, but I am not going to save you."

She was staring intently at her dead sister's doll lying facedown in the pond water. My heart thumped; her face was becoming a mask again, her wrists beginning to rhythmically circle and her mouth twitch with silent counting. *Here comes the grief,* I thought to myself.

I knelt next to my little charge and began to try to soothe her back to me.

"Imogen, I can see that you are having big feelings at the moment. I think that these are about Maisie drowning and this makes you feel very sad and very anxious."

Without taking her eyes off the drowning rag doll, Imogen shook her head.

"Imogen, why don't we pull the rag doll out of the pond and go inside somewhere quiet where we can have a talk?"

Imogen shook her head again.

"Sweetheart, listen to me. I think it would be so sad for you if we leave Maisie's doll to sink to the bottom of this pond. This is Maisie's doll, isn't it? And now that Maisie isn't here to love her doll, you are doing that really important job for her."

Finally Imogen turned to me. "I don't want to save her."

I began to feel very cold. "Why not, darling?" I stooped down to pick up the doll. "Look, we can save her together."

"No!" Imogen grabbed my arm. She was shaking and beginning to pant. "No. No. No. No. No. No. No. No. No. No."

She threw herself down on top of me. As I held her, I could feel her heart racing, her entire body shaking. She was sweating.

"OK, sweetheart. Shh, darling. It's OK. I'm sorry, darling. I'm sorry. We will leave Rag Doll there."

I started to rock her as she sat into my body, her back against my chest, her legs inside mine. We sat like this for a while, both staring ahead at the rag doll swelling with pond water and getting heavier, beginning to sink. Time went by slowly and I began to relax, listening to the sounds of happy children at the party behind us.

But then I felt Imogen twitch and pull away from me.

"What is it, Imogen?"

"It's not fast enough."

"It's OK, darling—she's beginning to sink."

"It's not fast enough."

Imogen jumped out of my arms and waded into the pond. I scrambled forward on hands and knees, trying to catch her and pull her back. I was panicking; was she going to try to drown herself? I crawled into the pond, but then I stopped.

She pushed the doll below the waterline, ever so gently. She was whispering. I struggled to hear what she was saying.

"It's OK now, Maisie. It will all be OK. I love you, Maisie, and you are now safe. Nothing more bad will happen. I promise, Maisie. Immy promises."

Imogen was drowning her sister.

I felt sick. What was I seeing here? Was this a fantasy reenactment? Was this a reality reenactment? Or simply a way for Imogen to find some closure—to deliver the rag doll back to its rightful owner?

That was it, I told myself. Imogen was drowning the doll slowly and gently, so I had time to think this through.

Rag Doll for Imogen was Maisie, or at the very least a transitional object that connected her to her dead sister. When she came into the unit, she was mute and regressed—a distressed neonate without words, communicating extreme despair and acute distress in her behavior. She suckled the doll at night and held her next to her body by day to comfort her, to keep her sister near.

Over time we helped Imogen heal, right? She had expressed her grief, and her family had come to a new place of understanding and acceptance. They all had a bright future, with a new little baby to come. Life would now move on.

That was it. That made sense. Now I felt back in control. All we needed to do was let Rag Doll sink to the bottom and then Imogen could be at peace.

The rag doll was by now fully submerged and Imogen placed her foot on it. It was time to move on.

"Sweetheart? Is it done? Is Rag Doll with Maisie now?"

Imogen turned to look at me and spoke in a calm, clear voice. "Yes. And now he can't touch her anymore."

Suddenly she vomited into the pond. She wiped her mouth, and then she began to talk. The rest of the story followed, not clearly, not in the right order, but I understood every word of it.

Imogen had helped Maisie drown when she turned five, the age she herself had been when Jake, her stepfather, had started sexually abusing her.

She had watched her sister fall into the swimming pool at their home and had then gently placed her foot on top of Maisie's head to keep her under the water.

In order to protect her sister from sexual abuse, Imogen had been making herself available to her stepfather; she thought that if she always let him enjoy their "special friendship," he would never go near Maisie.

But it was getting harder. Imogen realized her stepfather didn't want her anymore, she was growing up, becoming less attractive to him. He wanted only the very young. Imogen knew that she had been passed over for her little sister.

"I didn't mean to let her die. I didn't plan for it to happen, but when she fell into the pool and I couldn't pull her out, I realized what I could do to help her."

The air smelled of pond water and puke.

"I killed my little sister, Maisie. Please will you tell the police and take me to prison?"

I scooped Imogen into my arms and walked her out of the pond as she laid her exhausted little head into my neck.

As we walked into the unit, the analyst met us at the door and wrapped us both in a large, warm blanket.

Three

PRACTICE TALES

Martin was uncomfortable. Red-faced, looking at the floor, he was doing the best hand-wringing that I had ever witnessed, while his partner, Elise, sat bolt upright and struggled to explain their difficulties. I wanted to reassure them, but the air in my new office was crackling with collective embarrassment. Martin and Elise had come to see me for sensate focus sex therapy—a brilliant and effective technique, but a bloody scary one to administer. This would be a long session.

I had been at Market Street GP Practice for only three days. I hadn't figured out how the coffee machine worked, I was still struggling to remember the names of my new colleagues, and I felt completely freaked out by the pile of thick brown patient notes on my desk— referrals all waiting for me.

It had been a few weeks since I had last seen Imogen, but I hadn't shaken her off. She remained with me—I even sometimes dreamed about her. I knew that she was safe, that her stepfather had been charged, her mother was divorcing him and relocating to America so Imogen could be nearer to her own father when the new baby arrived, but I missed that little girl and felt I needed to see her from time to time, to check on how she was doing. Clinical training, with its six-month chunks of placement, felt very brutal, and I vowed not to get too attached to my next batch of patients.

I couldn't believe it had gotten to the point where I felt I needed to be so cut off from my patients that I had started referring to them as a "batch."

I was glad I was in a GP practice. I think the university had felt sorry for me, finishing such a harrowing child placement without the support of my supervisor, and so they had put me somewhere less challenging. I was grateful.

The practice felt more comfortable and familiar than my previous two placements. This GP clinic was just like any other based in a large city: slightly dingy, too small, always cramped with waiting, coughing patients, crying children banging grubby toys, phones ringing endlessly for appointments to see the six overworked GPs. I felt I could do this.

The only challenge, I thought, was going to be seeing Chris again. She had returned to work, and I was trying to pick up from where we had left off without showing her how abandoned I'd felt. I wanted her to see how strong and capable I'd been. I had helped Imogen on my own, hadn't I? But I still felt like Chris had let me down. Being left without her support in a difficult placement with such an unwell child had made me incredibly anxious. It was as though she had dumped me. I was pissed off that she could make me feel so vulnerable.

At the end of my first week at the practice, I went to meet her in the Market Street café near the surgery. It was a bright autumn morning, and the market stalls were being put up all along the street. The windows of the café were fogged up. When I entered, I saw Chris was already there, sitting at a table near the back. My heart was pounding.

Our greetings felt stilted; she was perfectly polite, even pleasant—she was smiling—but guarded. She bought us coffees and then insisted on buying the next round too.

"You look well, Chris. Really well."

She looked down into her espresso cup. "Yeah. Thanks. I feel pretty good."

This was bloody uncomfortable. I didn't know whether to talk about the big elephant sitting on the chair next to us. Chris broke the silence.

"So, I hear you did an amazing job at the end of the adolescent unit placement."

"Really? Who from?"

"I have my sources." Chris chuckled.

"No, really, Chris—who'd you hear that from? I mean, I finished the placement on my own."

Chris frowned. "Well, not on your own exactly . . ."

"Yeah, actually, I think I did."

Shit—I was getting angry. I knew I should just move on and get down to the business of this new placement, but I just couldn't help myself—I needed to hear her explanation, an apology, something.

Sipping my second coffee, I burned my mouth.

"So, where did you go exactly?"

"Pardon?"

"You know, during my last placement. Where were you?"

Chris's eyes hardened. "I believe that you were told I was off for personal reasons."

Blowing into my coffee, I nodded.

"So what else is there for me to tell you?"

My heart lurched. Chris was doing her staring, non-blinking thing. I knew I couldn't face this down.

"No, nothing else. I mean, I just wanted to know that you were OK."

"Didn't you just tell me I looked really well?"

I nodded, feeling sick. "You do."

"Well, then there's nothing more to say." Chris smiled at me, raised her eyebrows and stirred a sachet of brown sugar into her espresso.

I struggled with the uncomfortable silence.

"Right," she said. "Let's get on, then. So, between a quarter and a third of patients who visit their GP surgery have mental health difficulties. But I expect you already knew that."

Bloody hell, this woman raced all over the place. Clearly we'd moved on to business. I was still lagging in recriminations. I snapped into trainee mode.

So, between a quarter and a third of patients who visit their GP surgery have mental health difficulties. I didn't know that; blimey, that was a lot.

"Yes, I was aware of that. Hope I am not expected to see them all over the next six months!"

Why was I trying to be funny here? Why did I feel

like the naughty kid in the room trying to make Mummy like me again?

Chris continued to sip her espresso. "What do you think about the Goldberg and Huxley model?"

Shit.

"I'm not sure I know that one."

Give me a break, lady. I'm only a year into clinical training. I've already dealt with a sociopath and a suicidal kid—on my own.

Chris slapped a brown folder on the table; it was filled with academic papers. "You need to read these."

I saluted. "Yes, boss."

"OK, well, I'm off. Good luck."

What?

"Hey, hold on! What's the plan for this placement? Who am I seeing? What are the problems?"

Chris stood up and looked at the brown folder. "You'll find it all in there." She walked off, and as she reached the café door, she turned. "Shame you didn't think to prepare."

The bell jingled as the door shut behind her.

Unbelievable. This woman had reappeared in my life after buggering off for "personal reasons"; she refuses to give any kind of explanation, no congratulations for my work with Imogen, manipulates the conversation so that I end up looking like the idiot, and then tells me off—in public.

Thanks a lot, Chris. Bitch.

People in the café were looking at me. An old lady at the next table reached her mittened hand over to me and patted my arm.

"Ooh, dearie. I think you just got a scolding. Never mind."

She offered me a plate with cake on it.

"Have some Battenberg—that'll cheer you up."

Fantastic. Placement number three and already screw-up number one.

Sensate focus therapy works from the point of view that sex infused by anxiety requires a systematic desensitization program. It's a stepped, gradual approach to sex that is directed by the therapist and enables couples in a sex rut to retrace their steps, start from the beginning and move forward slowly. The boundaries set by the therapist are deliberately frustrating.

A heterosexual, sexually disengaged couple frantically trying to penetrate when she is tight and dry and he is soft is a recipe for disaster. Martin and Elise were in exactly that position.

The sensate focus program enables a couple to "rediscover" each other sexually. You begin with over-clothes touching and kissing, and you're rigidly forbidden to move on to the next step (over-clothes massage, plus upper-body caressing) without the therapist's permission. The theory is that a couple instinctively want to push against the restraints. But if you hold them back and let them progress to the next stage only with the therapist's permission, they'll soon be on fire again.

In a way, my role was to help Martin and Elise become teenagers trying to get away with what they could do on the sofa at home—to make their sex "naughty" and fun again. I was to be their sex guide, their controlling dominatrix.

All this was beautifully psychologically justified within the evidence-based theory of phobia management. Step by step, I would desensitize them to their anxiety related to sex. But in practice, of course, it was bloody weird to do.

I cleared my throat. "Would anyone like a glass of water?"

They both shook their heads.

I did need a glass, but I felt unable to move, pinned to my seat by two pairs of anxious eyes.

"OK. Let's get going."

Martin shifted in his seat.

"I am sure this feels a bit odd, you know, talking about your intimate, er, behavior with a total stranger, but"—I gave a strangled laugh—"we'll all muddle through."

Muddle through?

"So, Elise, just so that I am clear I have understood what you have told me: You and Martin have been together eleven years?"

Elise nodded.

"You are engaged and getting married next summer?"

Another nod from Elise.

"Congratulations!"

A couple of small, coy smiles.

OK, getting somewhere.

"And, well, it seems that you are struggling with sexual intercourse and want some help to get things back on track, as it were."

Martin closed his eyes and exhaled softly. Elise took his hand and nodded again.

"So tell me a bit about yourselves."

Elise looked at Martin, who raised his eyebrows.

"If you don't mind, Martin, it would be great to hear from you."

Martin went white. Elise squeezed his hand.

"I think I'll do the talking for the moment if that's OK. He doesn't want to be here"—she turned to her shiny-faced partner—"do you, darling?"

He shook his head.

I smiled at Martin; he flicked his eyes away.

"Of course."

"Well, we are both thirty, aren't we, Martin?"

A painful nod.

They've got seven years on me.

"We met at university. We lived in the same halls in the first year."

"Oh! Which university?"

"Cambridge. I was doing English literature, and Martin—you read history, didn't you?"

They're cleverer than me.

I didn't even wait for any kind of response from Martin.

"Anyway, I now work in publishing, and Martin's a—"

Martin sat up in his chair and made eye contact for the first time. "I'm a political journalist."

"Well done, darling!"

Elise beamed at her fiancé; he looked puce. I could barely breathe.

"So, how can I help you?"

Martin began to speak, but Elise cut across him.

"We are very happy, aren't we, Martin?"

No response from Martin.

She carried on. "And very excited to be getting married. And very content with our lives." Elise glanced at me.

I nodded and smiled.

"Sex, however, is a bit of a problem." She gave a small laugh. "Not a massive problem, but one we'd like to sort out now. I mean, we like to do things well, don't we, darling?"

Martin had his eyes closed. This was hellish and so time for an intervention.

"Maybe it would help," I suggested, "if I told you what your GP, Dr. Abrahams, has told me in his referral note." I opened the file. "So, it seems that, Elise, you presented with vaginal dyspareunia—pain during intercourse—which after examination was not found to have any underlying physical cause. And also, Martin, you are struggling with erectile dysfunction and premature ejaculation. So, psychosexual issues that can be dealt with. I am very happy to meet you so we can get going," I finished with a flourish.

The silence in the room was stony.

"Well, that was a beautiful example of a mistimed intervention."

I was on the phone with Chris.

"What do you mean?" I asked.

"What I mean is, a therapeutic foot in mouth."

"Thanks, Chris. I had already worked that out. I need your help here."

Apart from some chomping, salivary noises, there were no words from the other end of the call. I hate people who eat while on the phone; they make me feel homicidal.

"Listen, Chris, before we carry on talking about this couple, I've got to ask you something. I mean, seriously. Why did you walk out on me in the café?"

More slurping. My stomach muscles clenched.

"You need to prepare," she said finally.

"Easier if I know what I am preparing for."

More slurping. I wanted to head-butt the phone.

"You didn't know Goldberg and Huxley."

"So shoot me! Perhaps I was too busy recovering from the abused suicidal child that I had to cope with on my own to be able to switch my head into Goldberg and bloody Huxley."

"You had time between placements to do some reading from the book list you'd been given."

"Yeah, but no one to debrief me after the Imogen situation. For God's sake, Chris, I still haven't let her go. I can't stop bloody worrying about her all the time. You weren't there."

A large swallow, then a sigh. "Do we have abandonment issues here?"

"Sorry?"

"Are you angry with me for not being there for you at the end of your last placement?"

Oh, so she's noticed. Yes, of course I'm angry. But what am I supposed to say?

"Well spotted, Chris. Yeah, I suppose that you could say I am."

More chomping from the other end of the line.

"I mean, I get that we all have lives and stuff, but it

just seems like you disappeared. I was left high and dry, and there was no explanation, no apology, nothing."

The chomping stopped abruptly.

"You want me to tell you about my personal issues?" Chris's voice was icy in anger—I'd never heard this tone from her before.

"Well, not exactly."

"You want me to *apologize* to you?"

I raised my eyebrows and nodded to myself. "Well, not apologize exactly, but at least have some kind of conversation to help me feel less . . ."

"Abandoned?" Chris spat that word out.

"Yeah. Abandoned. You and the university let me down and not only put me in a tough position but potentially endangered Imogen and the other kids I was treating."

Chris sighed loudly. "So you think there was no discussion about how to manage things, no thinking about what would be best for you while I was away. No talking to senior staff at the adolescent unit?"

"Well, given that I'm not a mind reader, I suppose I wasn't able to guess that."

"Watch your tone."

And you bloody watch yours, lady. I took a breath.

"Sorry."

I could now hear Chris drinking, her gulps loud and steady. I wanted to kick something.

"I decided that it would be best to let you carry on with as little fuss or interruption as possible. It was clear that you were working well and engaging with all staff, including the analyst, in a productive and sensible way. I believed in your ability to continue, and I didn't want there to be a big song and dance about my temporary absence."

I was dumbfounded and angry. "Sorry, Chris, can I just get this right? Despite the fact we both work in a profession where we champion open communication and honesty, you are telling me to accept that actually it was all carefully thought through? Just that no one had the decency to include me in the thinking?"

"Yes. That is what I decided. And when you are one day supervising a trainee, you can decide how transparent you want to be when your issues arise during their training."

I snorted derisively. "If I get that far!"

"Pardon?"

"Well, if I decide I want to stick this out and qualify."

Chris paused, and when she spoke, her voice was icy. "And of course if I decide to qualify you."

Now she's threatening *me? Sod this. I'm done.*

"Chris, I want another clinical training supervisor."

A long pause. "So, you're firing me?"

I said nothing.

"OK. I'll tell the university," she said.

The phone went dead.

So I fired my supervisor. This was a good thing, but I also felt annoyed that she'd let me do it so easily. And I still needed someone to talk to—all my girls were away from London, doing their own thing. Rosie was off finishing her degree in Scotland, Megan had a research secondment abroad, and Ali had taken a "career-enrichment" break and was backpacking around Southeast Asia with a businesswomen's collective. I needed a new friend.

And then one found me.

"Hi! I'm Henrietta. Practice nurse. Can I help you with the coffee machine?"

"Oh God, yes, please."

Henrietta turned a gauge and flicked a switch. Soon rich brown coffee was dripping into the pot.

"Ooooh! I love that smell!"

Henrietta, very short and in her mid-twenties, was sweet—and also rather loud.

I introduced myself.

Henrietta giggled. "Hi! And oh my God, I love a clinical psychologist."

"Well, not quite a qualified one yet."

"Oh well, you'll do!"

Henrietta, still giggling, handed me a cup of coffee. I took it gratefully.

"And I love practice nurses!"

"OK. I will make you coffee for the next six months. Relax!"

What an absolute sweetheart.

We laughed and shook hands warmly. Our friendship was sealed.

Henrietta was a star in the rather run-down, drab, overpopulated firmament of a GP surgery. As she showed me around, I began to feel more at home. The GPs were all reasonably pleasant and welcoming; the reception staff was tough and uncommunicative, apart from Mrs. Chatterjee.

"Mrs. C," said Henrietta, "this is Dr. T."

The lenses in Mrs. Chatterjee's glasses made her eyes look huge in her small face. We shook hands.

"Actually not 'Dr.' T yet. Not for a while."

"You should meet my son! He is a proper doctor."

"Gosh. Well done him," I said. "And you."

"I will introduce you sometime."

"OK, Mrs. C. I'll look forward to that." I gently extricated myself, walked into my office and shut the door. With everything else ahead on this placement, I really didn't need an arranged marriage.

Martin and Elise came back for another session. My heart sank, but I tried to be upbeat.

"How are things?"

They looked at me blankly.

You are a bloody idiot. How can things be? Nothing has happened.

"Sorry. Actually, I know there hasn't been any progress because last session was only a 'getting to know you' session." I took a sip of water. "How did you feel after our last session?"

Elise looked at Martin. "You tell her."

Silence in the room.

Elise tried again. "Tell her."

I was confused. "What?" I looked at Martin. "What do you want to tell me?"

He stared at me blankly.

Elise sighed. "He thinks you are too young."

Shit.

"Martin, I can only understand this if you explain to me."

Elise burst into tears.

Martin stood up and suddenly found his voice. "How can you help us? This is really bloody awful. You are barely trained and really . . . come on . . . what do you know?"

Elise was sniffing into a tissue.

"Well, Martin, I know sensate focus therapy and that's what we could work on together."

Now I was wishing I hadn't fired Chris. I could have used her help right about now.

He looked blank.

"It's an evidenced-based approach to managing sexual dysfunction."

Martin spluttered. "Evidence-based?" He shook his head and looked at Elise. "This is bullshit! It's smoke and bloody mirrors. You're not even a proper doctor, for God's sake."

"No. I am not a medic. I am training to be a clinical psychologist."

"And what the hell is that?"

I explained, trying to keep my voice even. "Clinical psychology approaches difficulties from a humanistic perspective. We help people to make positive changes in their lives by using an eclectic range of psychological therapies. The sensate focus approach works from the idea that anxiety that underpins sex is challenged using a step-by-step—"

"Christ. I can't deal with this." Martin rubbed his face. "With *you*. In fact, you know what you are?"

I didn't answer.

Elise sat up. "Martin, please."

Martin pushed his face toward mine. "I think you are a fraud." Martin rubbed his sweaty bald head.

I took a breath; I could understand his point. "OK. Fair enough, Martin."

Martin looked surprised.

"I mean, if you don't feel comfortable with me and the fact that I am still training, then I probably won't be able to help you."

Martin looked at his fiancée triumphantly. "There you go."

Elise buried her face in her tissue and wept.

Martin looked at me, eyes flashing, as he gathered his coat and bag. "Well, that seems to be that, then. Sorry to waste your time. Come on, dear."

Elise didn't move.

"Elise, I said that we are going."

She stayed still.

"Elise? Are you listening to me?"

Elise looked up and wiped her face, which was smeared with makeup; she had wet-mascara panda eyes. "I'm not leaving."

"Yes, we are."

Elise stared straight at her fiancée. "No, we're not."

Martin looked shocked. "I said that we are."

"I know what you said, Martin. I have fucking ears. And I said that I am not leaving." She started to weep again. "If you want to, then you must."

Martin looked furious.

"He does this every time, you know." The panda eyes were now fixed on me. "You are our fifth therapist."

"And she's the least fucking qualified."

"Actually, Martin, I am not qualified at all yet."

Martin smiled at his fiancée. "See! She's not bloody qualified! She's a fraud."

I pushed myself up in my chair and took a deep breath. "Martin, what I am qualified to tell you is that if you continue shouting, I will ask you to leave this office. I can completely understand that you feel angry and threatened by this process, but there are kids and elderly people in the waiting room who will be very frightened by the noise they hear coming from this room."

Martin sat down, blinking. Elise looked stunned.

"I'm sorry," Martin said to me, beginning to cry. He turned to Elise. "Elise, darling, I am so sorry."

She took his hand.

Martin looked up at me as I handed him the tissue box. "Thanks. And again . . . sorry."

"Martin, it's OK. I understand how deeply difficult this must be for you. For both of you."

Through his tears, Martin nodded and gave a tiny smile. "I just feel entirely impotent."

Dr. Jarvis was my temporary supervisor while the university did an internal investigation into the breakdown of my relationship with Chris. I liked Dr. J. He was a leading researcher in memory and a kind elderly man who ate a lot of Garibaldi biscuits.

"So," said Dr. J, "tell me about your caseload."

I told him.

"Good. Sounds good."

"I have a new referral that I'd like to talk through with you."

"Go ahead."

"I don't know where to start."

Dr. J looked sleepy. He raised an eyebrow.

"OK. I have been referred a lady in her sixties called Marion. Her GP seems to think that she is anxious and depressed."

Dr. J nodded.

"She has had some shocking news and is presenting as highly anxious. Before her GP puts her on meds, he asked me to see her, thinking that perhaps she's in the midst of a psychological trauma that I can help her process."

"What's the trauma?" asked Dr. J.

"She has just found out who her biological mother is."

Sweet Dr. J seemed to be struggling to stay awake.

"The irony is that her biological mother lives in the long-stay asylum where I did my last placement—the adolescent unit I worked at is on the same grounds."

Dr. J's breathing was now slow, soft, and rhythmic; he had fallen asleep. Such a lovely and brilliant man, but it was clear that he was not going to be able to support me. At least Chris could stay awake through our meetings. I wanted her back.

I scribbled Dr. J a note thanking him for his time and quietly left his office. On my way out of the university department, heading back to work to meet my new referral, I put a note into Chris's pigeonhole, feeling embarrassed that I was asking her to take me back and afraid that she wouldn't do it.

Marion sat opposite me in my office with her handbag on her lap. She unbuttoned her coat, but didn't take it off.

"It was Angela, my granddaughter, who found all this out. She's the one who discovered that my biological mother was in a mental hospital."

"Found out?"

"Angela found out about this woman. She's doing a genetics thing at school."

"Genealogy?"

"Yes, one of those." Marion blushed.

I shouldn't have corrected her.

"Sorry—carry on."

I hated how my lack of confidence occasionally turned me into an arrogant arsehole.

Marion smiled. "I'm not very educated, Doctor. Sorry."

"And I'm not a doctor. I was rude to interrupt you. I'm sorry."

Marion smiled. "You don't need to patronize me, Doctor."

I felt my foot rammed in my mouth.

"Marion, I have all of your mother's information in here."

"She is not my mother."

"I'm sorry. I should say your biological mother."

Marion nodded and I reached for the file.

"Would you like to know?"

Marion nodded. "Thank you, yes." She took a deep breath. "Perhaps a glass of water as well?"

"Of course."

We went through the file. The first page was a testimony that June, Marion's biological mother, had dictated to introduce herself; with Marion's permission, I started to read it.

As I read, Marion sighed. "Poor woman."

"Are you OK for me to go on?"

Marion nodded.

"'I got here on a hot summer day, a June day, and so that is what they called me and that is what I am known as now. Later on, when they found out who I really was, I refused for them to give me back the name that my mother had given me. I was June Day, and I still am June Day, and when I die soon, I will die June Day.'"

Sixty-five years ago, June, who'd been deemed "simpleminded," had arrived pregnant at the asylum. There she had an illegitimate daughter, who had been conceived when June was raped, repeatedly, by the father of the family for whom she worked and by his sons. Her daughter—Marion—was taken from her, and June had stayed in the asylum ever since.

The file also mentioned a man called Frank, aged eighty-four—June's boyfriend. Frank had entered the asylum as a sixteen-year-old boy, with learning difficulties and epilepsy. He too had spent his entire life in the place. June and Frank didn't want to leave their home; they were resisting rehabilitation.

"Would you like to meet them, Marion?"

She took a sip of water. "No, I wouldn't."

I had no idea what to say.

Marion went on, "But I wonder if you could?"

What?

"Could you meet them for me and then tell me about them?"

This wasn't what I was expecting and seemed an unusual request. I paused to think about it.

"I'm sure I could, Marion." I hesitated. "But how will that help you?"

Her eyes welled up with tears. "I never missed having a mother until I found out that I had one. Now I really don't like how it makes me feel."

I suddenly felt very young and inexperienced. I wished I knew more about Marion's life—her childhood and her upbringing—but I couldn't ask her to share anything she wasn't ready to. I had nothing to say, so I kept my mouth shut.

"You meet them," she said. "Tell me about them. Then perhaps I could meet her with you."

I felt a weird kick of nostalgia driving back onto the grounds of the old psychiatric hospital. It'd been a few months since I was there. I found myself thinking of Imogen, of course.

I passed the abandoned villas. In the distance was the overpass. I remembered running after Imogen in the rain. It didn't feel real.

A group of teenagers from the adolescent unit passed the car, on their way to morning roll call at the school. A few of them glanced in at me as I drove by, but there was no recognition. These weren't the kids I'd known in my time here. It stung, somehow.

It was autumn, and the day was bright and crisp. I glanced at my watch—shit, already late. I drove on until I got to the complex of refurbished villas. The elderly long-stay residents here were the opposite of the kids I'd just seen. They were completely institutionalized—no "care in the community" for them.

I was listening to "Bohemian Rhapsody." As I pulled up alongside the villas, Freddie jammed and I ejected the cassette. I parked. I am ashamed to confess that even though I was late, I spent time rewinding the shiny brown tape tightly back into the spools of the cassette; I was procrastinating.

To be honest, I was pretty freaked out. I wasn't used to talking to people with mental disabilities. We'd only had a few lectures covering communication strategies. I hated myself for my anxiety. It felt discriminatory.

The place wasn't what I was expecting. It seemed cottagey and homely. I couldn't see any staff, but I guessed that no one wore a uniform, and so when a very kind elderly gentleman came and greeted me, I was relieved.

"Welcome," he said. "How can I help you?"

I dropped my bags and extended a hand. "Hi. I'm here to meet June Day."

He shook my hand formally. He looked about eighty and reminded me of George from my first placement in the outpatient psychiatric department a year ago; I felt safe.

"So good to meet you," I said, "and sorry I'm late. Took a couple of wrong turns!"

"We are happy to have you here safe and sound. I think you should meet June." He took my arm and led me into the body of the unit.

I glanced around at the residents. Some were what I had feared: One seemed to be dribbling, rocking his head from side to side while biting the back of his hand;

another was standing facing the corner and moaning as he hit his head. A shriek made me jump.

The gent squeezed my arm reassuringly. "Don't mind Clive. He gets excited by new people."

"Not a problem for me. I'm happy to be appreciated." My heart was racing.

The wallpaper was a very 1970s brown-and-orange geometric pattern, but fresh. A TV was on, and a number of residents were sitting around watching a bland daytime program.

We got to the end corner of the room and stopped.

"Here's June."

June was well into her eighties and sitting in a chintzy chair with what looked like doilies draped over the armrests; one of her legs, which looked rather edematous, was propped up on a matching chintz footstool and clad in a skin-colored stocking.

Her voice was soft and croaky. "Who's that, Frank?"

"She's come to talk to us. New."

"Hello, dear." June patted the seat next to her. "Please do sit down."

I sat.

"Frank, some tea, please," June said.

Frank did another small nod of his head and went off, I presumed, to make tea. Shit, that was Frank, the boyfriend. I didn't know what to say.

"Well, you are very pretty."

"Thank you, June."

"We like pretty."

Then there was a very, very long nonconversational pause as June smiled and stared at me.

Frank brought the tea on a tray. It was beautifully presented under a tea cozy, with patterned cups and saucers.

"June," I asked, "shall I be Mother?"

"Yes, dear. Yes, please be Mother."

June and Frank turned out to be wonderful company and they told me everything.

As I knew, Frank was eighty-four and had been admitted to the hospital at age sixteen. That made sixty-eight years, but he was proud of those sixty-eight years.

"They thought you were the devil, didn't they, Frank?"

He nodded.

"They thought he was possessed!" June smiled and winked at me. "Tell her what you do here, Frank." June didn't give Frank time to speak. "I run this ward, but Frank runs the whole hospital, don't you, Frank?"

Frank gave a small nod and went a little pink.

June winked at me again. "What do you do, Frank?"

Frank said nothing.

"Shall I tell her what you do, Frank?"

Frank nodded.

"You deliver the post to the whole hospital, don't you, Frank?"

Frank nodded again.

I took a sip of tea from the dainty bone-china cup.

"How long have you been here, June?"

June cackled. "Forever, my dear. I have been here from the beginning."

I took another sip of tea. "Do you think you could tell me about how you came to be here, June?"

June looked at Frank. Once again Frank gave a slight nod.

"No one knew my name, because when I arrived

here, I wouldn't speak to anyone. I had been sent here because I was going to have a baby and so I was a fallen woman. I was pregnant because while I was a kitchen maid not far from here in a large house, I had been forced against my will to have relations with the man of the house and his sons. I wasn't the only girl who was forced regularly, but I was the one that had a baby. I was the unlucky one.

"I got here on a hot summer day, a June day, and so that is what they called me and that is what I am known as now. Later on, when they found out who I really was, I refused for them to give me back the name that my mother had given me. I was June Day, and I still am June Day, and when I die soon, I will die June Day."

I knew those words. They were exactly the same as those in the testimonial in her file. She was well rehearsed.

"June, I wanted to talk to you about your daughter."

"Yes, dear?"

"I was wondering whether you wanted to know more about her." I anxiously clutched the bone-china cup in my hand.

"No, thank you, dear."

I was stunned but felt I should try again. "June, you have been told about your daughter, haven't you? That she knows who you are?"

June stared at me and nodded.

"In fact, it was her granddaughter—your great-granddaughter—who traced you via a school project looking at family trees."

June smiled at me.

"I've met your daughter, June. Would you like me to tell you about her?"

June shook her head. "No, thank you, dear." June leaned right back in her chair and closed her eyes. "Time for my nap now. Thank you for coming. Good-bye, dear."

Frank turned to me. "Would you like another cup of tea before we go for a walk?"

Later that morning I met a very kind charge nurse who explained to me that he and other staff had spent a lot of time with June talking about her daughter and that June was adamant that she was not interested to know her at all. Afterward Frank took me for a short walk to a sister asylum down the road. Except there was no asylum anymore—it had been decommissioned and replaced with a redbrick estate of new-build commuter homes, each one looking exactly the same.

On the way Frank told me the history of his home for the last sixty-eight years. Even though I'd spent six months here, I'd never heard it before.

The asylum had opened in 1922 on the site of a Victorian manor house where there were airplane hangars. The airfield was abandoned after the First World War and nine male "lunatics" were sent there and given the job of setting up their own home by converting the hangars into wards. Frank, just a teenager, was one of the "lunatics."

Soon more male patients joined the site and more buildings were built. Dormitory blocks were erected alongside sports fields and a tennis court, a large recreational hall and nurses' accommodation. The site operated around a working farm with chickens, pigs and dairy cattle. The residents worked the farmlands, as well as operating the workshops, laundry, sewing rooms and kitchens. Here was a self-sufficient community where everyone had a role and felt they were part of something.

Women were eventually brought into the hospital, and so the site was segregated to accommodate the sexes and keep them apart. After the Second World War and with the formation of the new National Health Service, the "colony," as it was now called, expanded, and by the 1950s there were almost 1,500 residents. Male nurses joined the workforce, and an indoor swimming pool was built.

The "abnormal" were separated from the "normal" and they became their own distinct community. Sadly, due to urban expansion, the place soon became a dumping ground: Villages no longer existed, and the large towns that were being created had no interest in supporting their most vulnerable. Communities no longer looked after the "village idiot" because there were no longer any village communities. The asylum soon became over-crowded. Frank told me that in the male dormitories the beds were so close together that a person could ride a bicycle across them, and patients were dying because nurses simply could not reach them in an emergency.

Then in 1961 Enoch Powell gave his famous "Water Tower" speech, in which he questioned the efficacy of large institutions because they were expensive and over-crowded. Get patients out of the asylum and back into mainstream society, he declared, and the notion of "care in the community" was born, which Margaret Thatcher famously brought into effect in the 1980s.

It's a nice idea: ideologically sound but so ridiculously

unworkable. After so many years of segregating the "lunatics" from the rest of society, where was the community who would welcome these "social lepers" back with open arms and care for them again?

It was all about deinstitutionalization: Patients were put on "social skills" programs in order to one day blend back into the community—a community that just did not bloody care and was frightened by and intolerant of difference.

Our walk stopped as we reached the redbrick estate that had been built on the site of the sister asylum. Frank looked into the distance, and as I followed his gaze, I saw a person, head bowed, shuffling into the estate.

"Who's that, Frank?"

"That's his home."

I watched the small figure shuffle toward a house.

"I don't understand."

Frank said nothing and so for a long time we stood still and watched. And then the sirens wailed and the blues and twos came and scooped up the small figure and drove off.

Frank looked at me and shook his head. He didn't seem to want to talk about what we'd just seen.

Later I was told by the charge nurse on June and Frank's ward that the stooped, wandering figure was an ex-resident who made a regular pilgrimage to where he had once lived before the asylum had been demolished. Every time he returned to what he considered to be his home, he was taken away by the police, who were summoned by the anxious housewives living in the new redbrick estate.

As we walked away, Frank simply said, "This was our community."

I had a six p.m. meeting booked with Chris in my office and I was nervous. Two more patient sessions before her: my sensate focus couple and, before that, Daisy and her daughter.

Mrs. C. filled me in. "Daisy's child is a monster."

"How?"

"She screams all the time."

"Thank you, Mrs. C. Can you ask them to come in?"

"It's only her. Daisy didn't bring her monster."

"Thank you, Mrs. C. Ask Daisy to come in, please."

The door opened. It was Henrietta with a big mug of coffee.

Oh God, I felt smothered. Maybe there was something to be said for Chris's distant style.

I took my coffee and smiled at Henrietta. A few seconds later Daisy entered, all designer bag and whippet-thin fluster.

We introduced ourselves.

Daisy explained, "I have to get off to Great Ormond Street Hospital to run a charity round table, but I was so happy when Dr. Abrahams told me I could have a session with you."

She gave me her background, speaking at a hundred miles an hour.

"My daughter, Jocasta, is extremely bright."

"So how can I help you?"

"The thing is, she is too bright, and I don't know how

to handle her. My husband is getting very cross with me because I don't know how to deal with her."

"What is it that Jocasta does? Why does your husband get angry?"

"Jocasta is almost seven and knows she should sleep in her own bed."

I nodded. "At her age, she should be sleeping in her own bed."

"My husband and I can't sleep together in the same bed anymore because Jocasta won't let us."

That's one powerful child.

"Daisy, why won't Jocasta let you sleep in the bed together?"

"Because she insists on sleeping in the same bed as me. I have no idea how to deal with it. She won't let me put her in her own bed."

"She won't let you? But she's almost seven years old!"

"Do you have children?"

"No."

Daisy laughed in a "well, what would you know, then?" kind of way.

I plowed on. "Tell me what you try to do to get her into her own bed."

Daisy laughed again. "What have I tried to do? You mean, what haven't I tried to do!" She looked at her watch. "But I have my Great Ormond Street charity meeting in half an hour, so could you just tell me what to do?"

"Daisy, what I need to do is get a baseline."

"A baseline?"

"Yes, a picture of the current situation to measure against. I will give you a simple diary sheet so you can keep some brief information for me over the next week.

That will help me understand the problems you're having settling Jocasta into her bed."

"You don't need a baseline. She simply refuses."

"I still need to understand Jocasta's sleep cues and work out how your behavior might be reinforcing the problem."

I was standing on the safe ground of behaviorism. I was sure about this, but Daisy was having none of it.

"There is no pattern. Each night she simply refuses to get into her bed."

We were playing slightly tense verbal ping-pong. I needed another approach.

"OK. So what do you do?"

Daisy sighed. "She refuses. I try to get her into her bed, but she just screams, and so I have to put her into my bed and lie next her until she falls asleep. I get out, go downstairs, have a bit of an evening. Two hours later I have to come back to my bed and sleep with her, because otherwise she will be up all night screaming at me. That is your baseline."

Daisy glanced at her glittering watch and smiled brightly. "Well, we now have twenty-five minutes for you to tell me what to do. I just want to be a good mother, you know. My daughter really does need to sleep in her own bed."

"Daisy, I still need to understand the nuances of Jocasta's behavior. You've given me a summary. The devil is in the details!"

"There are no nuances. Like her father, Jocasta does not do nuances. Jocasta does what she wants to do and she will not go to bed." She paused and took a breath. "Please just tell me how to make her go to her bed and sleep in it all night."

The atmosphere in the room altered and her eyes began to glisten.

I pushed a box of tissues across the desk to her. She furrowed her brow and shook her head.

"Daisy, how much do you want Jocasta to sleep in her own bed?"

"Very much."

"Then it would really help this process if you could just keep a baseline diary for me for one week of all the ways in which you try to get Jocasta into bed. When and how she wakes, what you do then, including all the times you try to get her back to bed—once I understand all the ways in which you and your husband behave around bedtime in your household, I can then help you."

Daisy closed her eyes. "My husband? My husband has nothing to do with bedtime, except when he shouts at me for being a poor mother." Daisy opened her eyes and sniffed.

OK.

"Daisy, do you think this could be part of the problem?"

Daisy grabbed the diary sheet and stuffed it into her bag. "I'm sure it is, but that's not what I'm here for. So I'll keep your baseline and make an appointment to see you next week on my way out. I really do have to go now."

Hold on!

"Wait! Daisy, we still have time to talk. I am concerned that there are other issues underlying the problem. Bigger issues, perhaps concerning how you and your husband parent Jocasta."

Daisy stood up. "Yes, there are. That's why I'm doing

this on the bloody NHS. I don't want him to know that I am here. He'd find out if I saw someone privately. So, look, I have to go. I'll see you next week." Daisy extended her hand and gave me a smile. "Thank you for your time. Sorry to leave early, but charity calls!"

And she was off.

I banged my head on my desk slowly.

"Are you all right, Dr. T?"

Mrs. C was standing over me.

I sat up. "I'm fine. Daisy had to leave for another appointment."

Mrs. C smiled. "My advice, Dr. T, is that they take that child into her bed and hold her there until she doesn't leave. She'll learn that her parents are in charge!"

Henrietta popped her head around the door. "Coffee?"

"No! Dr. T doesn't want a coffee." Mrs. C turned to me. "Your next patient is here already."

I looked at my watch; Martin and Elise were early.

"They're early."

"No," said Mrs. C. "Not they. He's here already." She laughed. "Don't tell me. He's a premature ejaculator. They always arrive early for their appointments."

An hour later, after I had finished my appointment with Martin and Elise, Mrs. C told me that Chris had called and left a message canceling our appointment, our first meeting since I "fired" her. Chris said she would see me at work the following morning. No sorry. No explanation.

Great.

As I walked to the Tube, I felt odd; I just wasn't feeling comfortable in my own skin. This placement should have been easy—I was located in a busy, colorful part of London where the local population was diverse in every way, and being based in a GP practice brought nothing too difficult for me to treat. The cases were good. This was "proper" clinical psychology—much more straightforward than Imogen's case had been.

Mrs. C and Henrietta were very sweet, even if they were a bit pushy in their own ways. The GPs were great; referrals were coming thick and fast. But something didn't feel right.

The idea of squeezing into a packed Tube was making me anxious, so I stopped to watch the market traders pack up their stalls. It was an early evening in September. The light was fading, and the thickening cold air seemed to amplify noises.

I listened to the sharp, separate sounds around me: the scraping of metal bars as the awning frames were dismantled, the shriek and scratch of bristle brushes scrubbing at the pavement, the slosh of water around the fishmonger's stall. Voices were calling out to each other; crates were being jammed into the backs of small vans; distinct colors within the overall hum of a busy market street canvas ending its day of hustle and bustle.

Everyone was working hard, and the chat was low and friendly. Cups of steaming tea were being handed around. This was a community.

A few people were picking away at the leftover goods scattered on the curbside. I was sure I recognized the elderly lady searching through the old, unsalable, half-rotten fruit with her mittened hands. She was my friend with the Battenberg cake. But then she stood up, gently holding a bruised orange and an avocado half split out of its soft skin, and I realized I was wrong, I had never seen that face before.

I felt sad looking at her with her scavenged goods. Who was she? Where had she come from? Was she happy having to finding her next meal among the discarded leftovers? Was she an eco warrior or a woman reduced by poverty to searching for her food among waste? I felt desperate to know her story.

As I looked around, I noticed many other shadowy figures poking through the curbside detritus before the waste collectors came to remove the bounty. I wondered about them all.

When I was a child, my mother would constantly exclaim, "Darling, it's rude to stare!" I didn't understand that, because with the magical thinking of a child, I didn't think the people I'd been staring at had noticed me watching them; I was invisible.

It was getting cold, but I couldn't face the Tube yet. I felt both mesmerized and comforted by what was going on around me: a community, a network, a series of relationships united by a common goal. Each stall out to make its own profits but working with others to create the market atmosphere, to keep the tradition going. Stalls being run by the children, and grandchildren, of the original stall holders.

All so connected, and then further within the network, almost disguised and unseen but so very present, there were those tolerated as they scavenged, those who were linked to the community but were units separate and alone.

And then it all came together. I suddenly realized what I was feeling.

I was lonely.

My skin tingled. I thought about the three cases that were really challenging me.

Martin and Elise, so in love and happy in every way. "We like to do things well," she'd said, but his behavior suggested it was more complicated than that. Here was a lovely, clever woman wanting to do and be the best in a relationship with a man who was just too angry and passionate to accept "nice." She protected him from his performance anxiety and, in the attempt, dried up. He wanted anything but nice. He wanted raw emotion, passion and realism. That was sex, but it lived too far away from their baseline relationship and the anodyne world of "doing things well."

Daisy's baseline was her perceived failure at getting her daughter, Jocasta, to sleep in her own bed. Her husband had told her she was a poor mother, so the last thing she wanted to do was keep a diary in order to confirm this—especially when she would have to show it to me. The marriage seemed fractious. Maybe fractured? "Please tell me how to make her go to her bed," she had begged.

She wanted me to help her perform in the way her husband expected of her, as the mother at home, but she was a bright woman; she knew what to do. It wasn't rocket science, so why couldn't she get her child out of her bed?

Because the answer, I realized, was that she didn't want Jocasta out of her bed.

Why?

"I just want to be a good mother."

And then lovely Marion—she didn't want a mother: "I never missed having a mother until I found out that I had one. Now I really don't like how it makes me feel."

All of them, in different ways, lonely.

A couple that connected intellectually but intimately were poles apart.

A mother who didn't want to share a bed with the father of her child and so, in order to feel some kind of human connection, was allowing her daughter to share it with her instead. The little girl both comforted her mother and also functioned as a relationship contraceptive for both her parents.

A motherless woman who had created her own family, had always felt loved and valued and then whose life was blown apart by the notion of having her own mother.

All of these stories were about loneliness.

It was beginning to get dark, and the stalls had been packed away.

My parents lived hundreds of miles away in Yorkshire; my sister was doing her university year abroad; Rosie, Ali and Megan were all scattered far away; Chris and I were estranged, and she was playing hard to get.

Life felt very lonely.

The next morning I was drinking coffee in my office with Chris. I was nervous and felt I needed to address the issue of me "firing" her.

"Chris, before we start, can I just say—"

She cut me off abruptly: "No, you can't."

"OK. It's just that I want to say—"

Chris looked around. "Any brown sugar?"

"I'll buzz and get you some."

I couldn't read her. Was she angry with me or just her usual blunt, cut-and-dried self? I desperately wanted to acknowledge our disagreement, but my instinct was not to push it.

"Don't bother—I've got my own sugar. So, who are we discussing?"

So I told her about Martin's chat with me before Elise joined the session the previous day.

"He was remorseful. He apologized for shouting."

Chris was rummaging in one of her large, messy bags. I wished she had just let me buzz for the sugar. "And?"

"He told me it wasn't easy to talk when his fiancée was in the room, and Elise had agreed for him to have some time with me before she joined the session."

Chris pulled a packet of sugar out of her bag. "And?"

"Well, it was awkward. He opened up about their relationship while she wasn't there. I felt like I was betraying her by listening to him."

Chris was trying to rip the sugar sachet with her teeth and failing. I opened my desk drawer and found some scissors.

"Here, let me do it."

Chris grabbed the scissors. "Carry on."

I told her that Martin seemed to genuinely regret his aggression. He told me that he found the whole sex therapy thing really hard, and he meant it. He described his fiancée as a woman he loved deeply but for whom perfection was the required standard. Martin wanted "naughty and dirty," whereas Elise struggled with spontaneous unpredictability, and so her perfectionism caused him performance anxiety, leaving them both feeling as if they had "failed"—an impossible place to be for high-achieving Oxbridge graduates.

Chris stirred her sugar into her coffee with the end of a pen.

I went on to describe the whole session after Elise arrived. She had entered the room and I could see that she felt relieved to see Martin and me talking.

Chris took her pen out of the coffee. "Okay, she was relieved. But what else? Was she threatened?"

"Elise probably was a little bit threatened too—who wouldn't be wondering what had been said about her while she wasn't there?—but then she kissed the top of Martin's head and sat down. The thing is, it took me a while to stop feeling angry with him."

Chris looked directly at me. "You are allowed to feel angry if a patient attacks you, but then you move on from it. It's their stuff, not yours."

I wasn't sure about that, and I didn't like this part of me that was so quick to judge those I was working with.

Chris stirred her coffee again with the pen and then began to slurp at it; a trickle dribbled onto her chin. This woman really had a problem ingesting liquid, but this time I was so relieved to have her there that it didn't even bother me.

"Sensate focus really did seem like the way forward, but there was something getting in the way, so I had decided to let them tell me about themselves." I handed Chris a tissue to wipe her mouth.

"And?"

"And then they told me about Mickey Mouse and Minnie Mouse."

Chris looked up. I will never forget that moment: I

had startled the Ice Queen. She composed herself quickly.

"Chris, they are Disney freaks."

"Meaning?"

"They are going on their third Disney cruise for their honeymoon."

Chris put her coffee cup down and looked straight at me.

My sensate focus couple couldn't get past first base because they hadn't got their vocabulary right. His was Mickey, and hers was Minnie.

A toe is a toe. An elbow is an elbow. If they were ever going to have a happy sex life, they were going to have to communicate like adults. A penis needed to be called a penis, not a Mickey, a vagina needed to be called a vagina, not a Minnie. That's where I would have to start. Vocabulary.

"And," said Chris, "she needs to stop being his mother and be his lover so he can stop feeling emasculated."

A week later Daisy came back.

She slapped the diary sheet down on my desk. "I can't do it."

The diary told me what we already knew.

"See, he's right! I am a shit mother!"

I gathered my thoughts. "Daisy, is Jocasta toilet-trained?"

"Of course!"

"Does she feed herself? Can she read, write? Does she have friends? Can she talk to adults?"

Daisy laughed. "Yes. All of the above, very well!"

I screwed up the diary page and threw it into my bin. "So clearly she does not have a poor mother."

Daisy stared at me.

"Look, I don't have children and so I am not going to pretend that I can get my head into how tough it must be being a parent at times. But what I can see is that you 'know' how to parent, so the question is, why is sleep training so difficult for you?"

Daisy didn't say anything.

"I think you need Jocasta in your bed."

And then it all came pouring out—she spent the next twenty minutes telling me the story of her unhappy marriage. She managed to get through half a box of tissues.

"I think you will be able to get Jocasta out of your bed when you feel ready for her father to join you there."

Daisy wiped her eyes and nodded. "Then I think she'll be in my bed for a very long time."

"Why do you say that?"

"Because he and I don't like each other very much anymore."

"But how can you learn to like each other again if you have no intimate space together?"

Daisy sighed. "I think he has an intimate space with someone else." She hugged her bag. "And besides, I don't like being alone in that huge bed."

There was the loneliness.

We only had five minutes left of our session and I didn't want this poor woman to walk out feeling broken.

"Let's make a plan."

Daisy rummaged in her bag and pulled out a small compact mirror. "Oh God! Look at my eyes."

She started dabbing powder on her face, and as the mask went back on, we discussed the way forward.

I have always loved libraries. The university library was huge, beautiful and imposing, stuffed full of books, manuscripts and, one day, I hoped, my doctoral thesis—if I ever got around to doing it. Like a child in a sweet-shop, I didn't know where first to run to in order to start stuffing myself full of all the delicious treats shelved around me.

However, that day I had a clear purpose for my visit, so no settling into a small nook and gorging on whatever I fancied; I had to deliver some case report write-ups to the university and so wanted to do research about lone-liness, the theme that was coming up among a number of my patients.

As I walked toward the social sciences section, I thought about my favorite author, Sylvia Plath. Her book *The Bell Jar*, which I first read not long after my grand-mother was killed, was the one that cemented my interest in mental health and my desire to work with vulnerable people.

Sylvia Plath once said, "How we need another soul to cling to," someone to trust, confide in and share our-selves with.

Scrolling through the microfiched records of books related to *The Bell Jar*, I came across a story published in 1892 by Charlotte Perkins Gilman called *The Yellow Wallpaper*. It was a fictional journal account written by an unnamed woman with mental illness. It made me think of June.

Like June's, this woman's confinement and isolation started after she gave birth to a child. Suffering with what we would now recognize as postpartum depression, the woman was labeled as having a "temporary nervous depression—a slight hysterical tendency" by her physician husband, who locked her up in her bedroom in their summerhouse to recuperate. She could not leave the room, and the windows were barred. She was not allowed to read or do anything other than rest, and so she hid her journal from him.

The woman, vulnerable and alone, slowly began to hallucinate, seeing women creeping within the pattern of the yellow wallpaper on the walls of her prison. Over time she began to believe that she was one of them. As her isolation and loneliness increased, she slowly descended into her imaginary world with her companions, and her psychosis set in. The woman refused ever to leave the room again.

I needed to make my search more fact-based. Loneliness can lead to insanity, even to death, but how?

The obvious explanations were there: alcoholism, drug abuse, anxiety, stress, depression, suicide—all caused by loneliness, a psychological pain, a mental anguish that is powerful enough to break biological sleep rhythms, leading to problems with memory, understanding and learning. Loneliness leads to antisocial behavior: Children become delinquent as their lack of social connections makes them hostile and afraid. Lonely children—the thought made me shudder and then led me to reread material about the controversial Harry Harlow experiments of the 1960s.

Harlow, a man who died as a clinically depressed

alcoholic, showed that attachment was fundamental to living. He did it by running cruel animal experiments with baby monkeys that he raised in isolation.

After separating the baby monkeys from their mothers within hours of their birth, he noticed that when put in isolation with the choice of a wire "surrogate" mother with an attached bottle of milk or one that had no food but was covered in soft terry cloth, the babies would spend significantly more time with their cloth-covered mother: Comfort contact was more important than being fed.

A baby monkey placed in a strange environment with its cloth surrogate mother would explore that environment, occasionally returning to cuddle up to its "mother," to feel anchored and safe; however, if put in the room alone, without any form of surrogate, the baby monkey would rock, scream and cry.

Harlow watched his baby monkeys die of loneliness and then went on to do the same himself.

Loneliness kills via strokes and heart attacks: It increases blood pressure and stress hormones, elevates a blood chemical linked to cardiovascular disease and causes vasoconstriction. Social exclusion leads to a decrease in body temperature—literally, a chronically lonely person will feel "left out in the cold."

We are designed for social contact, for connectedness. If we don't have that in our lives, our minds and bodies begin the slow process toward death.

Loneliness is lethal.

The placement continued through the increasingly cold, harsh winter. Having Chris back felt good and I was glad that she didn't indulge my need for a big chat about the blip in our relationship—she was boundaried; it was business as usual.

It took only a few sessions for Daisy to enable Jocasta to sleep in her own bed. We opted for the "gradual retreat" method, whereby Daisy began lying with Jocasta as she settled her off to sleep in her own bed and then over consecutive nights sat farther and farther away from her until the little girl felt secure enough to fall asleep without her mother being present.

A better-slept child and a confident mother meant that Jocasta was much less a monster, and Daisy was better able to set boundaries around all other behaviors designed to dominate and undermine her. At first Daisy's husband didn't like this new, more assertive wife setting boundaries for him.

"How are you both getting on?" I asked Daisy at our last session together.

"Gosh. Well, we are getting on better."

I smiled. "So, like Jocasta, perhaps he is beginning to respect your voice, your needs."

Daisy smiled back. "Let's hope so."

"And is your husband back in your bed yet?"

"He was, but I have had to kick him out."

I looked at the clock; we had only a few minutes left and now this revelation. "Why?"

Daisy smiled again. "His bloody snoring was keeping me awake. He can come back when he's lost weight."

"Crikey!"

"Yes. So he's joined a gym."

Daisy had to rush off to a charity fund-raiser. Before she left, she gave me an awkward hug. "Thank you."

"I'm happy I could help."

"No, I really mean it. Thank you. I feel so much better. I feel like I've got part of myself back."

"Daisy, it was a pleasure."

And it really was.

Meanwhile Marion kept canceling her appointments with me, and the practice policy was that three consecutive cancellations meant off the list.

I tried to persuade Mrs. C to offer just one more appointment, but she was not having it. "I'm sorry, but this is the policy—it is how we work."

"I know, but I think this lady needs one more opportunity to see me, and this time I'll call her to make the appointment so I can talk to her, see if there's a problem."

Mrs. C was not going to budge. "This is what I am telling you. There will be no more appointments for this person."

I had to find another way. It was sweet Henrietta who pulled Marion's notes and got me her address and telephone number.

We spoke on the phone, and a few days later we met at her flat.

She opened the door nervously and ushered me into her small, tidy, cozy kitchen.

"Cup of tea?"

"Yes, please." I blew on my cold fingers.

"I'm sorry I didn't come back to see you. I hope I didn't waste the appointments for someone else."

"Don't worry about that, Marion. There's always something to catch up on."

"Oh good. Sugar?"

"No, thanks."

"I didn't like coming to the practice to talk about this whole business. It didn't feel right at all."

"I can understand that."

Marion opened a tin of biscuits and offered me one.

"Angela, my granddaughter, is not happy with me."

"Why's that?"

"Well, I suppose that I haven't finished her project off for her."

I sipped the lovely strong brew. "How?"

"You know. Genealogy. No big family reunion." Marion opened a knitted spectacles case and pulled out a packet of cigarettes. "Smoke?"

"Not for me, thanks."

"Mind if I do?"

"Of course not. This is your home."

Marion smiled and lit up.

"So, Angela wants you to meet your biological mother."

Marion nodded as she pulled long and hard on her cigarette.

"And what do you want, Marion?"

Marion sighed and rubbed her eyes. "I want that this had never happened."

"What? Finding out about June?"

"Any of it."

"Why, Marion?"

"Because beforehand everything was settled and I was happy."

Marion topped up our teas and told me her story.

Marion was brought up in orphanages and children's homes until she started work at the age of fourteen, as the Second World War broke out, as a maid in a large house in Belgravia. Working there and living in the attic, Marion described happy times when she felt valued and useful and well cared for by the family she worked for.

"Life was simple and I was happy."

Marion had a purpose and felt part of a family.

"And then he arrived."

Reg was the delivery boy who would hang about chatting to Marion as she scrubbed the backstairs. He was handsome and funny, and soon they were courting.

"I loved dancing, and my Reg was a brilliant dancer."

Reg and Marion fell in love doing the foxtrot and the waltz, and when she turned sixteen, they got married. After that life was filled with setting up a home, having their four daughters and running their successful fruit and vegetable market stall. The daughters were now all grown up and married with their own children, living nearby and running the stall in shifts for their elderly beloved parents. Reg and Marion ran the local barn-dance club.

Marion lit another cigarette. "It's all been very nice."

"You've built a lovely life."

"Yes, I have. In my time you accepted what you had and never wanted any more. Nowadays everybody is chasing what they don't have. The past is the past. No one can have it all. I am happy with what I have and accept what I didn't have. That's why I don't want her in my life."

Marion's statement shook me. I'd been so sure that, ultimately, she would want to know her mother. I was clearly from the generation that wanted it all.

"Do you want me to tell you about my meeting with June and Frank?"

Marion shook her head.

"Well, if it would help you, I could tell you what her caregivers think about you and her meeting up."

"No, I don't want to know. Thanks."

I drank my tea. "OK. Why did you agree to see me, then?"

"It wasn't for your psychology. I just wanted to apologize for wasting your time."

"Marion, that's not necessary."

Marion went to top up my tea.

"Actually, I'd better go."

She looked up at me. "I've never had a mother, and I don't need one now."

"That's okay, Marion."

"Is it? Shouldn't I want to know her?"

"Only if it feels like the right thing for you and for June."

"Would it be the right thing for her?"

"I'm not sure. I think perhaps she feels the same way as you do."

Marion looked relieved.

A gust of wind blew against the small kitchen windowpane and made it rattle.

"Will you be all right getting home? It's bitter out there."

"I'll be fine. Thank you. And thanks for the tea."

We walked to the front door of the warm tiny flat.

"One more thing before you go. I was just wondering . . . are they looking after her OK?"

"Yes. June is well looked after."

Marion nodded. "Is she happy?"

"Yes, I felt she was."

"She'll never just appear out of the blue one day—
you know, knock on this door or something?"

"No, I don't think June will."

"Good."

I turned to leave.

"Here. This is for you."

I was handed a large brown bag stuffed full of fruit
and vegetables.

"No, really, Marion, that's not necessary."

"Please. I insist. It's the least I can do after all you've
done for me."

As the door shut behind me, I pulled my jacket together and walked into the wind, having just no idea
whether I had done anything at all for Marion or June.

As I sat on the Tube going home, I thought about my
stupid assumption that they would want to be reunited.
I was the one who was lonely. I wanted to fix that by
bringing them together.

God, I felt drained by not getting any of this right. I
had helped Daisy and Jocasta, but this whole placement
felt so disjointed and odd. I'd had a year of drama and I
think I had come to this placement believing it would be
a rest, nothing too dramatic, perhaps less important,
less relevant.

What an idiot.

I needed a break, but I still had to sign off with Martin and Elise, who, as it happened, were going great guns.

Just before starting the placement, I had visited Rosie,
who had just finished the second year of her second degree and had got a summer job running a theater at the

Edinburgh Festival, managing the season and all of its star acts. I stayed in her overcrowded flat and met a nice bloke who was good at sex; it had been a fun few days.

The main attraction at Rosie's venue was the one-woman show by a well-known dame who had run an English "party house" in the seventies and eighties where sex was on the menu. Rosie told us that this woman was warm and funny, small and frumpy, but hated having anyone putting her body microphone on her: She couldn't bear to be touched. A body-phobic madam, she told me when she met me that with my height and cheekbones, I'd make a great sex worker.

When Martin and Elise appeared in my office, life had started imitating art.

While the earlier sessions with Martin and Elise were deeply embarrassing for them, the later ones—the ones where they took pleasure in reporting back their progress through the sensate focus stages—were more difficult for me. I struggled to manage my embarrassment at their frank disclosures.

After the big session with Martin and then the split chat, they both went off and decided to swap roles. Martin encouraged Elise to be naughty, while she relied on her fiancé to protect her. We then worked on vocabulary and had a hilarious session brainstorming all the words for Mickey and Minnie. After Martin managed to say the word "cunt," we all looked back at our two lists and marveled at how few words there were for "vagina" and how many there were for "penis."

"Do you know," said Martin, "that Hamlet spoke about Cunt-ry matters?!"

Elise laughed and flushed. I felt like a gooseberry.

The systematic desensitization program, though, worked a treat.

Take something that makes you anxious and what do you do? You avoid it and reinforce your belief that you can't deal with it. So you try to deal with it and then, literally, push too hard and too early and fail.

So, take a psychological deep breath. Step back, think and plan. Identify your long-term goal and then break it down into smaller stages.

"Imagine," I said to Martin and Elise, "that you are climbing a mountain. Don't look at the peak, because if you do, you will fall over. Let's plan each staged base camp until we get to the top."

And so we did. Martin, Elise and I built a hierarchy of steps that enabled her to loosen control and get naughty, while he let her lead and took his focus off "the act."

Eventually they got to the climax of the mountain. Thankfully well before their wedding day.

Chris and I met in the Market Street café for our final session of the placement.

"So, what have you learned?"

I smiled. "Well, I've learned that I can't do without you."

"OK."

Not the response I wanted. I wished I hadn't been so sentimental.

"And I've learned that I've got a lot to learn," I added.

"Such as?"

I handed Chris the sugar bowl. "Such as don't discard the people whose problems seem less dramatic."

Chris threw three brown cubes into her coffee. "You did well with Imogen."

What?

"Yes, you did. Well done. But here's the thing—Imogens don't appear in our clinical lives every day."

She was right. I nodded.

"I think you felt alone this time," she said.

I swallowed hard. "Yeah, I did."

"So did your patients. That's life."

Not the response I wanted.

"Lack of drama doesn't mean lack of importance," she counseled. "Don't get compassion fatigue. If you do, then this isn't the job for you."

As I left the café, a small, mittened elderly lady winked at me. I couldn't be certain, but I was pretty sure she'd been the one who had offered me cake a few months earlier. I thought of June and Frank, the dignified Marion and the newly assertive Daisy. And Martin and Elise? I had to push my thoughts of them out of my mind: They were now in a private space where I didn't belong.

I got onto the Tube, and looking up at an animal sanctuary poster, I began to tear up wondering about Harlow's baby monkeys pining for their mother and choosing to die of starvation in wire arms covered with soft terry cloth.

Four

HAROLD AND THE NAZIS

I'd hated Sundays since I was a small child. Before the days of video games, American-style bowling alleys and shopping malls that stuck it to any Christian notion of a day of rest and reflection, Sundays were bloody boring.

My Sundays were often spent wandering aimlessly around the house. My grandmother would be watching wrestling—not that she was a particular fan, but there were only three channels in those days. At some point Mum would tell me to tidy my room or help with the gardening or write in my diary.

My mother was a stickler for a daily diary entry—a reflection on the day: what we had learned, what we could improve on—and every entry had to be finished with the phrase "Tomorrow I must try harder."

Boredom was the Sunday curse of the 1970s childhood. It was elevated into despair by the realization that the next morning meant the end of the weekend and school would resume for another five days.

Having left the GP practice, I was about, yet again, to change gears and was preparing for my next six-month training placement. I spent the Sunday before my next placement wandering around my flat, bored and agitated. And pissed off, actually: The placement was to be with the elderly—geriatrics, or, in PC terms, older adults—a population I had no clinical interest in what-soever. I flicked through TV channels. Nothing at all to watch, not even wrestling.

Viktor Frankl defined "Sunday neurosis." A brilliant psychiatrist who survived the Holocaust, the camps and the loss of his wife, Tilly, Frankl pinned it down per-fectly. He described an emptiness, a void, and the mis-ery that comes from boredom. He described a feeling of apathy, and by God, Viktor was right: "Sunday neurosis, that kind of depression which afflicts people who be-come aware of the lack of content in their lives when the rush of the busy week is over and the void within them-selves becomes manifest."

I just wasn't fired up about this new placement, not the way I'd been about the other three. Discontent de-fined the Sunday neurosis. I was experiencing the Frankl effect.

I told myself that tomorrow I must try harder.

I applied my mascara on the Tube, but I was still really bloody late; also I was totally ill prepared.

With my head bent, I attempted to speed-walk down the long drive toward the large mock-Tudor building where the care home for the elderly was housed. I had been delayed by an early-morning telephone conversation with Rosie, who was now in the final year of her second degree and trying to decide whether to apply to do another degree or join the world of work.

I glanced up to see Chris grinding a cigarette into the ground. She didn't look happy.

"Where have you been? You're late."

"Hey, Chris. How are you?"

"You are bloody late."

Hot, pissed off and out of breath, I swallowed back my impulse to point out the hypocrisy of Chris's complaint.

Really, perpetually late lady? You of the world-famous disappearing act. You chastise me?

"Sorry. Problems on the Northern Line."

Chris wasn't impressed. "And why the ambling? This is work time! Come on, head down, on time."

"I'm sorry. It was a girlfriend thing—you know how they can be."

"Actually, no, I don't." Chris snapped herself around and strode through the large wooden door.

I scampered behind.

Chris was looking really well, despite her abruptness and rudeness. She was attractive, tall and slim, and today seemed even more carefully dressed than usual. I was still trying to work her out, and I guessed that she was probably in her mid-forties. She intrigued me—she'd never mentioned a relationship of any kind, and as there were no rings on her fingers, I assumed she wasn't married. But getting to know her personally wasn't something I felt that I had any kind of permission to do.

Since her time off "for personal reasons," Chris had remained changed for the better—her skin brighter and her green eyes less puffy; even her shoulder-length dark blond hair seemed alive and bouncy. Something else was different, but I couldn't put my finger on it—she was crackling that morning with a sort of restless energy, and not just because she was annoyed with my tardiness.

A few minutes later I was still sweating as I sat down on the chair in the airless doctor's office opposite Dr. Anne Gee, who didn't even look at me.

"Chris, you can probably guess what my schedule is like today—I just don't appreciate being kept waiting."

"Anne, chill out," Chris responded. "What can I say? I was late—bloody Northern Line." Before I could intervene, Chris went on, "And there was no way I was letting her near you until I got here."

The room was tense. I began to feel trapped in a surreal world where two alpha females were rearing up against each other. They continued their quick-fire banter, each trying to establish seniority. They were sparking off each other and they seemed to love it. Being the onlooker made me feel uncomfortable.

The only other time I'd met Dr. Anne Gee, a psychoanalytically trained psychiatrist, had been early in the last term in the support group set up for my clinical training year group. These groups were a nightmare for me. I could barely contain my frustration at sitting and pontificating when I could be doing the same thing far more productively in a clinical setting, with my patients. Against my will, I was expected to "openly share the experiences, the concerns and emotional challenges of training" with my cohorts.

I wasn't the only one who felt that way. For everyone

sitting in the circle of chairs, this was hell. It was all self-conscious silences and endless analysis of one another's footwear, while desperately trying to avoid the glacial gaze of Dr. Gee.

Dr. Gee had a reputation for being cold and analytical. She was neat and precisely dressed with a short dark bob and minimalist makeup. She was an attractive woman, very much in control and impenetrable. So the gossamer white shirt revealing her lacy bra underneath was a bit of a distraction.

She was as hard as nails and as boundaried as hell if anyone came even only a couple of minutes late for the support group. I remember her once saying to me, "So, this is how you would treat your patient? You'd turn up late? You'd make them feel like you didn't want to be there with them? Their distress not worth your punctuality? While ordinarily I'd not permit you to join this group because you are late, my instinct is in fact that you do need to be here." Dr. Gee had turned to the rest of the group. "So how many others of you don't want to be here but are too afraid to show it?"

We'd then spent a whole hour exploring our defenses to being in this navel-gazing circle, each of us wishing we were somewhere else. The group hated me. I hated Dr. Gee.

"So, Harold Samuels, aged sixty-nine and in cognitive decline—what are you thinking?"

I snapped back into the room. Harold Samuels was the first patient I was due to see at the care home, later that morning, and I didn't feel ready.

Chris said, "I'd say we'll look at the neuro angle here first: a definite case for assessment and differential diagnosis." Then she turned to me. "What do you reckon?"

I recovered myself. "Yes, sounds good to me. I'd really like to spend some time with Mr. Samuels and also interview those on the nursing team who know him, if that would be OK."

A frosty, lacy-titted nod.

"Also—again with your permission, Dr. Gee—I'd like to have access to Mr. Samuels's charts."

"Why? What's that going to tell you? You're not a medic."

She was making me sweat. I saw Chris reach for a cigarette.

I licked my lips, tried not to let my voice shake. "Dr. Gee, I'm not looking for medical incongruities. It's just that it would be helpful for me to chart changes in medication and physical function against the changes seen in Mr. Samuels's cognitive function."

"Changes in function?"

"Appetite, sleep, bowel function—those kinds of things."

Chris sighed. "Look, Anne, don't make this any harder than it has to be. I know you hate us clin psychs coming onto your patch, but here we are. And you know what? There seems to be a need for our skills in terms of the ongoing management of this elderly chap in cognitive decline." A long drag on the cigarette and a slow exhale. "What is being proposed by my trainee sounds entirely appropriate. Can we just get on?"

"Indeed we can, Chris. Happy to support the learning of those helpful professions allied to medicine. But would you mind very much taking your cancer stick outside?"

Dr. Gee's assessment of Harold: "Mr. Samuels has only just joined us, although his wife, Sarai, who is suffering from Alzheimer's, has been with us for almost two years. His current functioning is stable in some areas, but it's compromised in others: His short-term memory is becoming poor. For a very highly educated, articulate man, he now seems to have more difficulty finding words than one would predict, even for a gentleman for whom English is not his mother tongue."

I nodded. "How have you assessed the short-term memory impairment, Dr. Gee?" I asked.

"I've done a quick screen using the Mini Mental State Examination, but no specific testing—that's what you're here for, isn't it? But I do occasionally have to reintroduce myself to him. He forgets who I am."

Jesus. No one could forget Dr. Gee. I worried about Harold's brain.

Harold Samuels was sixty-nine years old and an Auschwitz survivor. A retired professional, he was educated to doctoral-degree level. With no significant alcohol issues or depression, he had become subjectively aware of his memory problems: He'd become a little repetitive, was having difficulties finding words and seemed to show some spatial disorientation.

My first job on this placement was to assess Harold

using a battery of cognitive tests and to determine whether he was showing early signs of dementia.

Harold believed that he was following his wife, Sarai, who was already a resident of the home, into dementia.

"Why did you come? Go, go before it's too late," Sarai would warn her husband when he came to visit her in the care home. "They're killing people here. You don't understand."

Alzheimer's had sent Sarai back to Mauthausen, one of the concentration camps in which she had been held during the Second World War. She was reliving the Holocaust on a daily basis.

"You can't approach Sarai from behind," Harold told me when I first met him. "She'll ask, 'Who are you here for?' because she's reminded of guards entering her concentration-camp barracks." Reliving the roundups, selections, starvation, brutality and the killing of her mother and three sisters in front of her, Sarai had become acutely anxious, paranoid and suspicious.

Because her temporal lobes were shutting down, Mrs. Samuels was living on her limbic system: perpetually anxious and hypervigilant to threat, ready at all times to snap into fight-or-flight survival mode.

I read the clinical notes. Throughout their long marriage Sarai had comforted Harold through the flashbacks and nightmares that brought his time in Auschwitz back to him in the middle of the night. She would reassure him, as he feared her abandonment, and lightly brush over uncomfortable moments where he would read anti-Semitism into the innocent comments of others. And because Harold had always found it difficult to stand in a queue or deal with uniformed personnel, Sarai ran every aspect of their lives and their household. Sarai was "my princess," Harold said, and indeed she had been named so, after the wife of Abraham and mother of Isaac in Genesis.

Two survivors. Sarai had been Harold's rock as they built their life together. He had to watch her crumble and slide into dementia. She hoarded food, stockpiling it in her room, and she continually blocked the air-conditioning vent, convinced that noxious fumes were coming in to poison her and her husband.

Eventually Harold had to move Sarai into the care home, where he would come spend every day with her. Her long-term memory was intact, but the dementia ate away her ability to remember one minute to the next.

Sarai would become hysterical when showering: "Harold, Harold, we have to go. This is no place to shower—they are killing us."

And so Harold would wash Sarai himself, standing at a sink, while she tried to put a damp cloth over his nose and mouth.

I put down the notes. My hands were shaking.

When I went home that afternoon, Harold was still very much on my mind. I felt out of my depth. That evening the girls came around and I decided to practice my professional skills on them over a bottle of wine and a number of cognitive tests.

"OK, girls, I'm going to talk about cognitive reserves." Laughter, conversation: No one was taking me seriously.

"Come on. Listen! Tomorrow I'm going to assess an

elderly man who is possibly in cognitive decline an have no idea how to do these tests."

"So is he losing his mind?" asked Ali, freshly returned from her travels round Asia; she took off her suit jacket and kicked off her black pumps. "Sorry, girls, my feet stink."

As Ali went over to rummage through my fridge, I gave them Harold's background.

"But he won't know about it, will he? If his mind is going?" Rosie, my girl who was visiting from university, looked anxious. "I've never known anyone with dementia. Have any of you?"

Ali and Megan shook their heads.

"The thing is, Rosie, he does. These cognitive reserves he still has mean that when he is present in the here and now, he knows that he is losing his mind. And given that he has seen his wife losing hers, he has a sense of exactly what is happening to him."

"You can stop him sliding into that place, right?" Rosie asked.

All my girls, even Megan, the one with the research science background, looked anxious now. Wine was poured.

"You can stop him going into that place if you know he's going there, can't you?" Megan, ever the scientist, was looking for a solution.

I shrugged. "This is dementia. You know how it is, Megan: big clumps of beta-amyloid protein forming plaques in the brain; neurons tangling up like broken spider webs; connections getting lost. The here and now is being eroded, so the brain relives the past. For Harold, reliving the past is going to be worse than brain death."

"Why?" asked Rosie.

Ali passed the wineglasses around.

"It means he knows that he is slowly being consigned to relying on his long-term memory to try to make sense of the world, which in his case takes him back to a time and place so bad that you'd only want to be put down."

I loved Rosie because I could see, suddenly, that she was as afraid as me. She knew that what I had to learn would lead to a diagnosis. When I passed that diagnosis on to Harold, he'd be left with nothing to do but wait to slip below the surface, into darkness.

"Are there any other explanations?" asked Megan.

"Yeah. We're testing him in the hope we can make a differential diagnosis."

"Meaning?"

"I am trying to work out whether this is dementia or delusion or perhaps a B_{12} deficiency or even—get this—constipation."

"B_{12} deficiency?" Megan was in territory she understood.

"You have to rule out all the physiological stuff because physical problems can affect memory. Vitamin B_{12} deficiency would do that. So would an underactive thyroid gland."

"And constipation?" asked Rosie.

"Because being chronically constipated when elderly is so toxic it sort of poisons your brain. The symptoms can masquerade as a pseudodementia."

"OK," said Rosie. "I will be your subject, but let's just *please* find out that all Harold needs is a bloody big enema."

I unwrapped my testing materials and laid them all out on the table.

To begin with, I explained that premorbid functioning— the way Harold's brain worked before the cognitive problems had begun to kick in—had to be established if neuropsychological test interpretation had any chance of determining the extent of intellectual changes caused by a possible organic disease.

So I first practiced the "hold tests" that would help me work out Harold's predementia cognitive function.

"A hold test will help us tap into cognitive abilities that are the last ones, the least likely, to show cognitive decline. This can tell us how a person functioned before the brain erosion kicked in.

"So," I said, grappling for my testing manual—I had no clear idea what I was saying, "I'm going to administer a word reading test because that will test those brain capacities that are the most resilient to atrophy. So, in this test . . ." I quickly scanned the manual to get the explanation right. "Sorry—bear with me . . . OK, I will get you to read and pronounce words that have an ir- regular grapheme-to-phoneme translation; so if you don't know the word, you can't guess it by how you sound it out. What you know in terms of your vocabulary size indicates your IQ."

Rosie looked blank. I took a slug of Chardonnay.

"OK, sorry, I have no real idea what I'm saying here. I'll try again."

Another quick gulp of wine.

"So the thing is, you can only really find out if some- one's brain function is declining because of organic decay if you are able to work out what is called their premorbid level of functioning—how their brain worked before problems started. So what we do is assess their known vocabulary, by using test words that are unguessable. Words they just know, that are hardwired and stored in the long-term memory and the last to be affected by a diseased brain. So, the more educated, the greater the vocabulary, the higher the IQ. Dementia doesn't take that away until the very end. These hardwired capacities are the last to go."

"Come on, I really, really want to help you understand this. Get testing," Rosie said, eager to help me learn how to assess Harold.

"OK, sweetie, let me just set up the tests."

"Hey! No, no, no, if you can be the doc that does the testing, I am not your sweetie; I am your patient! So bloody hell, Doc, please talk to me in a way that feels like I am your patient."

And so I did. My lovely friend Rosie may not have been the most successful of all of us in applied IQ terms, but by God she outdid us all in her emotional intelligence.

I talked to her in a way that felt clinically appropriate and she responded as best she could. That, fundamentally, is how I learned to navigate Harold through the threatening testing process that I was to administer to him the next day.

Harold placed his hand over mine.

"Tell me what you are doing here with this. This testing. What do we have to do?"

I thought about how to answer this.

"Harold, can you tell me what you have noticed in terms of what you are finding difficult for you?"

"My memory is now very poor. I can't always find the word I want. Sometimes my concentration lapses and I lose my way in a conversation. I offend people I already know, without meaning to. They think I don't know who they are, but I do—I just can't remember them."

"Why does this worry you, Harold? Maybe you're tired. You spend every day caring for Sarai."

He looked at me for a moment, with a slight smile. "Sarai loves sharon fruit, and every week I would visit our friend Moshe the grocer in Stamford Hill to buy her some. This has been a familiar route for over thirty years. The last few times I have been to Moshe, I found myself confused about how to get home again."

"Can you describe what happens?"

"It's a familiar place to me, but I get *überwältigt*. Sorry—how do you say this?" He rubbed his tired face. "*Überwältigt?*" Another pause. He looked up at me questioningly.

I shook my head.

He sounded the word out slowly. "*Über-wäl-tigt*. Ah yes. I get overwhelmed. Yes, overwhelmed and feel lost, even though I know I am not. I know to turn right at the synagogue and walk toward the tall elm trees that sit behind our house, but I find myself asking whether this is the synagogue. Are those the elm trees? I even question whether my elm trees are those I see in front of me or perhaps there are others around the corner from another synagogue. In familiar places, and with familiar people, I am feeling lost and overwhelmed."

Harold sighed and rubbed his face hard again.

Überwältigt. Lost and overwhelmed. I shared that feeling with Harold.

"So, Harold, let me get this right. You know what the landmarks are, but begin to doubt whether the ones you are seeing are the right ones?"

The big man took a breath and looked up at me with a kind smile. "Doctor, thank you for trying to make sense of this for me, to give me a rational—how do you say?—narrative. I am sure you are right."

Harold was describing visuospatial disorientation, a key marker in dementia.

"That's what I'm here for, Harold, but please don't call me doctor."

Another smile. Why was this dear man trying to re-assure me?

"So I couldn't get home from Moshe's and so I stopped buying the sharon fruit for Sarai because I would be no good to her at all if one day I got lost and disappeared. That's when I knew it was happening."

The room was hot. I opened my testing case.

"And that's when I began to let her down."

Because I was relatively inexperienced at this job, there would still be words spoken by those I was work-ing with that would punch hard—turns of phrase that encapsulated everything that was so tragic about their psychological difficulties.

I swallowed and took a breath. "I see you care for Sarai every day. How can you feel that you are letting her down?"

The old man said nothing. He smiled and patted my hand again. His actions conveyed to me that he knew that my lack of a relationship, even life experience, meant that I had completely misunderstood the significance of his not being able to get to Moshe's and back to buy Sarai's sharon fruit.

Harold was too much of a gentleman to point this out to me, but his silence taught me a lesson I've never forgotten when I've worked with others in psychological distress. As human beings, we can mostly sweat out the big stuff—it's the smallest changes in function that often have the biggest meaning and cause the greatest despair. For Harold, it was not being able to buy Sarai's sharon fruit reliably.

I just didn't know what to say and so I stuck to the script.

"Harold, I have to test you so we can see how you are functioning at a cognitive level, how your memory is, what you're doing well and where you might be having difficulties."

I hated this job.

I knew from the notes that Harold was a research scientist. After the end of the Holocaust he had repatriated to England with Sarai, whom he had met in an internment camp after the war. Sarai made money teaching German to students, while Harold took night-school after night-school course. He earned his degree, followed by a master's and then a doctorate, and when he qualified, he had an impressive career. Up to his retirement he had run an award-winning research science faculty at a London teaching university.

He was a scary man to assess: He knew assessment protocols; I was just learning them.

"I need to establish the presence or absence of cognitive impairment to provide explanations for misunderstood behaviors. I need to establish a baseline of premorbid functioning and then test your current ability, so I can monitor change. Most of all I want to describe your strengths and needs."

"Misunderstood behaviors? Ah yes, I understand. So now tell me what you need to exclude."

He was used to mentoring his students and now he was mentoring me. This was the beginning of a process that would end with me telling him what we both knew already. I just didn't want to have to do this.

"OK. First I have to make sure that even if English isn't your first language, you speak it well enough for my testing to be valid and culturally fair."

Harold told me that his mother was highborn—from the German "aristocracy"—and he had had an English governess. Harold spoke English better than German—in those days the governess was the main caregiver and Tante Agnes had encouraged him to speak English only.

"It was all 'cup of tea' and 'God save the King!'" said Harold.

We both laughed.

"OK. English no problem. And next . . ." I tried to glimpse my pretesting assessment checklist without Harold noticing. He did notice—I was sure of it—but he played along to save my face.

"Alcohol?"

"Ah, *Alkohol: der Nektar der Götter.*"

Nectar of the gods.

"Aber nur Nektar?" I asked.

But only nectar?

Where had that come from?

"Ja, mein Liebling. Alkohol war nicht zu vergessen, nur zu genießen!"

Despite having a German grandmother, a German father and a decent O level in German, and apart from understanding that he had called me his *Liebling*, his darling, I had no idea what Harold had said.

"My darling, I don't drink to forget, only to enjoy," he explained.

Fair enough—me too. But if anyone had a good reason to want to forget, it was Harold. I made a note on the assessment form.

"OK, *Liebling*. Next?"

I hesitated, so Harold took my list and read it. "You need to ask me if I am isolated?"

I nodded.

Harold looked down and the pause seemed like forever. "Yes, I believe I am. I have no anchor except Sarai, and now she is . . . What do I say here? She is *hilflos schwebend*."

He knew I didn't understand but couldn't ask.

"*Hilflos schwebend*. She is floating away from me. How do you say it? She who is my anchor floats adrift."

He paused. No sound, just a moment. He passed the broad back of one hand over his bright blue eyes. Then he looked back to the list, focused again.

I knew the next question. Is the patient bereaved?

Bereaved? This was a man who had lost his entire family in concentration camps, had watched his wife become another person.

Harold started singing softly:

Wenn ich Dir die Wahrheit sage, meine Liebe,
Meine eigene Trauer ist dein Geschenk an mich
   Trauer allein.

Wilde Leidenschaft um Mitternacht,
Wilde Wut im Morgengrauen.
Doch wenn Du abwesend bist, wein' ich dich weg.

This I knew. My grandmother—she of the frontal lobes on the baseboards, a native German—sang this Kurt Weill song to me and my little sister when we were tiny girls.

If I tell truth to you, my love, my own,
Grief is your gift to me, grief alone.
Wild passion at midnight,
Wild anger at dawn,
Yet when you're absent, I weep you gone.

That night, after I left Harold, I went to Heaven.

In the late 1980s a gay club called Heaven was the place to go. It was all about music and sex, sex and music: a London club that let those who were made to feel they didn't "fit in" feel part of an awesome tribe of belonging.

Rosie, Megan and Ali took me there: They knew what I needed and I bloody loved them for knowing that.

It was a wild place, a place of heavenly debauchery. Beautiful men wanting beautiful men and beautiful women wanting those excellently sexy girls who wanted something more than the sexy boys.

Rosie, with her endless degrees and her immense emotional intelligence, had already told Ali (she of the world of human resources) that she knew that Ali wanted all the girls of the world. There had been endless dis-

cussions about Ali's sexuality, but they were going nowhere and so we decided to do the scene and help Ali be
comfortable in her own skin. And after my day with
Harold, I needed to feel comfortable in mine.

After assessing Harold and knowing the results—
even if I couldn't tell him before I'd scored them and
run them past Chris—I needed to blow my head off. I
needed to be so out of my world that the only place I
could be was in Heaven.

The idea was that we would stick together, but soon
after we arrived, Ali dispatched herself among the
glamour-girl tribe and then we were three. And then we
were two, as Megan, after a disastrous day in the research
lab, drank one too many tequila slammers and needed to
puke onto the curb outside the club. Sweet Rosie went
to hold her hair back and then get her home in a cab. So
then there was only one: me.

I looked at the room: tall girls in sheath dresses and
the occasional leather peaked cap; butch girls being
tough and sexy at the same time; small girls in killer heels
with death-defying stares. I was intimidated, so I escaped
to the loo.

"Hey!"

I turned around as I washed my hands. "Hey?" I said
to a small blond pixie behind me.

"Hey yourself!" the pixie answered.

I didn't know what to say next, so I didn't say anything. The jammed towel dispenser gave me welcome relief from the pressure to respond; I tugged at the roll.

The pixie ignored my towel-pulling and asked, "You
new here? First time to Heaven?"

"Yep. First time."

"Welcome! Let me be your guide!"

She and I spent two hours dancing. She was gorgeous and fun. She blew my Harold head open, emptied it of death camps and dementia.

Debbie Harry filled the room. I danced and sweated. Eventually the pixie grabbed my hand and gestured toward the bar, but while I wanted to party on, I knew that I had to go home—to sleep and then wake to score Harold's test and to then talk to Chris and, I hoped, have her tell me I was wrong in my assessment, that Harold was fine. I said good night. She wasn't happy, but as much as I hated disappointing, I had to go: Harold took precedence over a pixie in Heaven.

I walked across the dance floor, sweaty and tired, and then, on the other side of the room, I saw Chris and Anne Gee slow-dancing. I was transfixed, my magical thinking telling me that while I stared at them, they wouldn't see me. And they didn't, because they were looking only at each other. They kissed.

Dr. Chris locked lips with Dr. Anne, while Dr. Anne pressed her mouth to Dr. Chris's. I was rooted to the spot.

Actually, though, I'm not sure I was entirely surprised; thinking of my first meeting with the two of them, I remembered the crackle in the air between those two powerful women.

Tomorrow I had to tell Harold that he was losing his mind. I needed Chris, my mentor, as a buffer against the world of people with dementia descending into the horrors of their long-term memory that Dr. Anne had introduced me to. I needed her to be truly objective in her dealing with Dr. Anne on my behalf.

Reality was not what it seemed; those you trust to be on your side let you down.

The next day Harold told me his story. He did this because he knew that dementia would turn him into a different person and he didn't want me to misunderstand him. He needed a reliable account of who he really once was. He wanted documentation before he became whatever his long-term memory would make him as it took him back into the camps.

"In dementia, Sarai only wants to save me; she protects me, as she thinks we are living together in Mauthausen. She is kind. She is afraid, but she is still my protector. I, sadly, will be nothing like her." He looked out of the window. "When my mind goes, I will not be me."

"How do you think you will be, Harold?"

Sitting up, Harold fixed his red-rimmed bright blue eyes on me. "I am sorry to tell you, but I will want to kill you and all those who want to look after me."

"Why would you want to do that? You are a kind and compassionate man."

But I knew why, of course. I knew where he would be.

Harold had faced his past honestly and with courage—I had to be honest and courageous in preparing him for his future.

I found myself thinking about another patient.

When I was working with Imogen at the adolescent unit, there was a boy called Paul who had been in the unit since he was twelve. The unit was a fully staffed, medium-secure multidisciplinary team setting for children and young people aged between twelve and sixteen for whom life was so unbearable and challenging that their psychological, emotional, psychiatric and behavioral difficulties made them impossible to contain in the community.

Some of these young people came from the backgrounds anyone would expect to legitimize their desperation—they were poor, unloved, neglected and abused. Others came from backgrounds where their neat aspirational families provided a mask of sanity, until the child cracked and broke open a dysfunctional system. Paul belonged to the first group.

When Paul's milk teeth came through, they were black stumps. The back of his head was flat because he spent most of his early life lying down. No one picked him up or cuddled him. This had caused the soft bones of his skull to become flattened against the cot mattress.

A silent boy who had stopped eating, washing and living, Paul had the appearance of a human being but nothing more. He had arrived at the adolescent unit in a sleeping bag smelling of feces, his eyes tightly shut. He was brought in and placed on the floor of the admission room, where he curled into the fetal position, stinking and silent. He made it very clear that he had no intention of continuing his life. By the time we saw him, he'd tried to kill himself twice. Then he embarked on a hunger strike. I had never seen this in someone so young. None of my more seasoned colleagues had either.

To begin with, before we could even address the what, why and how of Paul's helplessness and despair, we agreed that we needed the skills of the wonderful and nurturing nursing team to coax this vulnerable boy out of his sleeping bag and into our care. These nurses were some of the most incredibly empathic people I had ever met.

Paul was put in his room in his sleeping bag and placed on one-to-one observation. That meant he had someone near him at all times, only an arm's length away. The nursing team would sit by this young man in shifts, day and night, and suggest gently and very occasionally that he might want to eat or drink. None of us wanted him to end up being nasogastrically fed—we wanted him to make that decision for himself.

To begin with, Paul rejected all foods, but he'd drink water. Occasionally other young people in the unit would come past his room and say hello, and we left his door open so he could hear their music and the sound of laughter in the recreation room as they played pool, chatted and watched television.

One day a song was playing loudly from across the unit—I can't remember which one—and Paul started humming in his sleeping bag. The nurse who was sitting quietly and patiently by his side joined in. In time Paul asked what the song was. He was told, and then, after a few moments, he asked if he could be helped to have a shower. Without fuss the nurse called for a colleague and they took him into the shower room. The rest of us, who had studiously pretended not to react when they took him out, stood in the nurses' office and silently cheered and high-fived.

After a week Paul was beginning to join the unit and become a member of our community. While he spoke little and made no eye contact, it was possible to see him smile occasionally, a wonky, reluctant half upturn of his mouth, as he listened to the chatter of the young patients and the staff team around him.

He was a good-looking boy, with thick chestnut-brown hair and deep dark eyes. I found it very difficult to meet his gaze. Having read his history in the many files compiled by social services and other agencies over his twelve years, I knew that behind those eyes was a past I couldn't bear to think about: mother with mental health problems, alcoholic father, domestic violence, physical abuse and abject neglect to the degree that he would often be seen rummaging for food in dustbins near his flat.

Eventually Paul moved out of his sleeping bag. He would allow himself to be washed. In time he began to wash and feed himself, but he struggled to engage any further. So one day we, as a staff team, decided we needed to give him a nudge.

The day had started normally with breakfast, and then Paul was told that he would, after breakfast, brush his teeth and go into the unit school—just to sit and take the community roll call, with no expectation that he would engage in the school day, although he was welcome to sit in the main area and listen to the lessons going on in the rooms around him. I was to accompany Paul to school, sit next to him and be near him until he felt he needed to return to the safety and containment of the locked unit.

Paul and I joined the group of young people and stepped into the sunshine. It was a bright late-spring day and the air smelled of cut grass and roses; I was happy.

Paul walked next to me, his head down as we made our way across the courtyard to the school building. He said nothing.

In the school, Paul and I sat next to each other in the large circle of chairs and listened as the head teacher, an ex-professional rugby player, reassured the young people with his structured roll call and his large but calming presence. Everything felt right.

Each young person acknowledged their name and spoke about their goal for the day. The bright, perfectionist, eating-disordered, self-harming girls and one boy were easily able to set out their coursework goals, and the teaching staff quickly jumped in to encourage them to reduce their overelevated expectations.

The angry pupil-referral-unit kids, those who had been kicked out of school, sat back and laughed at the thought of a "goal." One was excluded back to the unit for a lack of respect, and the others quickly fell into line and managed to find something that they were interested in accomplishing that day.

The sweet and talented psychotic girl with an autistic-spectrum diagnosis rocked and bit the back of her hand while the staff showed her yesterday's drawing and asked her if she would like to complete it. She had sketched most of London in perspective and to scale, but she had still to finish each carefully outlined turret of the Tower of London. She grimaced, shrieked and nodded.

Then it was Paul's turn and we all paused, but only briefly, ready to pass on by him. He spoke.

"I want to do English—to read stories."

It was a good moment, a great moment. The teacher

smiled. I teared up and had to look away. This was what I was training for.

Roll call ended and all dispersed to their classrooms. Paul and I sat together. He looked at me and gave a wonky smile.

We sat in silence as I wrestled with my next move. Other team members passed me, smiling and nodding encouragement, because they knew that this brittle, broken boy was only ever going to make the next step forward toward them if I was there to facilitate that. I was the person he trusted, maybe the first person he'd trusted in his whole life, and I knew I could and would bring him on to the next stage of his recovery. I felt so high.

He was looking at me questioningly.

"Paul, let's think about the next move."

No response, just that smile.

A considered, therapeutic pause and then: "Paul, you have made a big step. Let's make it bigger."

The classroom was quiet. I had the odd sensation that everyone was waiting for me to do my stuff.

And so I did.

"Paul, you are a beautiful, bright boy. You are better than you think you are. You came into the unit in a sleeping bag, wanting to die, and we were worried about you. We thought you were going to die and we would have to do drastic things to you to help you live. But you proved us wrong."

Paul stared at me, unblinking. My heart was racing. This is why I did this job.

"Paul, now is the time to make the next step, and I will make it with you . . ."

I had to reach out to him, to hold his hand and help him learn to take his first few steps back into life.

Time stopped. I went to place my hand on his . . .

Half an hour later I was sitting in the critical incident debriefing. My eyes were bruised and my nose was bleeding. I felt broken.

"Why did you encourage him to go into the classroom?" the now rather scary head teacher asked me.

"I thought he wanted to. The time felt right."

"Right for whom?" The head looked really unimpressed with me.

"For Paul."

"So you weren't aware that the care plan had specifically laid out the first step in his systematic desensitization program to school—sit, do roll call, come back to the unit?"

"Yes, I was aware."

"Why didn't you follow it?"

"We all knew he was ready to join in."

"Who is 'we'?"

"Me, the staff, the other kids."

"No one saw this. No one understood why you did what you did. What did you see?"

What did I see? I saw a boy who needed me. I saw a boy who had never been understood, and I knew I understood him. I thought that he was telling me, with his smile, that he was ready to take the next step.

But maybe that had all been wishful thinking. The reality was different. What I had played out in my head was not what was going on in the school: There was no anticipatory silence. I had dreamed it all up and had seen what I wanted to see as I sat in my reverie of salvation, my rescue fantasy.

"Paul has known nothing but physical abuse. You made a physical move. You touched him without warning and without his permission." The teacher told me off sternly.

I got it: Paul had only responded to my physical gesture of compassion in a manner that he understood. When anyone approached him physically, they beat him.

Paul punched me hard between my eyes and almost broke my nose; this was the physical language he understood. I had expected him to understand mine because I needed him to validate my desire to rescue him.

Paul taught me that my rescue fantasies were my problem. He was my professional salvation. Some people you can't save. Rescue fantasies are just that; they're fantasies.

As with Paul, it seemed that with Harold I had encountered another person I wouldn't be able to save.

Harold's reading test score—the test of premorbid IQ—had indicated that he was intensely bright.

His verbal IQ score, a measure of crystallized "hold" abilities, was provided by two types of measures: the vocabulary subtest for measuring word knowledge, verbal concept formation and fund of knowledge; and the similarities subtest for measuring verbal reasoning and concept formation.

The performance IQ score was provided by two different types of performance measures: object assembly for measuring spatial reasoning and visual-motor coordination; and block design for measuring the ability to analyze and synthesize abstract visual stimuli, nonverbal concept formation, visual perception and organization, simultaneous processing and learning.

Harold's verbal IQ was good, but his performance IQ was very poor.

But it was his memory that really troubled me. Harold's immediate memory, working memory and delayed memory scores were all significantly lower than I had predicted. To add to this, his visuospatial memory was shot.

I met with Chris, who was on time but all out of any kind of compassion. In fact, she seemed short with me, irritated. Had she glimpsed me at Heaven?

"The results speak for themselves. So why the urgent meeting?"

"I just wanted to double-check. It's big news to give and I don't want to get it wrong."

Chris put on her spectacles and ran her fingers down Harold's raw scores, checking them against the scaled scores, which indicated where his results sat among the "normal population" of his age.

"Come on, it's pretty obvious. There is a significant difference between premorbid and current functioning, and the most impaired capacities sit around those we'd expect in an early but established Alzheimer's-type dementia—visuospatial, short-term recall . . . Do I have to carry on? Haven't you had your neuropsychometric testing lectures?"

"Yes, but . . ."

"But what?"

I knew I was wrong to like her at the beginning of this God-awful placement. She defended me against that ghastly bloody woman only because it turned her on—and I had evidence to back that up.

"OK. I'm sorry for wasting your time. I'll leave."

I started to pull the testing papers together.

Chris lit a cigarette. "Stop the tantrum. I'm here, so let's get on with it. Just tell me what your problem really is."

"Look, there's no problem—I'll go. Sorry to bother you."

Chris started smiling as she continued to drag on her cigarette. I wanted to punch her in the face.

After an interminable silence I felt like I was going to explode. "What? What do you want from me?"

She took another heavy drag on her cigarette. "Don't bullshit me with the 'I think I've got my scoring wrong' malarkey."

Malarkey? Who says that? This woman was from another age.

"'Malarkey'?" I couldn't help myself.

Chris smiled again. "Yes, malarkey. Nonsense. Drivel. Rubbish."

"OK, Chris, my malarkey, as you call it, is that I don't want to tell him what the results show."

"Why not? That's your job. That's what you are paid to do."

"It's not as cut and dried as that."

A pause. "Well, I disagree. It is 'as cut and dried as that' because if you don't tell Harold, who will?"

"Why does he have to know?"

"Know?" Chris was getting angry and I began to feel

like a naughty little child. "Know? It is his right to know. He consented to the test because he wanted to know. In fact, given what you have already told me about this man and what his results show, he is way too intelligent to not already know."

I couldn't speak and just sat there feeling red in the face and uncomfortably vulnerable.

Chris seemed to soften. "Look, breaking bad news is never easy, but it's part of the job, and the skill is in doing it well."

"Are you serious? How can this kind of news be broken well?"

"It can be done with compassion, with respect and with care."

"I don't think that I am the girl for that job."

"Well, I think that you bloody well are." Chris mashed her cigarette into the ashtray and stood up. "And next time you want to tell me that you are afraid of what the job is asking you to do, tell me straight. No pretending not to know how to do the scoring. OK?" She picked up her bags.

"No malarkey, you mean?"

"No more malarkey, thanks. You can't pull it off."

Leaving the room, Chris squeezed my shoulder.

Harold was screwed. I had to tell him. I poured us both a cup of strong, thick, fresh black coffee, sweetened as I knew Harold liked it; my grandmother drank it the same way.

He took a sip and blew on the hot liquid. "OK, *mein Schatz, gib mir die schlechte Nachricht.*" He asked me for the bad news. *"Wann wird sich mein Zustand ver-schlectern? Wie schnell?"*

When will my decline happen, and how quickly?

"How about you tell me how you think you did, Harold?"

Harold just smiled warmly; I sensed he knew I was delaying the difficult conversation.

"Well, Harold," I said eventually, "your lifelong abilities are well above average, and your verbal test scores indicate that they are still well preserved. But you did have greater than expected difficulties with tests of memory and nonverbal reasoning."

Harold continued to wait patiently.

"Harold, it seems that you have signs of dementia."

"I knew, *mein Schatz.*"

I felt awful. "Look, Harold, of course I can't say definitively that you have Alzheimer's because this is a diagnosis of exclusion and we need to continue to be vigilant that there aren't other explanations. However, your bloods are normal, you don't drink heavily, your thyroid is functioning well, and so the most likely explanation is that what you are experiencing is because of dementia."

"I'm sorry you had to tell me."

"I didn't want to. I'm so sorry."

I felt like crying.

"I am sorry you had to tell me, *mein Liebling.* I am so sorry that you have found this difficult." He patted my hand and I hope didn't notice me wiping away a tear. "There is one thing more you can do for me, though."

I looked up. "What is it, Harold? Anything you want I'll help you with."

"I want to tell you my whole story—*meine Ge-schichte*—so that you can tell others *wer ich wirklich bin.*"

Harold wanted me to tell others who he really was, so I listened and wrote it all down in a notebook.

After being separated from his family and put into a concentration-camp factory, Harold one day saw his emaciated brother standing behind the barbed wire that separated the camp from his place of work.

"I threw him my watch," Harold told me.

I was confused. "Why was your brother not with you in the camp factory?"

"He was ill before we got there. He had poor lungs and was physically weak. Our father was shot in front of him and from that point I think he stopped caring. *Er hatte keinen Willen mehr.*"

Harold's brother gave up the will to live. Again I felt tears prick my eyes.

"Your mother, your sister?"

"They were sent to another camp and we never saw them again."

And so Harold's story began with a watch—a precious watch given to him by his brother on the occasion of his bar mitzvah. This watch represented everything to Harold: becoming a man, his brother's love, being part of his family, his culture, his religion.

"I kept that watch hidden from them for a long time. They took everything from us—our clothes, our possessions—but I would never let them find my watch. There were times, you know, when my watch could have got me a better meal or stopped a beating, but to give them my watch would have been to give them my life."

From the window of the camp factory, Harold saw his brother standing behind the barbed wire; his brother saw him.

"It was an instinct for me to throw the watch at him. And so that I did."

I waited, pen poised.

"It fell to the ground in front of the wire."

"And then what happened?"

"And then I went back to work in the factory."

"And your brother, Harold?"

"I never saw my brother again."

Then Harold had to do awful things.

He built bridges for his kinsmen to walk over to their deaths into the gas chambers. He sorted cadavers into piles of those with normal teeth and those who had gold fillings, which he was required to extract.

Finally he was sent on a march with feet bleeding from ill-fitting wooden clogs.

Harold told me, "I saw those others die as they fell on the road and I just marched on."

One day, weak from hunger, he found himself in a wood next to a graveyard.

"I stood against the wall. The women were screaming and their children wailing. Men were praying."

Telling me this, he began to rock gently and softly chant.

I knew those words. The Kaddish: the Jewish prayer for the dead. My father had spoken it at his mother's funeral.

Among the terror and the wailing and the prayers for the dead, Harold at twenty-three years old and half dead from hunger and fatigue, somehow found the immense strength to jump over the high churchyard wall and into the cemetery behind.

"I heard gunfire. There were screams. I will never forgive myself for leaving them, but I hid behind a gravestone. Later an SS guard pissed near where I was hiding and I wanted to kill him, but I couldn't."

"Mein Liebling, ich bete zu Gott, dass Du nie dasselbe erlebst."

Harold asked God that the same would never happen to me. I loved him for that, but I knew then, and I know now, that all over our world the same barbaric shit still goes on.

It took me many weeks, a few days here and there at a time between working with other residents in the home, to chronicle Harold's stories as he had asked me to. Some of it was horrific, but similar in a way to what I had already heard from my grandmother and other relatives and, in a more sanitized version, from history lessons at school. But there were moments when I couldn't believe what Harold was saying. Reading about it is one thing; hearing it spoken by a man who has lived it is quite vividly different.

"Toward the end, when I was recaptured and put back into the camp, I became very ill. I had dysentery; I was malnourished, my body broken and covered in sores. *Sie haben mir den Geist gebrochen:* They broke my spirit. Then I gave up and I went to die in the infirmary, where I lay between two others waiting to die."

Harold took a sip of coffee. "You make this very well, *Schatz.*"

"My grandmother taught me. She was born in Hamburg."

And she also called me "sweetheart."

"Tell me about her while I drink."

"Well, she was an eccentric woman—an actress and a model; she was a cabaret dancer in Berlin before the war, before she met my *Opa*. They were Jewish and left Germany in 1937 when she was pregnant with my father. *Opa* had already been married and his first wife wasn't a Jew; she denounced them to the Nazis."

Harold continued to drink and listen. "Were any of your family in the camps?"

"Yes, many. I know about Dachau and Buchenwald."

Harold shook his head. "So what you hear from me you already know."

"Actually, not really. Those who survived never spoke much about it." I refilled the coffee cups. "They said nothing, but many struggled with depression."

We raised our cups to each other.

"Anyway, this is your story, Harold, no one else's."

Then I had a thought. "Children, Harold? Why didn't you and Sarai have children?"

Harold put his cup down slowly. *"Leider keine Kinder.* There were some experiments done in some of the camps and my Sarai was made to be unable to have children."

Christ, could it get any worse? I am ashamed to say I let that information drop without acknowledgment.

"Is your grandmother still alive?"

"No, Harold. She was murdered eight years ago."

He patted my hand. "So you too know of the senseless butchery of one you love."

I couldn't go there. I couldn't let this man become responsible for helping me through my still unprocessed grief.

"How did you survive the infirmary?"

"Ach, I have no idea. My bedfellows would die on either side of me and they would pull them off by their feet and drag them to join the pile of rotting bodies outside the infirmary window. As they dragged them, their heads bounced off the floor. This is a noise I will never forget."

I grimaced, feeling sick.

Harold sensed my disgust. "*Entschuldigung, Liebling.* Enough. Let's get to the end because we are now nearly done. So, the Americans came one day. They rounded up the Nazis, but there were some that were killed, some torn apart by those with enough strength to do so." Harold paused and wiped his mouth. "Some became savages like them."

"But that's understandable, surely, Harold?"

"Inhumanity is inhumanity whichever way you look at it. Somewhere it has to stop."

I struggled with this. If I'd seen my parents, my sister, tortured, starved, killed in front of me and if I'd made it through to get revenge, wouldn't I do it and feel justified doing so?

As if reading my thoughts, Harold asked, "Would you kill your grandmother's murderer?"

I was shocked. I'd honestly never thought about it.

"I don't know." I thought again. "I think if I had had the chance, at the time, when everything was so raw, I believe that I would have really wanted to have some kind of revenge. Perhaps I still do."

Harold placed his coffee cup down and shook his head slowly. "Then you have not accepted what happened. You have not grieved for her loss. You still have too much rage about her killing."

He smiled at me. "Did your grandmother sing this song to you?"

When Harold started singing, I got goose bumps.

Zog nit keyn mol, az du geyst dem letstn veg,
Khotsh himlen blayene farshteln bloye teg.
Kumen vet nokh undzer oysgebenkte sho,
S'vet a poyk ton undzer trot: mir zaynen do!

He paused, opened his eyes and looked at me.

"She didn't, Harold. I don't know what this song is."

"This song is called '*Zog Nit Keyn Mol*'—in English, 'Never Say.' It is written by Hirsh Glick and known as the 'Partisan Song.' It is a symbol of our resistance during the Holocaust."

"How do spell the name of the song?"

"Don't write this thing down, *Liebling*. I just wanted you to know this song."

There was no more coffee to pour, and the day was getting late. My fingers ached from writing.

"So finally the end. The Americans came and we were liberated. They gave us chocolate and good food, which was their kindness, and I believe in response to the horror of how they found us. Many more then died—the rich food was too much for them. Yes, the Americans killed some of us with their kindness."

I put my pen down and closed the notebook.

Why is it that the most highly stressed, overworked, heart-attack-waiting-to-happen people are generally more likely to die when on holiday relaxing than when at their desk? They work like buggery, sleep too little, eat, drink and smoke too much, yet somehow keep going until the day that they can pull on their beachwear, acknowledge their dire need to relax, and then they promptly die on the lounge chair.

This must be a phenomenon; it must have a name.

I witnessed a similar phenomenon take place in Harold. When he suspected he might be suffering from dementia but there was no official confirmation, he soldiered on and compensated as best he could to keep up a semblance of "normal." As soon as the diagnosis was made, his condition acknowledged, his descent into dementia was horrifyingly rapid.

Over the final months of my placement I visited Harold as often as I could when I was in the home and struggled once or twice with having to reintroduce myself to a suspicious man. He found nights difficult and became a real problem for the staff to manage— sometimes aggressive and occasionally violent, he often had to be sedated.

One night I decided to do a night shift and realized that Audrey, the kindly Jamaican care worker, needed to change her clumpy shoes. As she walked between rooms checking on the residents as they slept, Harold heard jackboots. A conversation with Dr. Gee resulted in a change of uniform policy and all staff wore rubber-soled shoes. Harold soon slept again, under his bed.

To compound Harold's deterioration, Sarai was fading fast. She refused food, drank little and gradually lost all bodily function, becoming bedbound.

I started smoking. On my final day at the care home, I sat on the terrace with Chris, both of us puffing away.

"Sarai knows Harold is changing."

I didn't want to tear up in front of my clinical supervisor, so I took a long drag on a Marlboro Red.

Chris, who had turned up early for our final, end-of-placement meeting and had spent some time with Dr. Gee in her office beforehand, dragged on her cigarette companionably and nodded while listening.

"She kept herself functional in order to look after him, I think, but once he moved in and began to deteriorate, she had nothing to save anymore. I think she gave up."

Chris continued to smoke.

"In fact, Chris, I think she gave up when he did, and then he had nothing else to live for, so he joined her by rapidly declining. Now, I think Sarai is releasing them both. I think she is shutting her body down so that Harold will then be released to die as soon as he can."

I coughed. "I hate this job, Chris. I've hated this placement. I want to help people live better. I want to relieve them of their mental distress and free them up to a quality of life—a life worth living."

"Well, good thing you did this placement, because now you know it's not always possible."

I took another long drag. "Fuck you for saying that, Chris."

A tense pause.

Shit—now I've failed the placement because I've dissed my supervisor. Shit, shit, shit, shit, shit.

"Oh bloody hell, Chris. I'm really bloody sorry."

Another pause, another drag.

"No apology necessary," she said finally. "Your sentiment about this part of the training is noted."

Noted? Noted how? Noted as in "You've crossed the line, trainee. I am going to fail you"?

Chris stubbed out her filter. "In fact, I agree with you. Fuck this and all the misery it brings to those you work with and to you yourself."

Then I started to cry.

"You've got to face down the shit and learn from it," Chris said then. "Don't forget, you've managed a suicidal girl—that was a great job, and well done for someone so young and inexperienced. But . . ." Chris lit another two cigarettes and handed one to me. "But after the easier ride at the GP practice, I decided to put you here because you needed to learn that you can't save everyone."

My nose was running.

"Wipe your nose."

I took the tissue that Chris handed to me.

"You did better here than I expected you would—and I knew that you would do well. Despite the malarkey."

We both smiled.

Somewhere behind us from deep within the building a series of shrieks ran out. Someone was running from the SS dogs or screaming as a bath was being run.

The early-evening sun was setting.

"Thanks, Chris."

"I don't want thanks—if you'd been shit, I would have told you."

We laughed and smoked on.

"So, where are you sending me next?" I asked then.

"OK. Next you will do six months in an eating-disorders unit."

"For women who won't eat and have panic attacks over pasta?"

"And men too."

"Great. We'll have nothing in common."

Chris smiled as she began to pack up her bags.

Dr. Anne Gee drove around the back of the home to where we were sitting and beeped her horn.

"Gotta go. Oh, and well done—great placement. Dr. Gee respects you, and I think that's a first."

Chris began to march off toward the waiting car.

"Hey. Thanks—and Chris?"

She turned around.

"You and Dr. Gee?"

Chris rearranged her bags on her shoulder. "You can say 'fuck you' to me, but never ask me about my private life."

And off she went.

I finished the cancer stick and watched the sun dip behind the trees.

Eating disorders? As a woman who, like every other I knew, was too aware of what I ate and how tight my clothes were and constantly questioned whether losing a few pounds would make me feel better about myself, I wondered how I was going to empathize with those making a career out of restrictive eating. I made a mental note to nail my personal-professional boundary on this placement.

That weekend I canceled my arrangements with the girls and sank back into my Frankl effect. I wallowed in self-pity and forgot about the privilege of the job I was training to do.

On Sunday afternoon as I was reading some research papers about anorexia and bulimia, my phone rang.

"Hi. It's Anne Gee."

I was stunned. Soft jazz was playing in the background of where Dr. Gee was calling from.

"Hello, Dr. Gee."

"I just wanted to let you know that Sarai died in the night."

"Oh no. I am so, so sorry to hear that. How's Harold?"

"We found Harold this morning lying with Sarai, holding her, although we believe she had been dead for some time."

My heart raced. "And Harold?"

"He hasn't been speaking. I think he has removed himself from any kind of reality."

"Is he having flashbacks? Is he confused?"

"Nothing. He is doing and saying nothing."

I was stunned, could say nothing.

"Are you there?" she asked.

"Sorry. Yes. Just a bit shocked, to be honest."

"Yes," said Dr. Gee. "It would have been so much better if they had died together."

"Will he die soon, do you think? From a broken heart?"

A pause; jazz still playing softly in the background.

"Physically he isn't anywhere near death. He's a very fit man. And as for dying of a broken heart? Well, that would be the right thing, wouldn't it? But I'm afraid that in my experience that kind of thing mostly only happens in books and films."

I lit a cigarette, breaking my "no smoking in the flat" rule.

"Thank you for calling me, Dr. Gee."

"No problem. By the way, you did the right thing by Mr. Samuels. And for what it's worth, I think that Sarai died as they both wanted her to."

I could only croak, "Thank you. Yes."

The phone call was ending and I was done in.

"OK, thanks for calling to let me know, Dr. Gee."

"No problem. You did a good job. Oh, and Chris is here and asks me to say hi."

And then I had a sudden thought. "Dr. Gee?"

"Yes, I'm still here."

"Could you find the Hirsh Glick song called 'Zog Nit Keyn Mol' and could it be played regularly to Harold? I know he'd want that."

Dr. Gee paused. Oh God, I didn't have the energy to argue.

"Yes, I'll make sure we do that."

I put down the phone.

I sat and thought. Sarai died in Harold's arms and so they were together in the way they wanted, in the way they should have been. For all the years of their long marriage, she had guided him through times when he was afraid and unable to cope, yet here, at her end, she gave Harold permission to hold her, to be her protector and to guide her on.

I didn't believe in an afterlife, but I hoped that one day they would be together and free from persecution and fear—certainly that is how they have always lived in my mind.

As I made a pot of strong, sweet coffee and put on my Broadway show tunes CD to accompany my next placement reading, I suddenly felt so perversely happy that

Sarai died when she chose, with dignity, being held by the wonderful man whom she loved, doing what he needed to do for his wife.

I was beginning to look forward to my next placement. It was a Sunday; Viktor Frankl would have been proud of me.

Never say this is the final road for you,
Though leaden skies may cover over days of blue.
As the hour that we longed for is so near,
Our step beats out the message: we are here!
    "Zog Nit Keyn Mol" (Hebrew: זאָג ניט קיין מאָל)
                                            Hirsh Glick, 1943

Five

THE SKELETON CUPBOARD

An all-girls private school is the best training ground for perfecting the sport of the eating disorder, and by the time I was fourteen years old, a number of my friends were winning the Olympic gold.

"Did you know," asked one, "that you can eat what you want when you want but not get fat if afterward you poke your fingers into the back of your throat and puke it all up?"

We were all gripped. Really? Was it that simple?

"Yes!" she said. "And if we all eat some raw red pepper before we eat everything else, my sister told me that apparently we can work out when we've chucked everything up because the red pepper skin will be the last thing to come up! It's difficult to digest!"

So after lunch we all trooped to the toilets, took up our positions in the individual cubicles and heaved and retched our way to weight loss.

To be honest, I was rubbish at it. A proper coward, I hated being sick. As much as I tried, I just couldn't go through with it. My instinct to pull my fingers out of my throat was stronger than my gag reflex. It felt like almost drowning and then pushing up to the surface and taking a big gasp of air.

However, because we went to the sort of all-girls school where success in everything is paramount, my friends offered all manner of helpful suggestions, and so I armed myself with pens, toothbrushes and even a tongue probe that one girl had stolen from her dentist father. None of them worked for me, but my fear of being a failure made me an expert at fake retching, which, combined with a water bottle poured into the toilet bowl at strategic intervals, reassured my friends that I could do it.

We were the champions!

The problem was that while my friends were all getting thinner, I was staying the same weight. They became suspicious; we were not allowed to fail at anything, not even being naughty eating-disordered girls.

One day in a really boring music class led by the small, round amateur opera singer Miss Giddens, I decided to be properly naughty and so rather pathetically took my shoes off and placed them facing outward from underneath the long curtains in the music study room.

Oh, ho, ho, look—there's a girl behind the curtains. No! It's only a pair of shoes. Too funny!

Miss Giddens was deeply unimpressed; she told us that we were in the top 5 percent of the population and if we were going to prank, we should either make it a bloody good one or not bother.

I was so terrible at self-induced vomiting and pranking. Even before my rather poor A-level results, which definitely did not place me in the top 5 percent, I was already a failure at that school.

To put my suspicious friends off the scent of my poor performance in the purging department, I got into actual sport. I worked out that exercising can get rid of calories as much as puking can, and that strategy worked better for me.

I played for the school field hockey and lacrosse teams and was goal defense on the first netball team. I got fit and ate what I wanted, but sadly never really lost that sense that my school imbued in me: I could and should do better. I was never satisfied with my body and often battled thoughts about what I "should" and "shouldn't" have eaten.

Tomorrow I must try harder.

And so working on an inpatient eating-disorders ward became the hardest and most frustrating of my training placements. I had to put my own "shit" aside and be a success.

Within forty-eight hours of being on the ward, I had decided that I could never work full-time with women who wouldn't eat. There was a sort of carbohydrate-induced panic in the air.

My first day was spent sitting at a table of anorexic young women who were lunching in the most painful and excruciating way. They had to be monitored constantly to make sure that they didn't either fill up with fluids before the meal or manage to secrete their food about their person. Have you ever seen an anorexic girl trying to hide a pea in her knickers? Trust me, you don't want to. Sitting at that table, I just wanted to grab their plates and eat the food for them to put them out of their (and my) misery.

Based in a large London teaching hospital, the ward was huge and bright but seemed to me to be peopled by figures painted by Lowry—little matchstick people, like tiny, lonely islands within a vast expanse of space. To be admitted onto a specialist ward like this, you had to have a body mass index of less than 15, which indicates a body weight that is dangerously low for the height of that body. To calculate BMI, a weight in kilograms is divided by height in meters, and then that figure is divided by the height again. A BMI between 18.5 and 24.9 is deemed healthy. Anything over that moves upward from over-weight to morbidly obese. A BMI under 17.5 would be considered an early indication of anorexia nervosa, and everyone who had been admitted desired and worked re-ally hard to achieve a BMI of 14, 13, 12—even though once you've hit those numbers, your blood pressure is dangerously low, your core temperature drops below 95 degrees Fahrenheit and the body grows downy hair, lanugo, to keep it warm. Basically, you're staring death in the face.

Death via self-induced starvation is hideous, as the brain and organs shut down and open sores leak pro-tein, while, perversely, the body becomes edematous, filling with fluid and leading to weight gain. To see a young person head toward that hideous and painful end of life is truly tragic.

One of the worst staff teams I felt that I had ever worked with ran the ward—the kind of team where meet-ings were always tense because of interdisciplinary rivalries. The doctors were rarely present, the lead psychiatrist was a red-cheeked, purple-nosed alcoholic and most of the nurses, I thought, seemed a bunch of female-hating, power-crazed, mostly overweight women. This was the placement where I saw that we, the clinicians, could easily be them, the patients.

"I am," I had told the nurses, rather arrogantly, "a clinical psychologist in training and would love to take some cases for cognitive behavioral therapy."

"Great, go for it!" they had all chorused as they tucked into the multilayer box of Belgian chocolate biscuits left in gratitude by the family of the last patient to be discharged.

Noting that the staff team seemed just as eating-disordered as the patients, I had shoved a couple of praline chocolate surprises into my mouth and left the staff room.

Mollie did not attend the communal lunches. When I met her, she was too weak to feed herself and too stubborn to be fed. In the end there had been no choice but to give her the nasogastric special delivery, meaning a tube was put up her nose and down her esophagus and into her stomach, feeding her a cocktail of isotonic fluids.

"Watch out for that one," Linda, the ward sister, had said as I reviewed her notes. "She's tougher than she looks."

I'd looked at Linda quizzically.

"It takes a lot of self-control to food-restrict like she does. Mollie may look 'butter wouldn't melt,' but she's got a core of steel."

I was beginning to think that these nurses really didn't

like their patients. I understood that iron-clad control was key to a "successful" eating disorder, but I wondered whether years of working with such young people had left the staff battle-weary and cynical.

Mollie sat up in bed looking paper-thin and fragile. She was beautiful and vulnerable.

"Hi."

Mollie smiled and I saw her skin stretch over every bony contour of her face. "Hello."

Her voice was tiny, and a tear trickled down one of her cheeks. Long arms and thin fingers stayed still by her sides.

I grabbed a tissue and dabbed at Mollie's cheek. I didn't know how hard to dab—she was so fragile I was afraid I'd tear her skin.

We talked.

She was your textbook eating-disordered young woman: fiercely bright and from a well-off, aspirational family. Mollie, who was seventeen, was doing her A levels and on track to get top grades and a place at medical school. She was cheerful and funny and hugely talented at sketching and drawing. Here was a girl who had everything to live for but wanted to starve herself.

"I just want to be tiny. Small."

Mollie helped me understand the anorexic mind. She wanted to be a wisp.

"It's a part of me that I hate but can't control. I want to be happy but can't until I am thin."

"Mollie, wouldn't you say that you are already thin?"

She sighed. "Look at this." Tiny little birdlike fingers plucked at the minutest layer of flesh covering bone. "Look, see that. It is just too gross."

An entrenched dysfunctional belief of breathtaking magnitude; I wasn't sure my cognitive behavioral therapy skills were up to the task of helping Mollie shift it.

Mollie had started to have problems with food at school. What began as a slight anxiety became a full-on phobia of the school lunch hall; the smell of the food would cause her to become dizzy and nauseated, and the sight of the dinner ladies made her retch. Eventually she couldn't go into the lunch hall at all and tried to hide in the library. Once they discovered that, the staff tried to make her take her meals in the nurse's room. It didn't help. The smell of the school food was intensified in the small confines of that office, and just being in there made her throw up. Her parents were called in and she was sent to see the first of many doctors. Three years on, Mollie was finally admitted as an inpatient to this unit.

She leaned her head back against the headboard and sighed. "So many doctors checking my blood, testing for allergies, sticking cameras down my throat."

"Sounds grim."

Mollie raised her eyebrows at me. "You have no idea."

She shuffled up the bed slightly, the exertion causing small beads of perspiration.

"At first, my school was really supportive, but when all the tests showed nothing, they began to get really irritated with me. I remember a meeting with my parents where my headmistress and form teacher seemed frustrated with Mummy and Daddy that they couldn't make me just get on and eat at lunchtime like everyone else."

"How did your parents react?"

"Well, seeing as I couldn't eat at home either, there wasn't much they could do about it."

I imagined the helpless and frustrated adults trying to manage this quietly tough and determined girl who was immovable in her determination not to eat.

"At first I was put on a 'behavior program.'" Mollie laughed wryly. "You know, incentives for eating small amounts, consequences for not—like I was some naughty kid who wasn't doing as she was told and needed to learn the rules."

"Well, isn't eating a fundamental rule of survival?"

"That wasn't what they were worried about."

"Who, your parents?"

"No, the school."

"Well, I can imagine that it might have felt like that, but . . ."

"They were worried about other girls copying me. They said they didn't want my behavior to lead to an 'epidemic' in the school, like I was a contagion they had to control or eradicate."

"'Eradicate' is a strong word, Mollie. What made you think that?"

I could feel her anger. Mollie began to flush.

She sighed and stroked the nasogastric tube lying across her body. "I felt patronized."

"Why?"

Mollie fixed me with her eyes. "Because they were making me do something that I couldn't do."

I shifted in my chair. "Sounds like it became a battle."

Mollie smiled to herself. "You could say that."

"But why? Surely everyone was concerned and just wanting to help you?"

Mollie started laughing, and the laughter became a coughing fit.

When she'd recovered, she met my gaze again. "Help me? How can it be help when you are being forced to do something you can't do?"

I paused as I sensed a battle between us beginning. "You couldn't eat, Mollie, or you wouldn't?"

Mollie closed her eyes and sighed.

"Why the sigh?"

She shrugged her shoulders.

"Have you had this conversation many times before?"

Mollie nodded.

"OK. So how can we have it differently?"

Mollie opened her eyes. "You tell me—you're the psychologist."

Mollie's parents came in every day—her father was loud and charming, her mother well coiffed and reserved. They sat by her bed and held her hands as they chatted about their days and asked her about hers; they loved their daughter. This well-functioning family with such a troubled child confused me.

One bright Friday afternoon, sun streaming in through the windows in Mollie's half of the ward, we introduced ourselves.

"Robert. I'm dad." A firm handshake and a warm smile.

"Good afternoon. I'm Eleanor." A small, thin smile.

"She's my mother."

I drew the curtain around Mollie's bed and pulled up a chair.

"So," said Robert, his voice and size filling our tiny space, "when will you get this little minx to bloody eat?"

Mollie winced. "Dad . . ."

Robert ignored his daughter and continued, "Seriously. I know this wanting-to-be-thin thing is all the fashion these days—our other two girls were the same, but not to this degree."

Eleanor cut in. "Robert, neither Poppy nor Tilly had anorexia nervosa. It's different." She leaned forward and stroked her daughter's tiny hand.

Robert laughed. "Oh, here we go again. Dad just not getting it! Sorry—I suppose I'm one of those old fuddy-duddies of the 'just get on with it' generation."

Mollie closed her eyes and squeezed her mother's hand.

Robert continued, "I mean, surely a label like anorexia, or whatever you all want to call it, just makes it valid and allows a person to give in to it."

"Robert!" Eleanor's tone was sharp.

Robert sighed loudly and sat back in his chair. "Sorry, love. Me being a bull in a china shop yet again."

The silence felt tense, so I decided to jump in.

"Mollie, you've got two sisters. Tell me about your family."

Eleanor shot a look at me. "Surely you've read the notes?"

She was an understandably protective mother of a very ill daughter.

"I have, Eleanor, but I would love to talk this through as I get to know all of you."

Eleanor looked at her daughter, whose eyes were still closed. "Shall I speak, darling? Are you too tired?"

Robert thumped his chair arm abruptly. "For God's sake, love, let the girl talk. Mollie, please answer the question."

With eyes still shut, Mollie spoke. "My eldest sister is Poppy. She's twenty-eight and is a finance director. Then there's my brother, Rupert, who's a barrister. He's twenty-six. Tilly is twenty-five, and she's in the US doing her doctorate in international politics."

Robert patted Mollie's hand vigorously. "Well done, darling."

"Robert. Gently, please."

"It's OK, Mummy."

"So, Mollie, there's quite an age gap between you and your siblings."

Before she could reply, Robert spoke again. "Ah yes. You're our little bonus ball, aren't you, love?"

Mollie smiled and looked at her father. "I am, Daddy."

Robert beamed; he clearly adored his daughter. "Yes, and this little bonus ball is going to be the most successful of all, aren't you, love? My little girl off to train and be a doctor."

Mollie smiled at her father, whose voice boomed on.

"Once we get some flesh on those bones, of course!"

Robert guffawed. Eleanor remained stony-faced. Mollie closed her eyes.

It was feeling increasingly tense in our little curtained-off enclave.

"Robert, I understand your concerns about Mollie's weight, but I wonder whether we need to think past that and consider *why* she is so afraid to feed herself."

The booming voice now conveyed irritation. "Oh, come on. Let's not overcomplicate matters. With all due respect, we've had conversations like this for the last"—he looked at his wife—"how many years, love?"

Eleanor's tone was terse. "Three."

"Yes, three years. We've seen this bloody therapist and that one. Family therapy, Mollie has seen counselors, had outpatient treatment . . ." His voice trailed off, his face red.

"I can understand—"

"No. With respect, you can't. Our daughter needs someone to talk some sense into her and get her eating again. What's it called? Refeeding. Yes, that's it. Refeed her and help her learn to feed herself so she can get on with her life. No diagnosis, just some good old-fashioned 'pull your socks up and get on with it' therapy."

I turned to Eleanor. "Do you agree with your husband?"

Eleanor, a remarkably beautiful woman, stayed composed as she stroked her daughter's hand.

"Mummy just wants me better, don't you, Mummy?"

Eleanor smiled at her daughter. "I do, my darling. And so does your father."

Chris was tucking into a ciabatta. It was a big sandwich. Some of it spilled onto her blouse.

"Bloody hell, look at me! I'm the one with the eating problems!"

I laughed and sipped my coffee. At last the woman was demonstrating insight.

"So, what are your placement goals?"

Goals? Oh shit, here we go again.

"Well, I thought it would be helpful to review what I have learned across the other placements and look at what I need to get some more experience of in this one."

Chris munched on and nodded. "Well said. Also how's the dissertation coming on?"

Bloody dissertation. As if the clinical placements, case study reports, lectures, essays and termly exams weren't enough, I also needed to start my thirty-thousand-word dissertation, which was due at the end of my final year of training in order to qualify.

"Bloody dissertation."

Chris smiled. She seemed in top form. "Yep, but got to be done. Have you made a decision on your subject yet?"

I hadn't. I shifted in my seat. "I've been thinking about studying the treatment of stimulant users in an outpatient setting. I saw a few cases during the GP practice placement, mostly young people, though I ended up referring them to a drug-dependency unit."

Chris raised an eyebrow. "Why the interest? Be wary of choosing something you may not have had much hands-on experience with. You've only one more placement after this and it's not been firmed up yet—it may not be in a DDU setting."

"Drug abuse is so bound up with social issues. I want to study ways to give outpatients extra support, stop them from falling back into old patterns. And rave culture is everywhere. This feels like the zeitgeist. I've done some reading—we don't yet know the long-term effects of all these stimulants on young people's brains, and generally there is no pharmacological alternative." I shrugged. "It feels like territory for psychologists rather than the psychiatrists and their prescription pads."

Chris smiled. "A psychologist rescue fantasy?"

I shrugged. "Dunno. No, actually, a need to get in somewhere where I think psychologists may be the ones to make a real difference."

"Remember, we can't—"

I interrupted. "Yes, I know. We can't help everyone. Not unless they want to be helped."

Chris smiled. "That's right."

"The thing is, Chris, that I think that many do want to be helped, but they have too much stacked against them and also don't know how to accept help. Being cared for is alien to some people."

Chris smiled to herself, into her coffee. "Their choice."

"Don't agree. Most hard-core drug users I've met have been born into poverty and violence. They don't ask to learn to self-medicate. It's the shit they have to grow up with and live with, and it's the one thing we can't help them with."

I took a breath; that came out a little stronger than I'd intended.

Chris sighed and looked up at me. "Be careful—if you see any of the people you treat as victims, then they *will* be."

"Sometimes they are!"

The sharpness of my tone caused others around us in the small coffee shop to look around. Slightly embarrassed, I picked up my empty coffee cup and concentrated on draining its last drops.

"So let's talk about this placement and the goals." Chris paused and took a slurp of her coffee. "This young woman. What's her story?"

"Bombastic 'pull yourself together' father and a reserved mother."

"Reserved how?"

"Controlled. Protective of her daughter. I feel some passive aggression toward her husband."

Chris drained her double espresso. "And the girl? Millie?"

"Mollie."

"Sorry. Mollie."

"Bright, tight and controlling. Talented and self-destructive. Wants to be a wisp."

"Wisp?"

"Yeah, kind of there but not there. Smoke, not solid." Chris nodded.

"The thing is, Chris, this young woman frightens me. She's so intent on her own destruction. And so bloody bright. But she's almost deluded about her body, how underweight she is. I have never met anyone as controlled in my life."

Chris wiped her mouth with a serviette. "What are you afraid of?"

I had to think about that. What was I afraid of?

"That her need and ability to be in control are greater than my ability to help her get better."

"This powerful young woman reminds me of that little girl you saw in the adolescent unit on your second placement. What was her name?"

"Imogen."

"Mollie is powerful like Imogen. This behavior serves a purpose. How's your systemic family therapy?"

Shit.

"I don't know. Three lectures and a workshop?"

"OK. Not enough. So here are the goals for your placement. Number one, get a first draft of your literature review and the beginning of the empirical paper to me by the end of next week."

That was about twelve thousand words, and I'd only

written about a third of that so far. Plus it was Rosie's birthday the coming weekend. I'd have no time.

"OK."

Chris nodded. "Good. Next, I want a breakdown of the stats you are using to crunch your data so we can get that out of the way."

Oh massive shit.

"Chris, stats and me. I . . ."

Chris smiled. "I know stats. Send them to me and I'll work it out."

Really?

"Really?"

"Yeah. You are a clinician, not a statistician. If this is your hurdle, I'll get you over it. I can do stats."

"Well, if you're sure . . . I mean, I will have a viva—I will have to explain my stats to the exam panel."

"I can coach you. Just shut up and trust me. I want you to read the following papers relating to systemic and structural family therapy so that you can get on top of this family and finish this placement with a flourish."

This all seemed too much—it was my final year and I was totally overwhelmed, more than at any other time in the past two years of training. Chris stared at me while I wrote down my reading list and broke into a cold sweat.

The grind of the ward continued. Mollie and I would meet and talk regularly in order to, as Mollie once pointed out, build "our therapeutic relationship." She always seemed to need to be up there with me pointing out the process of the therapy, the psychology of what we were talking about, interpreting my questions. Clearly this was because she was a therapy veteran, quick-witted and intelligent, but it also felt very controlling.

Some days she wanted to debate the ethics of enforced feeding. Then there was the endless curiosity about my relationship with food. Had I ever food-restricted?

"Why," Mollie asked me sweetly, "should I trust you if you feel unable to let me know something about you?"

"How would it help you to know something about me?" I asked.

"Why wouldn't it?" Mollie replied with a smile.

While our conversations were challenging and interesting, I often left them wanting to tell this young woman that she needed to stop talking, listen and accept my challenges rather than throw them back at me. I had an urge to reprimand her, to say I was the grown-up and that's all there was to it. Yes, like her parents, teachers and the ward staff, I was struggling with this powerful young woman.

The following week the girls were given spaghetti for lunch and I discovered just how threatening pasta could be, as I walked into a ward of crying, hyperventilating young women. The nurses seemed barely compassionate; the head psychiatrist was sleeping off a hangover in the ward clerk's office.

It was another lunchtime of plate-scraping and food hide-and-seek, and I briefly considered braiding the cold, congealed strands of spaghetti and hanging myself with them.

But then it was action stations! Victoria, the career bulimic, was doing her after-dinner trick of self-induced vomiting. She was a pro: no fingers down the throat, no trying to break into the toilet or the cleaners' cupboard to hide and purge. This girl just blatantly stood in front of us after clearing her plate of pasta and made her diaphragm and core muscles dance.

"She's off!" cried Linda, and, joined by her other nurses, she tried to hold the heaving young woman. Spaghetti vomit thundered poetically out of Victoria and found its way through the smallest window opening and onto a tree below.

I needed to be with Mollie. Sitting upright in her bed, tube up nostril and down into gullet, she was the only sane person in the place.

Curtains pulled around the bed, I sat down.

Mollie smiled. "What was that all about?"

"A postmeal incident."

Mollie reached for her sketchbook and opened it. "Look at this."

I looked. It was me, perfectly drawn.

"Blimey, Mollie! Why this picture?"

Mollie shrugged her tiny shoulders. "I dunno."

I paused. Was this bright girl manipulating me, or was I just being an idiot who needed to catch up?

"You dunno, Mollie? But you are so bright. I'm sure you know."

Mollie closed her eyes and took a huge breath in. "Well, d'you know what? Work it out."

Feeling stumped by this intelligent, articulate, yet tight-lipped young woman, I was relieved when the doctor and a nurse arrived to remove Mollie's nasogastric tube.

"Good afternoon, my dear," said the doctor.

Mollie nodded, and the nurse smiled.

"So, the day has arrived. Nice steady weight gain— well done, you—and time to get going on proper food."

It was all very businesslike.

"Would you like me to leave?" I asked the doctor.

Mollie grabbed my hand. "No, please stay."

Oh God, I really didn't want to.

"Sure, no problem. That OK?"

The doctor nodded while he looked at Mollie's charts. Mollie went pale, and I started to feel sick.

"OK, Mollie, I'm going to pull out your tube very gently, OK? It won't hurt, but you will feel a tugging and you may cough or gag a bit. OK?"

Mollie shook her head and her eyes welled up.

"Great!" said the doctor. "Let's go."

The doctor washed his hands and put gloves on, while the nurse laid a towel across Mollie's chest.

"You OK?" I whispered.

Mollie looked at me wild-eyed and shook her head.

"Come on now, it'll be over in a minute."

I did not like the jolly bedside manner of my colleague.

The tube was unpinned from Mollie's gown, and the tape securing the tube to her nose was removed. Mollie winced.

"Oh come on, that doesn't hurt!"

How does he know?

As if reading my mind, the doctor continued, "I had this done to me at medical school, so I know it doesn't hurt."

Well, that's that, then—if it didn't hurt you, it won't hurt any other mere mortal, especially not a frail, frightened seventeen-year-old. Arrogant man.

The nurse turned off the suction and disconnected the nasogastric tube, while the doctor pinched it near Mollie's nostril.

"OK, deep breath and now breathe out . . . and out . . ."

The tube snaked out as the doctor pulled it and Mollie erupted into violent coughing and gagging. I had to swallow back my own nausea.

A brisk wipe of the nose and face, a sputum bowl offered and they were off.

"Make sure she sips water, won't you."

"I guess that final instruction was for me, Mollie."

Mollie nodded. "He's a moron."

Soon she was lying back on her pillow, her breathing calming.

"Thanks for staying."

I smiled.

"Disgusting, isn't it?"

I nodded. "Pretty grim."

The sound of footsteps approached and then the curtain was flung open, revealing the arrival of Robert with Eleanor behind him.

"Well, well, look at you, love. You're tubeless!" Robert boomed into the space, and gave his daughter a bear hug.

"Careful, Robert!" Eleanor was poker-faced. "Be gentle, can't you?"

Mollie smiled. "It's OK, Mummy—I won't break."

"That's my girl!" Robert squeezed Mollie again, setting off another fit of coughing.

"Robert, stop."

As Eleanor pulled her husband off their daughter and pushed him aside, Robert grabbed her hand and, squeezing it, said to his wife in a low voice, "Eleanor, you have to let go."

What a multilayered comment.

"So," said Robert, sitting heavily in a chair next to his daughter, "how's she doing?"

That was a question for me.

I looked at Mollie. "How are you doing, Mollie?"

Eleanor smiled to herself.

"I'm doing fine, Daddy."

Another nurse appeared with what looked like a large toddler sippy cup full of thick beige liquid; the process of weaning was to begin immediately.

"Bottoms up, darling!"

Mollie smiled and looked at the cup.

"Come on now, Mols, down the hatch!"

"Daddy, I'll drink it later."

Robert sat forward; he was a big man. "Mollie, you will drink it now."

"Daddy, I . . ."

Eleanor stood up. "Robert, a word, please."

Robert sighed and sat back in the chair, closing his eyes. "No, Eleanor, no 'word, please,' love. Let's just get our Mols to drink, shall we?"

Eleanor was still standing. "Robert, I said I'd like a—"

Robert's heavy hand thumped on the arm of the chair. "Sit down, love."

Eleanor stood still.

"Please, love. Sit down."

Eleanor sat.

Robert sat forward again to address his daughter and took the cup from her hand. "Let me try some of that." He took a sip. "Delicious. A good 1972 vintage, I think."

Mollie let out a tense, strangled giggle.

"Come on, love. Get it down."

Watching this was worse than seeing the nasogastric

tube come out. As much as I wanted to, it felt wrong for me to intervene, as I needed to see this scene play itself out, although somehow I felt horribly voyeuristic.

Eleanor remained expressionless as Robert sat forward coaxing his daughter to drink, and she did. It was excruciating.

"Come on, love, keep going."

Mollie wiped her mouth as she gagged slightly. "I am, Daddy. I'm just not used to doing this."

"Well, the quicker you drink it, the easier it'll become."

I couldn't stay silent any longer.

"Robert, it's great that you are encouraging her, but . . ."

"Back off?"

He was quite intimidating.

"Well"—I laughed—"not the words I would use, but it would be OK for Mollie to take her time here and drink it without anxiety—you know, so she feels comfortable feeding herself again."

"Fine." The big man stood up and leaned down to kiss his daughter. "Darling, I've got to go—business calls. Well done. Keep it up!"

With a nod to me, Robert left the curtained area, patting his wife on her shoulder as he passed. You could have cut the atmosphere with a knife.

Mollie was tired and needed to rest, so I took Eleanor to the small counseling room on the ward. She sat down stiffly and accepted a glass of water.

I knew that I had to proceed boldly.

"Eleanor, I am concerned about you. How are you doing?"

A tiny, thin smile. I felt that I had gone in too fast, too abruptly. This beautiful poised woman patted nervously at her throat.

"Is Mollie doing well?" she asked.

"She is doing better. She has put on a little weight. Independent eating is a good next stage. But how are you?"

Eleanor smiled and patted her pearls. "I'm fine if my daughter is doing well."

Long silence. Eleanor looked intently at me.

I couldn't sit this out.

"She is doing well, but I wanted to talk about how you are doing."

The hands continued to flutter one minute at the pearls, next in the lap.

"I am fine. Why do you ask?"

"I ask because you seem . . ." Words failed me.

Eleanor's hands fluttered again.

"I am concerned you might be struggling and I want to support you."

Hands stopped fluttering.

Again silence. I tried a different approach.

"You have a wonderful daughter. Mollie is so bright and beautiful, and, well, I just love spending time with her."

Suddenly hands were sat in lap. Body upright. Total focus.

"What do you love about her?"

"I love her brain. Oh my gosh, she's so challenging!"

"Yes." Eleanor smiled broadly. "She doesn't suffer fools gladly! She is challenging, always has been, the most of the four."

That last statement felt passive-aggressive. Who thought I was the fool, Mollie or her mother?

"How have you found her challenging?"

"Mollie was born at thirty-four weeks. She wanted to come out early. She was ready for the world." Eleanor took a drink and I noticed that her hand holding the glass was shaking. She continued on: "She was tiny but the most lusty. Oh my goodness, that girl could cry for England!"

We exchanged a smile.

"As you know, she wasn't planned, but when I held her, I knew she was very special. She was my little gift. A tiny present."

"Wasn't she in pediatric intensive care for two weeks?"

Eleanor looked down. "Yes. I couldn't feed her. She was so tiny, and my milk just didn't come in. She latched on, but I didn't produce enough milk for her, and so she lost weight."

"That must have been hard."

Eleanor stared straight at me. "Do you have a baby?"

"No, Eleanor, I don't."

She nodded and smiled. "Yes, that was very hard." Eleanor looked away as she continued. "It was so hard because I fed the other three very well."

Another layer to the story. I made a mental note: early maternal feeding anxiety; eating-disordered daughter.

"You felt guilty?"

Another long, long pause.

"I felt guilty. And I felt old."

"Old? You gave birth to a beautiful little girl. Your body was still . . ."

Eleanor put up her hand. "I wanted her, but Robert

didn't. We were too old. The other three were doing well and so he quite rightly reasoned that there was no need. But I wanted her." Hands patted pearls. "He was too busy for another one, but I wanted another one and so I made it happen."

This felt huge.

"How?"

Eleanor looked at me and gave a small snort.

I reddened.

"I don't mean how, but . . ."

She sat up. "But you mean how. Well, how was, he believed I couldn't and so I duped him. I told him I couldn't and then I did."

"But you knew you could?"

Eleanor took a long drink of water. "Of course I knew I could. What woman doesn't? Of course I could." Her tone changed. "For goodness' sake, what did he know? When was he there to know? For ages I told him I was menopausal because that explained my lack of interest." Eleanor blushed but doggedly continued. "But then I thought I needed another and so I made another happen."

I shifted in my seat. Whose discomfort was I feeling?

"Another?"

"My Mollie. Another one for me."

I jumped at a sudden knock at the door, a reminder of the ward round. I brushed them away. *Shit, the atmosphere had been broken.*

"So what's Mollie's prognosis?"

Shit. Damn that knock. I'd lost her.

"Please carry on, Eleanor. What you were saying was really interesting."

"What's Mollie's prognosis?"

"Why was Mollie another one for you?"

String of pearls clutched. Knuckles white. Voice firm. "What is Mollie's prognosis?"

I was stuck. She wasn't going to answer me.

"Her prognosis based on her developing insight and ability to self-feed is good."

Eleanor stood up. "Many thanks."

And then she left.

Shit. Shit. Shit.

A couple of weeks later I got to work and for the first time noticed that I was actually looking forward to my day there. As I arrived, the ward was alive with music and everyone was dancing—I felt like I'd walked into a big party. When they smiled, the young women looked alive, their hollow pink cheeks radiant with the exertion. Even the nurses were smiling.

Mollie was sitting in her chair tapping along to the music.

"Hi! What's going on?"

She looked up and smiled; her face was filling out and she looked beautiful. "Dunno! Everyone woke up happy."

I dumped my bags and coat by her bed and sat down.

"Are you feeling happy?"

"Yeah, I am. Today when I woke up, I wasn't crying. That's got to be a good thing, right?"

"Sounds like a good thing to me, Mollie."

Mollie looked down. "Can I ask you a question?"

"Sure, go ahead."

"I was wondering. Why did you choose to do this job?"

Blimey, another question requiring me to self-disclose. Do I tell her about my grandmother?

"I guess I'm nosy."

Mollie grinned. "No, really. I mean, don't you get depressed listening to people's problems all the time?"

I thought for a moment. "No, I don't get depressed as in depressed depressed. But sometimes I do feel sad when people tell me about what makes them feel so unhappy or confused about their life."

"Do you ever cry?"

Mollie was looking hard into my eyes.

"No, I've never cried, but I have felt tears in my eyes sometimes."

"That's because you're human."

"I suppose so, and also I haven't been doing the clinical work very long."

"Yeah, but do you worry that you might hear things that will just really upset you and you won't know what to do to help that person?"

"Well, we have a lot of support from colleagues and I have a supervisor who I can talk to about my cases and she helps me think them through."

Mollie looked down. "Have you told her about me?"

"Would it bother you if I have?"

"No. What does she think about me?"

"It doesn't really work like that, Mollie. You know, the whole point about supervision isn't for my supervisor to tell me what to do but to help me with what I am thinking and feeling, and make sure my treatment plans are evidence-based and robust."

"What's her name, your supervisor I mean."

"Dr. Moorhead."

"What's she like? Do you like her?"

Well, there's a question. I paused.

Mollie quickly cut in. "Sorry, now I'm being the nosy one!"

We laughed.

"That's OK. I can understand you must be really curious about us and how we work."

"Yes." Mollie smiled and nodded. "But as you once said, 'How would it help me to know about you?'"

The tea trolley came around and I ordered a strong tea with milk and one sugar.

"I'll have one too, please."

"Way to go, Mollie!"

Mollie gave a small tight smile and in that moment looked just like her mother.

She took a sip of tea. "Am I the most difficult person you've ever seen?"

"Difficult how?"

"I dunno, just difficult. You know, I don't really tell you much."

"Well, we've not known each other long."

"Yeah, I know, but I do like you, you know."

"I'm glad about that because I like you too, Mollie."

She grinned.

The music on the ward was switched off—party over. The girls were groaning, but the nurses were unrelenting, watching for patients doing a little too much exercise in the name of burning off calories.

"So, I was wondering—can we go out today perhaps to a café and have a snack and a chat?"

I was stunned.

"Well . . ." I hesitated; I wanted to give the right answer here. "Do you feel ready for that?"

Another small tight smile. "Of course I do. Otherwise, I wouldn't have asked!"

"Yeah, of course. Good point."

We shared another smile.

"Listen, let me ask the nurses how they feel about it."

"OK."

Mollie went back to sipping her tea and so I gathered up my things and walked into the nurses' office, wondering why, with Mollie, I so often felt like I was two steps behind her.

Ten minutes later, given the thumbs-up to a trip out, I made my way back to her room, where I found her mother. Today Eleanor looked pale; she was trembling. Mollie was looking at her with concern.

"Hi, Eleanor," I said. "Didn't know you were coming in this morning."

"Sorry—isn't it allowed?"

"Well, I think you have to call ahead, you know, if you want to come in outside visiting hours. I mean, just in case Mollie is in a session or something."

"Well, forgive me. Whom shall I sign in with?"

She was slurring her words and having obvious trouble focusing. She attempted to sit up in her chair before slumping back down and closing her eyes. I smelled alcohol.

Eleanor was drunk.

It was barely ten in the morning and she was absolutely off-her-face drunk.

"Mummy, are you OK?"

Eleanor smiled and patted her pearls. "Of course I am, darling. Very OK."

"Eleanor, let me get you a cup of tea."

Eyes still closed, Eleanor started to laugh. "Tea? Tea is not what I need."

This was awkward.

"Coffee?"

Eleanor snapped her eyes open and sat up. "I do not want a drink."

Her tone was sharp and abrupt.

"Mummy! What's wrong? Why are you being like this?"

Eleanor closed her eyes again and sat back into the chair. "Darling, you know I despise stupid questions."

"Mummy, you were being offered tea. That's not a stupid question. What is wrong with you?"

Eleanor wobbled slightly as she sat forward and took her daughter's hand. "Sorry, darling. Was Mummy being rude?"

Mollie nodded. "What's wrong, Mummy?"

Eleanor looked at me. "I apologize for my rudeness. Nothing to drink. Thank you."

I just did not know what to say; Mollie rescued me.

"Mummy, we are going out to a café for a snack today."

"Are we, darling? That's nice."

"No, Mummy, not me and you." Mollie gestured toward me. "We are."

Eleanor opened her eyes, sighed deeply and then pushed herself up unsteadily, wobbled slightly and fell heavily back down into her seat.

"Mummy!" Mollie looked horrified.

I leaned forward.

"Eleanor, can I help you?"

"No!"

The ward fell silent, everyone quieted by Eleanor's outburst.

Mollie, visibly upset, leaned back and closed her eyes, while her mother sat forward, patting her hair and adjusting her pearls.

"I shall go now. Thank you." Eleanor stood up stiffly, looking straight at me. "And of course next time I want to see my little girl, I shall phone to book an appointment. Just like I have to do with her bloody father."

The nurses were closing in as Eleanor staggered off toward the ward exit, but as she got to the double doors, she fell forward onto the ground. Mollie cried out as two nurses and I ran to her mother's aid.

"Please just let me be."

"Eleanor, let me help you."

Eleanor swatted my hand away, and as she pushed herself up off the floor, she caught her necklace and broke it.

As a nurse opened the doors for her and gently guided her out, Eleanor turned to me and pointed her finger into my face. "Just you make sure you get my little girl better. That's an order."

Eleanor stumbled out of the ward as her pearls rolled across the shiny linoleum floor.

A while later I was sitting in the nurses' office having a cup of tea with Linda, the senior nurse in charge.

"You OK?"

I nodded.

"Want a biscuit?" Linda offered me a tin.

"No, thanks."

"Listen, sweetheart, don't feel bad about what happened—you didn't see it coming."

"Actually, somehow I think I probably did."

Linda smiled. "What, you got some crystal ball that we nurses haven't?"

I smiled back. "No. But sometimes I wish I did."

Linda jabbed the tin at me. "Have one of these to cheer yourself up. In the meantime I'll contact the family GP and let them know about our concerns. Perhaps they can organize some counseling for Mollie's mum. We can talk about this at the case meeting with the consultant psychiatrist."

I took a chocolate-covered shortbread. "You mean ask his thoughts on the management of the alcoholic mother of one of the patients."

Linda laughed. "Well, you know what they say. When in Rome, ask a Roman. Or something like that!"

A couple of other nurses joined us to see how I was. They were all so nice. I felt grim. A traumatic experience for Mollie and her mother on my watch, and now the nurses I had so arrogantly despised actually turned out to be really nice, supportive colleagues.

But worst of all, I realized that the day had begun with Mollie checking on me to find out whether I was robust enough to hear what she wanted to find a way to tell me. Not for the first time I began to doubt whether I should actually be doing this job.

Mollie did not join the body-image group session I ran later that afternoon, and guessing that she felt upset and humiliated by her mother's episode earlier, I decided not to push her to come.

After the group ended, I finished my day packing away the chairs in a corner of the ward from which I could see into Mollie's bed space.

Sitting in her chair and bent over her sketchbook, Mollie was concentrating hard on what she was drawing. With her long hair flopped forward and her face determined, she looked like a little girl, all alone, and although she showed no emotion, her vulnerability in that moment cut straight into me.

Her parents were clearly unhappy and disconnected, and it struck me how when she was ill, they appeared more often together, united in their concern for her well-being. I began to wonder whether now that she was getting better, the chasm in the relationship had reappeared. Robert seemed always away on business and Eleanor more and more fragile and alone.

Was this what Chris meant by taking a systemic approach to the problem of Mollie's eating disorder? Was her anorexia the glue that held her parents together as their relationship fell apart?

I wanted to go and give this vulnerable young woman a hug, but that felt inappropriate and intrusive, so I finished stacking the chairs, and as I began to get ready to go home, Linda called me into the nurses' office.

"How you doing after today's incident?"

I yawned. "Knackered."

Linda laughed. "Yes, this place can be challenging, that's for sure!"

I smiled. "Listen, Linda, I just want to say thanks for being so supportive today."

Linda brushed my comment away with her hand. "How are you doing with our Mollie?"

"Mollie is gorgeous and sweet and brilliant, but you were so right when you told me she's tougher than she looks—and deeply unhappy at the same time. You know, I just struggle to get my head around how she seems just unable to let go of her compulsion to be really, really thin, even though it has almost killed her."

"Yes, she's tough." Linda sat down with a sigh, took off her shoes and rubbed her tired feet. "What's making her do it, do you think?"

I slumped down, also kicking off my shoes. "A need to be in control. An adolescent crisis of identity. A family in crisis. A society that champions thinness."

Linda laughed. "But to be fair, her BMI is getting healthier, which is amazing given that when she came in, it was so low that we had to NG-tube her."

I nodded. "Yeah, but I still need to get to the narrative of the problem. I mean, why would this girl with everything to live for risk her life? What is so urgent?"

"She doesn't eat because she has to show that something in her life is going badly wrong. She can't talk about it, so she shows it." Linda stood up and began to make tea. "Her parents are interesting, aren't they?" she said.

"Well, on the surface they seem nice, caring. Dad's a bit of the 'just get a grip and eat' school of thought . . ."

Linda chuckled. "Well, we can empathize with that frustration at times."

"Yeah, but given all the therapy they've had, he can sometimes seem really insensitive."

Linda handed me a cup of tea. "Compensatory parenting?"

"You mean his behavior compensates for Mum's?"

Linda nodded as she sipped her tea.

"Eleanor is terribly protective of Mollie, really attentive to her daughter, treats her like a fragile little wounded bird. Perhaps she's compensating for his bullishness," I suggested.

Linda shrugged. "I'd say it's a chicken-and-egg situation."

"Probably. Did you know that Mollie is the youngest, after a big gap, of four kids?"

"So we're talking about her youngest kid, her baby, right?"

I nodded. "Perhaps even a bit of a Band-Aid baby. Eleanor told me that she conceived Mollie against Robert's wishes: He didn't want any more kids."

"Wow. Ah, so now Mollie's growing up, Eleanor has the dread of the upcoming empty nest to deal with. I know the feeling—dreading it myself. My youngest is off on a gap year in a few months."

"Yeah, but would you stop them leaving you?"

Linda laughed. "'Course not! I'm buying him the plane ticket!" She put her feet up on a chair. "But you don't think Eleanor is stopping Mollie growing up and leaving home, do you?"

"No. Not consciously, anyway. But I think that she doesn't want Mollie to leave because she's afraid of being alone."

Linda offered me a biscuit.

"Oh God, I shouldn't," I complained. "I'm gaining weight!"

Linda laughed and patted her stomach. "Don't we all, working here? That's our compensatory behavior. It happens to the best of us. Weight gain in the face of starvation—you overeat because you register people around you living in famine conditions. It's automatic. Survival and all that."

Good fact. I now felt better about my newly acquired seven pounds in weight.

"Anyway, Mollie," continued Linda. "She's the one in hospital, so what's her part in all this?"

I thought as I continued to munch on my biscuit. "Well, I guess that by being ill, she unites her parents as well as enabling her mum to care for her and keep her at home with her as she recovers. You know—she lets her mum still be her mum."

Linda nodded. "Right, so via the anorexia Mollie delays becoming an adult and getting on with her life, leaving home."

Bingo!

"Yeah, Linda, that seems right. This young woman is ill, needs to be with her mum, can't go to school and get on with her life, and so her illness stops her from growing up and leaving home, which is exactly what Mum wants."

Linda smiled. "Sounds like a theory."

"Linda, what's the word for stopping your periods when you get anorexic?"

"Amenorrhea."

"Stop eating, get ill, need Mother to care for you, get thin, lose breasts and curves, and then periods stop . . ." My mind was racing. "Via her anorexia, the woman becomes the little girl again, psychologically, emotionally, physically and behaviorally, giving her mother more time in the role she can't bear to lose."

Linda smiled. "I think you're getting it."

"Mollie, the youngest child in her family and the last to leave home, is showing acute separation anxiety from her mother, whom she may be too afraid to leave because she's concerned that her mum won't be able to function without her. Her illness is symbolic of the unspoken role she has in her family. It serves a purpose by legitimizing her to not have to leave home. She also becomes, through her illness, a helpless dependent baby again. That allows her mum to continue the role that she can't let go of."

Linda raised her mug to me in salute and then sat back in her chair, smiling. "So, how are you going to help her grow up and leave the nest?"

As if she wanted to prove us all wrong, outwardly Mollie was doing well; she was attending group meals and eating independently, gaining weight and becoming part of the community on the ward. I had a theory, but we still hadn't established her motivation. What would stop her sliding back, once discharged?

Chris had given me papers to read by the family therapist John Byng-Hall—family mythology was his central theme. He described how families function in terms of the myths that they create around themselves, the implicit agreements we make about the role that each member of our family plays. I needed to understand Mollie's role in the family and how this contributed to her difficulties. I wanted to test some of my hypotheses about her mother's need to preserve her own role and Mollie's need to enable her to do so.

I hadn't seen much of her parents recently—Robert

was endlessly off on business. He had dropped by only once recently, with his rather pretty and attentive PA, on the way to an airport. Eleanor made daily visits but always very quietly, never speaking to me or any of the staff. Worried that she might be feeling embarrassed by her drunken episode on the ward, I decided to call her.

"Hi, Eleanor. I just wanted to check in, see how you are. We keep missing each other when you come in to visit Mollie."

"I'm very well, thank you. How are you?" Eleanor's voice was flat and controlled.

"Fine, thanks. How are you finding Mollie?"

"Mollie seems to be doing well. I am pleased. How do you find her?"

"I'm pleased with how she is really working to eat. She seems much less anxious at mealtimes."

"That's good."

"The thing is, Eleanor, I was wondering whether we could book an appointment to all meet up. You and Robert with Mollie."

"Why . . . would that be necessary?"

What a question.

"It would be useful to talk about the family—about Mollie's illness, how you all feel about what has happened over the last few years."

There was a pause.

"Why is that relevant?"

"Well." I had a sudden, almost vertiginous sense of how careful I needed to be in what I said next. "The thing is, Eleanor, as much as it is so vitally important that we enable Mollie to manage her urge to restrict her eating, it would be really useful to have some time together as a family, to think about how you all contribute to these issues."

Shit. Badly explained.

Eleanor laughed hollowly. "Well, as I think you will remember, Robert has had a bellyful of the therapy conversations, and to be frank, actually, so have I."

I could see from where Mollie got her controlling nature.

"I understand. I know that you've all been through many different therapists, but now that things have become . . . more *critical*, with Mollie having to be admitted onto a ward, it may be useful to look at those issues again."

I was pretty sure I heard Eleanor snort derisively.

"Well, I will do anything for my daughter. You might want to try to persuade her father, though, because I don't hold out much hope."

Oh God, where should I start?

"OK, to explain," I staggered on, "difficulties like Mollie's often serve a purpose that extends far beyond the individual with those difficulties."

There was still a deafening silence from the other end of the line.

"It is interesting—useful—to try to explore with the whole family why the young person is struggling in the way they are, and whether there are explanations that relate to the family structure and the family functions. Look, I feel it would be better if we met and discussed this face-to-face."

Eleanor sighed. "Neither Robert nor I would wish this on any of our children. We just want healthy, happy children who are able to leave home and make their own way in the world."

"Of course. I'm not suggesting that this is anything the family is wishing for in any sense. I guess it's just important to question why your youngest is finding the transition to adulthood so tough."

"Did you find the transition to adulthood easy?"

"Well, no."

"Did your family play a part in your difficulties?"

Shit, why was this about me? I was explaining things badly: Eleanor was getting defensive.

"I'm sorry, Eleanor, this is probably not the best way to have this conversation. Shall we book a time to meet up?"

Again a long pause.

"Eleanor, are you still there?"

"Yes. I need to check Robert's diary before we set up an appointment. I'll call his PA and get back to you."

She was firm, but afraid too.

"Eleanor, I hope that you do not feel embarrassed to come in and see me because of what happened the last time we met."

There was a strained laugh. "Oh goodness, no! I should have dropped you a note about that. I'm sorry I forgot. I wasn't well that day. Feverish. I'm sorry if my behavior was odd."

"Eleanor, it's—"

"I really do have to go. I'll get Robert's diary and call you as soon as I can. Many thanks."

The phone went dead.

Mollie and I had got to the point in our sessions where we were working on her "anorexic voice" and thinking about ways she could challenge it and learn to master it.

"So, it's all about anxiety?"

"What do you think, Mollie?"

"Yeah, I get it as in when I think about eating or know it's mealtime and I have to eat, I really start to panic, but otherwise I don't really do anxiety."

"What about school, exams, pressure?"

"God, no, I love that stuff. I just don't get some of my friends who get so pathetic and cry about work and stuff. I just love it."

"Maybe because you feel you are good at all that."

"Yeah, I do. I mean, you know—I'm sorry to sound bigheaded, but I know I can do it and it's like my brain slots into this calm place where I can just think and study and do exams."

"You don't worry about failing?"

"No, never."

"Have you ever failed?"

Mollie grinned. "No, never."

"Well, so here's a really great example of how your rock-solid self-confidence enables you to overcome anxiety and face down the challenge."

"I love the challenge of school and work. It makes me feel free."

"Why do you think that is?"

Mollie thought for a moment. "'Cos I don't have to think about food."

This girl shouldn't be doing medicine; she should do clinical psychology.

"I should do your job!"

"I was just thinking that. But anyway, let's take this self-confident student and think about ways that self-belief can shift into your anxiety about food."

"Yeah, but I fail with food."

"Why?"

"Because I have to eat it, and when I do, I totally hate myself."

"You seem to be dealing with it well at the moment."

"I know, but that's because I have to."

"What do you mean? Being here?"

Mollie looked down and her face became drawn. "No. I have to for Mummy and Daddy."

I could see Mollie's eyes beginning to shine with tears.

"Well, Mollie, of course they are concerned. Your dad is clearly anxious for you to eat and, in his own way, is trying to encourage you."

Mollie gave a small smile. "Yeah, that's because he wants a perfect final child. He just wants me to be the doctor. Gotta eat to be a doctor."

"Do you want to be a doctor?"

Still holding back the tears, Mollie smiled to herself. "Yeah, of course I do."

"Do I hear a 'but' there?"

Mollie shook her head. "Doesn't matter."

"I disagree. I think this matters very much."

The tears began to flow.

"I want to draw and paint."

I wanted to put my arms around her.

"But you feel your dad would disapprove?"

"They both would."

"Your mum as well?"

Mollie looked up and wiped her tears on the sleeve of her sweater. "I think Mummy would like me to be a doctor. You know, it's kind of been the thing in the family forever—Mollie will be the family doctor."

"Family doctor?"

"Yeah, you know. The only doctor in the family and also the doctor for the family."

"What, you mean the expectation is that you would treat your family?"

"Kind of. But it's always been a joke really. Poppy does the finance for the family, Rupert keeps us out of prison, Tilly changes the law to benefit us all, and I keep us well."

My heart was racing.

Mollie's role was to be a doctor, the family doctor. It was a joke, the sort of joke families tell themselves about themselves. But thinking about the story built up around the roles that each of the four successful children would hold in the family, I was suddenly struck that Mollie's role seemed the most significant in terms of her life moving forward into adulthood. She was at an age where her developmental task was one of individuation, of becoming herself, making an individual identity. But wasn't there a sense in which Mollie's role meant that she wasn't allowed to do that?

"So, your role, Mollie, is to keep the family well."

Mollie half smiled and shrugged her shoulders.

"It sounds to me like that could be sitting in all this somewhere for you."

"Perhaps. I don't know. But please don't hate my parents."

"Why would I hate them?"

Mollie shrugged. "Dunno."

"Do you sometimes hate them?"

Mollie paused and nibbled at a biscuit, taking ages to chew and swallow the small fragments in her mouth. "I don't hate them—I love them. I guess I worry about them."

"Worry about what? Letting them down?"

Again, I sat out a long, slow, masticated pause.

"Yeah, that." She smiled. "But I am doing a good enough job of that already."

I waited as more biscuit was nibbled.

"I think I worry most about Mummy."

"How?"

Mollie shrugged. "Dunno." More nibbling. "Well, I think she's sad."

"Why do you say that?"

Mollie looked at me incredulously. "You are asking me that?"

"Well, yes. What's the problem with my question?"

The atmosphere became tense.

"Come on. You're the trained one here. You've seen her."

"What have I seen, Mollie?"

"The other week, her necklace. When she fell over. She was drunk."

"Do you worry about her drinking?"

"I worry about why she drinks."

"What do you think is the reason for her drinking?"

"She's sad."

"Do you have an idea about what she's sad about?"

Mollie put the soggy nibbled biscuit down with a sigh; her face was red and tight as she looked at me directly.

"She's sad because when I leave her, she'll have nothing."

My heart sank. Unless I challenged Mollie's belief, I

realized that she'd always feel responsible for her family. She didn't want that. Of course she didn't.

A few days later I was racing around the streets of a small village suburb in North London, filled with panic. Mollie was angry—and she was missing.

Our lunch in the small bistro a few roads away from the hospital had started well. Mollie looked pink and healthy, albeit distracted, after our short walk and had confidently ordered herself some food. Our goal was to practice eating in public, something Mollie had an intense phobia of.

She was brilliant: focused and brave. If she seemed anxious, I put it down to the newness of the situation and pretended not to notice, to encourage her. As we ate, she was just an ordinary young woman having lunch.

And then it all changed.

"Mummy told me you spoke to her on the phone."

I nodded, my mouth full.

"Apparently you want a family meeting."

I swallowed. "Yes, we haven't had one and I thought it would be helpful."

"Why?"

I was aware that Mollie looked serious.

"Well, you are doing really well, and it would help to engage the whole family to think about how things will be when you go home and—"

"Mummy was upset. She told me that you wanted to discuss how the whole family is part of my illness. Why did you say that?"

I felt the familiar feeling of being pinned down by this bright young woman.

"I certainly didn't want to upset your mother, Mollie, definitely not leave her feeling that there was a need to apportion blame here."

"Who said anything about blame?"

Already I felt on the back foot, defensive.

"Well, this isn't about blame but just some understanding of how you all function as a family and how you can support each other when you are back home."

"Mummy said you used the word 'role.' What were you talking about?"

I paused.

"Seriously, you've upset her. Why did you do that?"

I looked up at Mollie, who was getting red in the face, tears of anger pricking her eyes.

"The word 'role' is not meant to imply blame, Mollie, and I am sorry for upsetting you and your mother. What I meant was for us to explore how the family may contribute to the difficulties that you have."

Mollie threw down her fork. "Yeah, in other words, blame. Whose fault is it that Mollie is the anorexic?"

I wiped my mouth on my napkin. "Mollie, are you more upset that it sounds like I am looking to blame members of your family or that I have upset your mother?"

Mollie snorted in exasperation. "You know how Mummy is at the moment. You've seen her at her worst. She can't be upset any more than she already is."

"It wasn't my intention to upset your mother, and I will make sure I help her see that. But given our recent conversation about your worries about your mother especially when you leave home, I think that your protectiveness of her and your anxiety about her need to be talked about within the family."

"Well, I don't."

"Well, why don't we spend a bit of time thinking about it together? Perhaps feeling you can't leave your mother is part of why you became so unwell."

Mollie looked at me incredulously. "How?"

"Well . . ." I paused as I chose my words carefully. "Perhaps your leaving home as the youngest is something you worry your mother would find so painful that you are struggling with making that next step in your life."

"But I'm getting better!"

"Mollie, why don't we pay and go back and talk about this somewhere less public?"

Mollie pushed her chair back from the table. "I don't want to talk about it, and I won't talk about it."

With that she ran out of the café, leaving me to pay hastily and then rush out onto the street after her. But she was already gone.

Forty minutes had now elapsed and I hadn't seen Mollie. This could be an almighty disaster—her first outing on my watch and now she was wandering the streets on her own.

There was so much that couldn't be talked about. Should I have had that conversation with Eleanor on the telephone? Was my psychology shorthand, the jargon of the profession, too blunt and insensitive, implying blame? Why did I get into the detail of Mollie's anxiety about her mother in a bistro? Was it a mistimed intervention?

My heart was racing and I was contemplating returning to the ward without Mollie when I saw her sitting at a table outside a café opposite the hospital. Relief flooded through me as she waved me over.

Mollie sat with two cups of tea. She pushed one toward me.

"I'm sorry," she said.

"Mollie, I was worried about you."

Mollie looked down. "Yeah, I know. I'm sorry."

"Look, no problem now. Are you OK?"

Mollie sipped at her tea. "Yeah. I just needed some space to sort out my head." She looked intently at me. "I know what you mean about all this, and I think you are right."

My tea was still warm enough to drink.

"What am I right about?"

"About Mummy, about me."

I stirred my tea. "So how do you feel about finding a way to talk about it as a family?"

"Like I don't want to, but I know we should."

"Why?"

Mollie paused in thought. "Because Mummy has to learn to live without me."

I left a meeting with Chris at her university office in a daze—she was really pushing me on my dissertation and I needed some space to clear my head before traveling back to the ward. It was a warm late-spring day and so I jumped on a bus and rode across London until I got to Marble Arch, where I alighted and walked into Hyde Park.

I had finally arranged a family meeting with Mollie and I needed to focus.

Everything about her felt fragmented in my mind—strands of thoughts and ideas seemed disconnected and muddled. I just couldn't pin a coherent narrative around Mollie, her restrictive eating, her need for intense control and her relationship with her parents.

The sun was bright and the air clear and so I walked to the lake, bought myself a coffee and sat watching the families strolling past, excited children throwing bread to the ducks and geese, concerned parents keeping them away from the water's edge.

A small child in a red duffle coat was insistent on running toward the large birds and scaring them. He found it hilarious, but his increasingly frazzled mother did not. She began by coaxing him back to the table she shared with other mothers and their more compliant children with promises of biscuits and chocolate milk. But he wasn't having any of it.

I felt sorry for the mother because I could sense that she was becoming increasingly embarrassed as her friends tried hard to ignore the struggle she was having with her child. The little boy continued to run up and down the edge of the lake, flapping his arms wildly as the birds scattered in all directions. The mother jumped up and ran toward her son, then knelt behind him putting her arms around his waist and clearly whispering in his ear for him to calm down. But again the little boy was having none of it.

The geese returned to the water's edge and, getting agitated by the presence of this exuberant child in a bright red coat, started hissing. At this point the mother had clearly had enough and abruptly stood up, grabbed her son under her arm and walked back toward the table. The little boy descended into the most almighty tantrum, screaming, kicking his arms and legs wildly, and as much as the mother tried to reposition him in her arms so she could hold him more elegantly, it was clear that this little chap was not going to play ball.

The mother glanced up at me, clearly embarrassed that her son was attracting attention, and so to spare her blushes I quickly looked away and leaned forward to pull some papers out of my bag. I took a slug of coffee and started to sort through the papers until I came across the one written by the family therapist and my guiding clinical voice, John Byng-Hall. Holding the paper that I had read many times, I gazed across the lake as Mollie's narrative began to coalesce in my mind.

Mollie was the glue that held her parents' marriage together; she had already helped me to understand that. I thought back to the early days of my placement, when she was extremely underweight and unable to feed herself, and remembered how often her parents would both be there together with her in the hospital, holding her hands and talking, as a family should.

However, as she had become healthier and changed from that helpless baby whom we needed to feed to a more independent functioning young person able to feed herself, the animosity between her parents became more apparent—in particular, her mother's vulnerability became more acutely visible.

Mollie was right. She couldn't leave her mother, because if she did, what would her mother have? Eleanor's role had been to be the mother, a role she had fulfilled with commitment and care. For her, the loss of her youngest child, the child she had to inoculate her against the loneliness of her role in her marriage, was clearly more than she could bear. With alcohol, I realized, Eleanor was self-medicating pain that must have been overwhelming for her as she contemplated the loss of her final child from her life and faced a future where she was both unhappy in her marriage and unclear about who she was and what her place in life was now to be.

This all began to make more sense—clearly the anorexic Mollie who became unable to function, could not feed herself, was unable to do basic tasks because she was so weak and therefore had to be helped to walk, to self-care and to eat, was regressing backward into her mother's open, needy arms. By being so underweight that her periods had stopped, she ceased to be a reproductive woman.

Mollie had become the helpless baby again, the baby that her mother had so longed for more than seventeen years previously. In being so, she was fulfilling her designated family role by managing their well-being. Mollie was providing her mother with the baby that she was desperate to keep and enabling her parents to unite around her critical illness, which helped them to function as a couple, united as concerned parents.

As the sun shone steadily onto the surface of the lake, I began to see things more clearly. How could this young woman be freed from the bind of the role that she had been given? It clearly wasn't just a case of helping her learn to feed herself again and providing her with the tools to challenge her underlying belief that she would only ever be a failure if she gave in to her body's instinct

to nourish itself. The family had to be helped to understand what Byng-Hall called their "script."

However, it then struck me, with a sinking feeling,
that Mollie would never be free of her anorexic self. If
she was too thin to go to medical school, then she would
never be a doctor. If she was too weak to look after herself, then she could remain at home and be cared for by
her mother. If she remained dependent and attached
to her mother, then she would also enable her parents to
remain married despite the groaning chasm within their
relationship. Although she was getting better now, as
the situation between her parents continued to deteriorate, with her father mostly away and her mother drinking
heavily, Mollie would have to stop eating again. She was
totally and utterly trapped.

My heart lurched. I pushed the paper into my bag,
gulped the dregs of my cold coffee and made ready to go
back to the ward for a meeting with Eleanor and Mollie;
Robert was, yet again, away on business. Christ. Why
had it taken me so long to pull this all together?

The Northern Line was, as usual, slow, and so I got back
to the hospital later than I intended. I looked at my
watch—shit, I was literally minutes away from my session with Mollie and Eleanor.

As I walked into the ward, I began to feel unsettled.
Mollie was not in her bed space, and the place was unusually quiet; it felt like a morgue.

"Where have you been?"

"Sorry, Linda, I got stuck on the bloody Northern
Line."

"Listen, we've got a situation and we're having an emergency ward meeting. You'd better come now."

Although I was desperate for the toilet, Linda's face and voice made me follow her into the clinical room immediately. Everyone was present—I'd never seen the whole ward team in one place at the same time. The consultant stood at the front of the room, his face completely ashen. I sat down.

The consultant nodded in my direction and then began to speak.

"Thanks for all getting here. I've just had a call from Mr. Richardson, Mollie Richardson's father, to inform me that Mrs. Richardson, his wife, was killed this morning in a car accident."

My heart stopped.

"Mr. Richardson was unable to give me any precise details, but it appears that no other vehicle was involved."

My brain started spinning wildly—had Eleanor been drunk behind the wheel?

"Mr. Richardson is currently on business abroad and attempting to get an immediate flight back. One of Mollie's siblings is coming back from the US, and the other two are coming in as soon as they can. Understandably, this is a tragic time for the family."

No one could speak. We were all stunned. Despite our combined years of training in a field where we often had to hear the most desperately sad stories told by those we treated, none of us seemed at all able to process this news.

The consultant turned to look at me.

"Mollie has not been told as yet, and Mr. Richardson specifically requested that you should be the one to tell her before her siblings arrive, and if you feel you can manage that. I think that given your relationship with her, that would be the most appropriate. Linda, perhaps you'll sit in too."

My mouth was dry. Everyone turned to look at me.

"OK," I croaked.

Linda leaned across and squeezed my hand. I was shaking.

Sitting at the back of the church, I felt guilty for being tearful. I hadn't really known Eleanor very long and it seemed selfish to indulge my own sorrow.

Looking through the sea of black in front of me, I stared at the back of Mollie's head at the front of the church sitting to the right of her mother's coffin. I could not see her expression except when she occasionally leaned forward to wipe her eyes or blow her nose.

I sat among the entire staff team and some of the young women from the ward. Looking around the church, I saw faces of people that I had never met, some probably relatives who bore the family resemblance, others pretty young women whom I had seen in the photos stuck around Mollie's bed space on the ward.

The priest stopped speaking and Mollie stood up to walk to the lectern. She looked so small and fragile as she walked past her mother's coffin without looking at it. My muscles twitched with the urge to run to her and envelop her in my arms, to rock her, to hold her.

Mollie opened the book in front of her and, in a strong voice, began to speak: "I am reading this for Mummy. 'Do Not Stand at My Grave and Weep.'"

I couldn't breathe as I waited for Mollie to compose herself and begin to read.

Do not stand at my grave and weep;
I am not there, I do not sleep.
I am a thousand winds that blow.
I am the diamond glints on snow.
I am the sunlight on ripened grain.
I am the gentle autumn rain.

As Mollie paused, the sound of her father sobbing loudly into the shoulder of one of his older daughters filled the hushed church. Sniffles and sobs began to echo from all directions as the collective grief was finally given permission to release itself.

Mollie continued:

When you awaken in the morning's hush
I am the swift uplifting rush . . .

Her voice faltered. She then took a deep breath and carried on.

Of quiet birds in circled flight.
I am the soft stars that shine at night.

And then her voice broke as her tears began to flow.

Do not stand at my grave and cry;
I am not there, I did not die.

That was what Mollie had screamed at me over and over again as I held her in my arms in the counseling room on the ward.

"She isn't dead. No, please—that's not true. Please tell me you're wrong. She is not dead. Please tell me Mummy did not die."

In that moment there was nothing for me to say. No cognitive challenge, no systemic interpretation, no well-timed intervention. In that moment, words were ineffective. As we sat together on the floor with her tears soaking my shirt, all I could do was hold Mollie and rock her until her family arrived.

Six

DODGING STONES

When I entered the working world, my mother, once a senior nurse, advised me sagely, "Darling, never shit on your own doorstep."

Mum warned me of the dangers in engaging in a relationship with one's colleagues, but I ignored her. At the drug-dependency unit, the psychiatrist and senior doctor was strong, sure and decisive. As I fumbled to understand my patients, he listened calmly, interpreted my meandering thoughts and congratulated me on my intuition. He was flirtatious and I allowed myself to be reeled in.

He wasn't my type physically, but he looked sharp and sexy in his charcoal-gray suit, white shirt open at the collar and Church's shoes. He had welcomed me to the DDU on my first day with an hour-long induction meeting in his office. He sat behind his desk with his feet up, leaning back in his chair, arms behind his head. I'd bloody read Desmond Morris's *The Naked Ape* and done a whole undergraduate degree module on body language, so why the hell was I mesmerized by this person trying so hard to be the alpha male?

I was finally in my last placement; I was splitting my time between the DDU and a palliative-care unit—a new center for the research and treatment of those with HIV and AIDS.

Leaving Mollie had been difficult. With Imogen, she sat in a place in my mind that I have struggled not to return to with sadness over the years. For Mollie, my feelings were more complex: I was saddened by her loss but I undertood what it meant. There had been no evidence in the accident report to indicate that Eleanor had done anything to cause the crash. But her sudden departure had perversely given Mollie the space she needed to move on in her life.

Mollie was discharged from the ward before I left the placement. She was back at school, still focused on the idea of being a doctor. I held on to an anxiety that she now had no choice but to fulfill the role expected of her—to train as a doctor and, even more so after the tragic loss of her mother, look after the family.

Before she left, we spent time working through her shock and grief, which she expressed in her sketches and drawings. Her art was her form of emotional communication, and I wondered how she would cope with life without being the artist she so clearly was. Would she periodically return to food restriction as a way of communicating her feelings when life as a doctor, as a motherless woman, became overwhelming for her? At our last session she gave me a sketch that she had drawn of me; I still treasure it.

I would never know what became of Mollie. Just as I

would never know what became of Ray or Imogen, or
Marion, or any of the other wonderful people I had
worked with. These unanswered questions were just
part of the job. As I was learning to do, I shifted my
mind into my next and final training challenge: drugs
and death.

The DDU was based on the ground floor of an old
hospital on a busy, polluted road that led into the center
of the city, opposite a large run-down estate, a notorious
den full of drug dealers. Corridors of offices ran off the
large open-plan waiting area where seats were bolted to
the floor and pictures hung so out of arm's reach that
they almost met the ceiling. I shared my office with two
other drug workers—both nice and friendly and not too
dissimilar-looking to the unit clientele. At the back of the
DDU were the counseling rooms, also containing bolted-
down chairs, positioned so that the panic button was
always in easy reach, and two larger group rooms.

The pharmacy/needle exchange was behind a locked
door at the back of the unit and looked like a bunker,
built in reinforced concrete and thickly plated glass.
This was the hub where methadone and all other pharmaceutical delights were dispensed under the highest
security to one patient at a time. Clean needles were exchanged for blunt, dirty, possibly infected ones, which
were swiftly deposited into sharps bins with one-way-
entry, self-securing lids. Laminated posters advising
staff on the immediate protocol following a needle-stick
injury were displayed everywhere.

The psychiatrist was the only staff member to have
his own office, and the biggest one at that. His pictures

were hung at normal height, his coffee brought to him in his own special mug.

The whole place was painted white; it was clean and completely characterless. As the doors opened every morning at nine o'clock, an endless stream of some of the most dirty and destitute people I had ever seen would come steadily trickling in. It took me a long time to get my head around the fact that this waiting room was housing a population that lived within one of the wealthiest cities in the developed world. In that room the malnourished sat alongside those covered in sores, the broken and the discarded.

The place, however, was calm. There was rarely any violence, and I soon realized that this was because the staff team treated those they cared for with respect. Within our white, characterless bubble, we provided a haven, a tranquillity and warmth where everyone was acknowledged and greeted; often we struggled to get people to leave as they snuggled into their chairs in order to catch some comfortable sleep where they would, for a short time, be safe, warm and dry. For many, this was home.

The psychiatrist seemed to make himself available to me whenever I needed him. He was charming. In the chaos of the early-morning walk-in clinic he was clearly "the man." The receptionists loved him, the nurses loved him and so did I—we were his pride.

Being a competitive kind of gal, I decided that I would be number-one lioness. He and I worked on some tricky cases together, and he always told me how he couldn't have managed them without me. I loved his validation and luxuriated in the envious glances of my colleagues.

After work I would spend time in his office. We would drink coffee and talk about the day's challenges. I was impressed by his ability to immediately see the problem, to specify the intervention. I wanted to be like him—to see, know and then fix.

"Why didn't you do medicine," he asked me, "and then specialize in psychiatry? A-level results not quite good enough?"

Actually my A-level results hadn't been great, especially compared with those of the brainy girls I went to school with. At my pushy all-girls school, which I had hated, I preferred hanging out with the boys from the local boys' school to spending hours rote-learning facts I had no interest in knowing.

My school was one of those where the girls who got into Oxbridge were asked to troop across the stage in assembly to receive a gracious handshake from our tough headmistress. I, and those other thickies like me heading off to some "inferior" university, sat at the back of the school hall and applauded. At a sixth-form parents' evening, my parents were told that I would never be a "highflier"; my mother later reported that she had wanted to slap that particular teacher around the face.

Academic elitism, I hated it—still do—and the head psychiatrist's comments reflected that very same culture. How transparently patronizing—he epitomized everything that was arrogant about the medical model. Pathetically, though, at that time and in that moment I was too busy being flattered by his attention to notice.

He took my hand; he said that "the deans of all the medical schools in all the land" should have met me.

"If I'd had the chance to meet you fresh from school," he said, "and was able to interview you, there would be no doubt in my mind that you'd have been on the medical training course straight away. A-level results notwithstanding."

He said all that as he looked directly into my eyes, and I knew that he could hear my breath catch in my throat. I wanted to kiss him. And so much more.

And so the flirtation continued until, a few weeks later, at the end of a long, hot, difficult morning, our relationship was consummated—in the most disappointing way.

The day started when I opened the clinic door and a woman fell in onto the floor. She fell so quickly I couldn't catch her. She was young and thin with dyed yellow-blond hair, strawlike from overbleaching, dark roots growing in at the hairline—not an unusual look in clinics in that part of town. The multiple gold hoops in her small ears jangled as her head bounced off the floor. There was dried blood under her nose and the beginnings of a nasty swelling on her left cheekbone. Her right eye was yellow and green with the faded remnants of a bruise that had been fresh the previous week.

Battered women are really awful to see, but not unusually shocking after your tenth viewing. In that clinic the fist seemed to be a common form of communication. But what I had never seen was a battered woman with the brand name and logo of an expensive on-trend sneaker stamped into her face. The trademark was etched in purple welts on pale, undernourished skin.

The other staff at the clinic knew this woman. Her name was Mo, and she came from a notorious local family. Everyone in the local health, social and educational services knew her, her parents, grandparents, aunts, uncles, siblings and cousins too numerous to name. Mo was often dropping into the clinic looking for "a few drops more of the methadone"—she'd been mugged for the last lot we gave her; it had spilled; she had had to share it with her ma.

She knew the drill in a way that at first I didn't, and for a while she would emerge from the toilet to hand me cold urine in a small plastic cup as evidence that "No, I swear on my late granddaddy's grave, I am not using"— and indeed a dipstick test proved her words true. In those early days I hadn't worked out that cold urine could have been anyone's smuggled in—her little sister's probably. I eventually learned not to accept urine from someone like Mo unless it had been deposited in the cup while in the unit and handed over body-temperature warm.

That morning, there was Mo, lying at my feet, facially branded like a gruesome sports advertising billboard. She was groaning, clearly alive, but not in good shape.

The psychiatrist examined her on the floor and then we scooped her up and took her into his office. A nurse came to deal with cuts and bruises, and then left once her task was over—I knew she wanted to be me, staying in the room with our alpha dog.

I spent a lot of the day with Mo: She had a full physical examination; ointments were applied to festering cigarette burns on her fragile skin; swabs revealed a sexually transmitted infection and pills were prescribed. She drank cup after cup of hot, sweet tea and ate her way through a loaf of bread, toasted, buttered and covered in thick layers of jam.

As she ate, her vulnerability touched me. She began to talk.

"I love him to bits," she declared.

"Why, Mo? He beats you and he burns you."

"He can't help it, bless him. He's not a bad fella. He came from a rough lot."

She gobbled her toast like a small, hungry child, her mouth covered in jam; I wanted to cuddle her.

"I am sure he loves you, Mo," I lied, "but he has a violent way of showing it, and unless he gets help to sort his anger out, you will always be his punching bag."

She looked up at me, one eye wide, the other slowly swelling shut. "Help? Help, you say?" Mo started to laugh. "Help from where? Who's going to help the likes of us?"

"I want to help you, Mo, so there's a start."

She stopped gulping her tea, and, with her head down, in a small, angry voice asked me, "How can you help me?"

Good question. How can I?

"How do you want to be helped, Mo?"

Head still down, Mo wiped the tears pouring from her eyes; she winced as she rubbed the now-almost-shut eye too hard.

"I want your life. I want to do good at school and have a job. I want to live in a nice place and make money for the family. I want to have a bank account with money in it. I want to be somebody."

The way she looked at me as she laid out what she wished for in her life touched me to my core and evoked in me deep maternal feelings toward this fragile young woman even though we were of similar age. She was asking for my life, and I momentarily felt guilty that I was the one who had it while she didn't.

"Why don't we start by getting you out of this abusive relationship, help you get clean and then take it from there?"

The sexy shrink came back from seeing other patients and together we tried to persuade Mo that she needed to leave the man responsible for her injuries, past and present, and go into a shelter until we could work out a longer-term plan. Many people had failed to convince Mo to do this before, but we were determined to get her to see reason.

We almost managed it. It was all going well—a shelter placement was found, and the police were coming to hear her evidence of assault. And then the perpetrator turned up and all our hard work unraveled. Mo fell into his track-mark-scarred arms, sobbing as he, also sobbing, thrust a cheap and tatty bunch of flowers at her, alongside all the remorse he could muster. Love was declared, vows renewed and then they were off, armed with clean needles and a few milliliters of the local brew: methadone.

So, what do you do when the plan fails but the pulse is still racing, the engine revved? You get passionate in the dispensary, of course. Or at least the sexy shrink and I did, and it was awful. Not just because he asked in a tiny toddler voice whether he could kiss me, or because when he did, his tongue felt like a motorized food processor in my mouth, but because I suddenly saw what a pathetic, needy, undignified idiot I was.

The shrink had played me using my vanity and my need to be his "top girl." I had demeaned my professional status by being sucked into the idea that psychology was somehow second best to psychiatry and I could have been a member of the elite squad, if only I'd done a little bit better at school. Of course, a really bad kiss can kill attraction in an instant, but actually it wasn't a real attraction in the first place, just a fantasy fueled by my own immature narcissism.

As much as I hated to admit it to myself, my mother was right.

I left the DDU after my half-day shift and walked down Tottenham Court Road to the new HIV/AIDS specialist center. While the virus united these two patient populations—one infected by sharing dirty needles, the other by having unprotected sexual intercourse—they couldn't have been more different.

Having spent a couple of weeks settling into the DDU, I was now, for the first time, about to meet one unique group of palliative-care patients I would come to know well. In those days, once someone was diagnosed with AIDS, that was it. There was no cure. There was no chance they'd get better. These patients were outdying everyone else on our watch. They were dying but alive; emaciated but often incredibly beautiful and well groomed; covered in skin cancer and cashmere. The boys with AIDS had come to town.

Working with gay men in the early 1990s, when the explosion of HIV/AIDS hit the gay community like a sledgehammer, was a strange, sad era. The time from diagnosis to death was often rapid and ruthless, while the virus was latched on to by those looking to fuel their homophobia and cruelly vent their prejudices as they rejoiced in the deaths of so many gay men.

Palliative care changed a lot: Suddenly there was a disproportionate number of glamorous young men among our patients.

Every time I left the dismal, dirty, hopeless world of the DDU and entered the HIV unit, I felt like I was on a completely different planet—a world of beautiful, emotional people crackling with the energy and the anger that came with fighting discrimination and watching their friends and lovers drop around them.

At the time, to get a diagnosis of HIV was a death sentence. Nowadays you die with the virus; then you died because of it.

As I entered the unit, on my first day there, I was greeted warmly by a small, effeminate man in green nursing scrubs. He was multiply pierced, had a crew cut reminiscent of an American GI and the most wonderful smile, revealing glittering white teeth.

"Well, hello, gorgeous. I'm Nurse Pete. Welcome to our happy home." Spreading his arms expansively, he turned three hundred and sixty degrees.

I felt very welcome and very much at home.

Pete took me to my small office at the end of the health advisers' corridor. It was the best office I'd had yet—wooden floor, a cream rug, pale walls and a matching desk, filing cabinet and chair combo.

"Everything to your liking, madam?"

"Beyond expectations, Pete!"

"Yes, you lot who have come from psychiatric services always react this way. Thing is, we feel that if we are going to value our patients, we need to value ourselves as staff. Anyway, you'll be talking to men who are dying in this room and they deserve a nice place to prepare for their death in. Don't you agree?"

I wanted to kiss that man.

A couple of health advisers came over with a cup of coffee and, because there was no other clinical psychologist there, told me about the place. In those days you had to wait an interminably long time between being tested for HIV and getting the results, and so the health advisers' role was to offer support before, during and after that hellish wait, while also providing condoms and safe-sex advice to the more vulnerable service users.

"More vulnerable?" I asked them.

"Those new to the scene, fucking everything they can and holding that 'it will never happen to me' attitude. Plus the rent boys."

"Rent boys?"

"Yeah—they get paid double if they allow themselves to be fucked without a condom."

Later that day Pete walked me across the road to the main hospital, where the wards were. He told me that more than a third of his friends were dead, another third dying. He wasn't infected, but had a test every three months.

"Do you ever have to nurse someone you know?"

Pete laughed. "Oh, sweetheart, you've got a lot to learn about the scene. Everyone knows everyone, and almost everyone *knows* everyone."

Yep, a nice serially monogamous girl like me had a lot to learn.

Walking onto the ward was as welcoming as walking into the clinic had been. Reception staff greeted me warmly, and Pete introduced me to the nursing team. Again a cup of coffee and an induction chat before Pete offered to get me acquainted with some patients. I couldn't wait to meet them.

There was no open ward—every patient had his or her own room and bathroom—but there was a communal space with sofas, magazines and a drinks machine so those who fancied company could come out and mingle. The communal space was empty, so Pete knocked on a door.

"Let's see if Tom is home!"

"Enter if you are naked."

We weren't, but we entered anyway.

Walking through that door into that room was like walking through the cupboard into Narnia. The room was dark but glittered with fairy lights strung across the walls; the air smelled of mimosa.

It took a while for my eyes to adjust to the dark. I could barely make out the outline of a body in a bed. Pete took my hand and we walked toward Tom.

"Hello and welcome," said the softest, smoothest voice I had ever heard. "Sorry for the lack of light, but I seem to have a degree of photosensitivity." If it's possible to fall in love with a voice, then in that moment I was smitten.

My eyes were adjusting and so I took the hand attached to the thin arm extended toward me; I shook it.

"Well, well, Pete, she's a formal one."

"Oh no, sorry!" I felt like such a klutz. I squeezed Tom's hand.

Pete chuckled. "I think this one could be a bit of a minx, Tom."

"Excellent. Thank you for bringing her to me. You may now leave us, Pete."

"Yes, my liege." Pete dipped into a deep bow and left the room with a flourish.

I was confused.

"Sweetheart, my mouth is dry."

I found the water jug, poured some into the tumbler with the straw and directed it to his mouth.

As Tom drank and my eyes finally fully adjusted, I was able to see his face—what a beautiful face. He had been sculpted in the most perfect way, his cheekbones hewn into dramatic ridges on a face that held the most perfectly almond-shaped green eyes. His hair was short and dark, tousled without effort into spikes; his mouth was a Cupid's bow and fleshy—entirely a mouth to be kissed and kissed. His neck was slim.

"I was actually once much more beautiful, you know."

What do you say to that?

"You look pretty bloody beautiful to me, Tom."

"Back atcha." Tom took a long drink from the straw. "So, what are you doing here?"

Good question.

"Well. Crikey, where do I start?"

"Name, rank and serial number will do."

So I told Tom who I was and about my training and what I hoped to do when I qualified.

"You want to make the world a more beautifully happy place?"

"Does it sound trite if I agree with you?"

Tom smiled gorgeously, and then with several grunts he shuffled himself up the bed. "No, not at all. Why not make the world beautiful? That's what I have spent my life doing."

Tom was a fashion designer of huge talent who, as he put it, "was now contaminated and rotting from the outside in and the inside out."

I knew his label; in my mind I could visualize iconic photographs shot by Mario Testino, Peter Lindbergh, Annie Leibovitz and Ellen von Unwerth in which Cindy, Linda and Naomi wore his clothes. This man was a fashion legend.

"I know who you are! I love your clothes!"

"Do you own any?"

I laughed. "Are you kidding? On my salary?"

Tom leaned forward with a small grunt and began to look me up and down. "Would you mind standing up?"

In the semidark room I hoped he wouldn't notice me blush.

"Don't be uncomfortable. Please stand."

I stood.

"Hmm. Tall. Check. Broad shoulders. Check."

That comes with having a Germanic father, Tom. You should see my sister—we were always called the Amazonian twins.

"Style. Oh, I'm sorry, darling. No check there."

I sat down, deflated. "What's the problem?"

"The man suit—vintage charity shop, right?"

"Yes. But a charity shop off Carnaby Street!"

"I've no doubt. It's a great suit, but it does nothing for you."

He stretched his head downward. "Oooh. Doc Marten shoes. Why?"

"Why not? I don't have to dress as defined by my gender."

Tom laughed. "No, I agree. But you don't suit the butch asexual look, and besides, this is your cover-my-body uniform. It would sit well if you were happy with the body hanging it."

I felt slightly crushed, but Tom was right, of course—I was dressing to disguise the many pounds gained on my last placement. However, I was also massively elated that this man was giving me fashion advice; I couldn't wait to tell Ali, Rosie and Megan.

"OK, sweetheart, here's the deal. You spend time with me getting my head around this fucking horror of a disease and I'll teach you how to dress."

Our contract was sealed with a less formal handshake and I left the room.

Pete met me on the other side. I blinked like a mole thrust into sunlight.

"Well?" he asked me.

"I think Tom wants to meet me again."

Pete hugged me. "Well done, gorgeous girl! You passed!"

I realized that Tom had been auditioning me to be his psychological support as he prepared to die. He wasn't in immediate danger, as his Pneumocystis pneumonia was responding well to treatment, but he knew it was only a matter of time. In return I would get a life-changing style makeover. While I wanted it, I wasn't sure if this was a contract I could honor. Was I experienced enough to support a man who was confronting his mortality so intimately? I had no idea what that would take.

The placement was busy. I flitted between the DDU and the HIV clinic.

Mo continued to make her regular pilgrimage to get her methadone. I found myself looking out for her and wanting to talk to her, to check in with her, as often as I could. To begin with there were no new bruises, and that made me hopeful. Unfortunately, I later found out that was due to the postapocalyptic honeymoon period so common in sadomasochistic relationships.

I began to get to know the DDU regulars and enjoyed the banter in the waiting room; it's funny how a place like hell can soon begin to feel familiar and almost normal. As well as the heroin users, there were those hardcore benzodiazepine "jelly" injectors—including a couple of regulars who had had to have a leg amputated due to chronic injecting. Also there were a few coke and stimulant users—they were easier to spot: cleaner, better fed, more functional, and, because prescribing pharmaceutical cocaine was not common practice, these patients were usually referred to me for work to untangle the psychological dependency they had on the white powder.

Charlie was a cheeky, nasty drug. An expert at tricking the brain, charlie would mimic dopamine and flood the happy centers so that life became one big pleasure cruise. Loads of people I knew used coke recreationally in the 1990s—it was *the* party drug. What was interesting was why the people who came to the DDU couldn't pick it up and then put it down again for a while, the way most of the people I knew who took it seemed to be able to.

Because the users all converged on the unit at the end of the working day, I eventually put them all together and ran a twice-weekly early-evening group. Group membership was varied: among the regulars were Jessica, thirty-one, a city broker; Sam, twenty-three, an up-and-coming professional sportsman; Isobel, thirty-nine, a club promoter; and Curtis, her fifty-four-year-old professional musician partner. With Chris's help I planned the group carefully: psycho-educational with some cognitive behavioral therapy thrown in and a huge element of sharing, listening and supporting.

Jessica came from an aspirational, high-achieving background, a superbright girl who had massive expectations for herself. Having carved out a career in a male-dominated world, Jessica was determined to be the best; she worked long hours, often sleeping at her desk and brokering huge deals.

The patients had a few minutes to introduce themselves to the group and tell their story. Jessica went first.

"Hello. I'm Jess. I'm thirty-one and I love coke!"

Those who'd done the Narcotics Anonymous program chorused back, "Hi, Jess."

She giggled. "Well, gosh, I don't know where to start. Actually, there's not much to say! I started using coke three years ago just after work, because the buzz of the job was huge and you didn't want to let that go, so you went on partying."

Chuckles and nods around the group.

"Yay, you get where I'm coming from!"

Curtis leaned forward and high-fived her.

I felt a bit uneasy; this wasn't supposed to be an af-firmation group.

"Thanks!"

Curtis bowed. I caught Jessica's eye and subtly tried to point to my watch.

"Sorry. Well, I loved the high. I loved the energy it gave me. And, God, I loved the weight loss."

Charlie really was seductive.

"Now I can't get enough of it. I snort for breakfast, lunch and supper. I race like mad throughout the day, and last quarter I exceeded my targets by over a third!" Jessica paused and smiled, waiting for another high five, but the group was silent; her face fell.

"I get the shakes before work meetings and have to snort to calm myself down. I spend all weekend in bed trying not to use but feel so bloody depressed. I hate myself."

Jessica started to cry; Isobel shuffled her chair closer to her and held her hand.

My university lectures, which barely ever kept up with what I was seeing clinically, had become interesting when they defined the role of the clinical psychologist. Despite my moment of vain madness with the shrink who said I could be a medic, I was now becoming more and more wedded to my brilliant profession.

I loved how as clinical psychologists, our role was to create a formulation—to assess carefully and understand the narrative, the story, behind the presenting problems. Patients presented via their symptoms—in Jessica's case, excessive, out-of-control stimulant use—and so rather than prescribe to get rid of the symptoms, we were training to look at why they existed in the first place. By understanding the "why," we could enable our patients to create a healthier narrative while challenging the dysfunctional beliefs that underpinned their behavior.

I wanted to take this powerful explanation and shove it up that pathetic shrink's arse. I felt bloody proud to be a member of a profession that did not merely reduce a person to a group of symptoms but dug beneath them in order to try to facilitate real long-term change; it was more than "see, know, fix"; it was a nuanced, humanistic approach to mental health.

Jessica was bright and articulate. She was aware that she had a serious drug problem but clearly needed to understand her narrative. With the help of the group, we pulled her story together.

Jessica was a perfectionist in every way. As a child, she received attention from her parents only when she performed exceptionally at all she undertook. So that was her focus: county cross-country champion, accomplished violinist, slim, fit and with a clutch of top grades, Jessica made her parents very proud of themselves.

Jessica grew up believing that results and top achievement garnered love and respect; to do and be the best was the emotional currency of her family. Over time this belief became entrenched and totally black and white: "To be lovable, I have to be the best."

This underlying belief drove everything she did, and because there was no room for slack, or, even worse, mistakes, her expectations of herself grew and grew until, when she joined the highly competitive and results-driven financial world of brokering, she couldn't be the best without being superhuman, and that's where charlie came in.

"I find that the better I do, the worse I feel. I always have to do better. Without coke I can't work as long and hard as I want to."

"What do you think about yourself, Jessica?" I asked.

"I like myself when I'm coked up. I feel free and funny and confident, and I can work nonstop."

Jessica needed support to recognize her limiting and dysfunctional underlying belief and then to have the courage to dismantle it and redefine herself and her worth; unless she was able to do this, charlie would always be her life partner.

Like Jessica, Sam, Isobel, Curtis and all the others in the weekly group had reached a place where their tolerance was so high that they had to use greater and greater amounts of coke with more and more frequency—their dopamine receptors couldn't keep up, and so when their brains crashed, the only thing to do was to reach for more.

Sam's narrative was interesting because coke had a paradoxical effect on him: It let him relax. A bright boy who couldn't sit still at school but was an ace on the sports field, Sam was only happy when he was moving at speed. Sam had to get up intermittently throughout each ninety-minute group session on the pretext of making another coffee for everyone or using the loo.

Reluctantly I discussed him with the shrink—after the day of the awful kiss, I had been avoiding him as much as possible, and our relationship was now cool and cordial. He agreed that Sam was possibly an undiagnosed case of attention deficit hyperactivity disorder, ADHD.

Kids with ADHD are prescribed a form of stimulant that seems completely at odds with their presenting symptoms, but the explanation is straightforward: They have an underfunctioning reticular activating system, RAS. With a lack of endogenously driven stimulation, these kids have to boot up their arousal levels by racing through life. Sitting still is impossible for them.

Luckily for Sam, he had found a career built around his need for speed on the soccer field. The shrink took him in hand and prescribed for the underfunctioning RAS and Sam was eventually able to let charlie go without losing his already well-established athletic prowess.

Isobel and Curtis were wonderful people, but I didn't hold out much hope for them. Though they were a loving couple, their worlds were tied up with using and partying. The using and codependency that united them also bound their relationship. In those days, I wasn't anywhere near experienced enough to help them unravel all of this. But I was grateful for their presence in the group because they were kind and compassionate, and knew way more than I did about the world of stimulants. They helped me out when I got stuck.

I enjoyed running the group, and by the end at least a third of its members were using less. Two people hadn't used for over a fortnight. Isobel's and Curtis's usage fluctuated. Jessica had cut down and began to see me for individual sessions, and Sam was now under the care of the shrink.

The final day of the group came and we all said goodbye with a hug. I liked these people and respected their honesty and was sorry to see them go. And then, in the final moments of the good-byes, Curtis had an explosive sneeze and chunks of his nasal septum whizzed past my right ear and splatted onto the wall behind me. That evening, leaving the unit to go home, I met another group familiar to me: Camped outside the DDU door were the local dealers.

"Come on, guys. You've got no business here."

My familiarity with the DDU gave me a streetwise confidence very new to me.

These guys were not threatening—in fact, they were rather charming.

"C'mon, Doc, give us a break. You're ruining business for us."

With acute entrepreneurial skill, the dealers waited for their vulnerable ex-customers to leave the DDU, gave them free samples of the finest on offer and quickly reeled them back in.

"Bugger off or I'll call the police."

My colleagues and I were fighting a losing battle.

The next morning I took a cramped Tube into town, looking forward to my time with Tom.

It was a bright, sunny, cold morning—my favorite kind of weather—and I wandered toward the unit, sipping a cappuccino. As I got there, I saw a small crowd holding placards gathered around the main door: One had a megaphone and was reciting something, but I couldn't make out what it was.

Pete was standing at the main door gesturing to me. He looked anxious, not his usual laid-back self at all. Worried, I started walking toward him. And then something hit me.

I instinctively put my hand to my forehead and felt warm blood. Then it happened again, this time on my cheek. Putting my head down, I pushed through the angry crowd and ran up the steps to Pete as my back was pelted with more small stones.

"Get inside, quickly." Pete grabbed my arm and pulled me toward him.

"What the fuck is going on?"

I staggered into the waiting area and peered out of the window.

"AIDS: God's punishment for homosexuality," said one placard. There were more: "Die, you gay bastards"; "Let the faggots burn in hell."

"The religious nuts. Let me have a look, sweetie. You OK?" Pete examined my cuts and called a colleague to bring some antiseptic wipes and plasters. "Fucking nutters. We never know when they are coming."

I looked out of the window again and caught the eye of a young woman, her face twisted with hate.

"Slag!" she screamed at me. "Homo-loving whore!"

I flipped her the bird as Pete pulled me away.

"Don't, sweetheart. That's what they want us to do. Ignore them and they'll soon go away."

To hell with them and their discriminatory religious ideology.

"Why should I die when this fucking disease decides it's the time? Why should I endure the pain or drown in my own Pneumocystis pneumonia, fucking PCP? I want to die now."

Tom, discharged from the ward, having recovered

from his PCP, was sitting upright and opposite me in my office. And what a way to start a session.

"I'm not sure I get what you're saying here, Tom."

He smiled. "Yes, you do. You know exactly what I'm saying."

How do you ask someone if they seriously want to kill themselves?

Taking my lead from Chris's approach, I asked, "Are you telling me you are thinking about suicide?"

Tom chuckled and then coughed hard, his lungs having just been cleared from the PCP that clogged them up on a regular basis. I handed him a glass of water.

"Thinking? Oh, sweetheart, I have so done thinking. I know what I have to do."

"So why haven't you done it, then?"

Again my comment was met with the most electrifying smile. "I like your style. Pete was right: You are a minx!"

I pressed on. "Tom, what have you planned to do?"

Tom reached forward and pulled a few tissues out of the box on the small table between us, and then, after dipping them into his glass of water, he started to dab his face; a layer of expertly applied Pan Stik concealer was wiped away.

What was revealed took my breath away but I tried not to show it. Tom's beautiful face was blemished by Kaposi's sarcomas—two small brown and purple tumorous lesions eating into his skin. He looked utterly vulnerable.

"Call me vain, sweetheart. Call me shallow. But the condom sex I can do, if and when I get it. The monthly monster dose of antibiotics is bearable. But this . . ." He gestured toward his face. "This is fucking monstrous. I have become the sodding Elephant Man."

"How you look on the outside doesn't define who you are on the inside."

"Oh, come on, sweetheart. You're not counseling a bloody anorexic here."

I wasn't going to back down.

"Tom, I just got stoned."

"Well, very nice for you, darling."

"No! Not *stoned*. I got stones chucked at me."

Tom nodded. "Ah yes. The compassion of the narrow-minded religious. Such horribly unattractive people. Were you hurt?"

"No."

"That's my girl."

"But here's the thing, Tom. They all want you dead. They love the virus: It justifies their prejudice. Why buy into that?"

"I'm not buying into what they want. I'm deciding what I want."

"Have you tried before?"

Tom pulled up the sleeves of his linen shirt and revealed thin scars on both of his wrists. "Take a look at those babies."

"So what happened?"

"What happened is that I'm a fucking coward. What happened is that I couldn't cut deep enough because it stung so much, and then I couldn't wait to bleed long enough, so I called a friend. I'm a fucking coward."

It had started raining outside. Tom closed his eyes. "I love that noise."

"Me too, Tom."

"When I was a young, arrogant buck, my first collection at London Fashion Week was shown outdoors. And oh fuck, did it tip it down!"

We both laughed.

"What happened?"

"My clothes clung to the most beautiful bodies; their shape was gone, but they outlined something far more beautiful. I was panicking, but the models went onto the open-air catwalk and what I had designed found its own beauty."

"So you started your career designing for a wet T-shirt contest?"

Tom clapped his hands. "Darling, you know you are right! Indeed I did! And that year I won 'Young Designer of the Year.'"

I wanted to take Tom, and if I'm honest, myself, away from his thoughts of suicide, so I asked him about his career; anyway, I needed to get to know him. He was an impressive man: talented, beautiful and one of the first "out" gay fashion designers.

"So you're an icon."

"Oh, darling, flattery will get you everywhere!"

"No, seriously, Tom—what made you come out?"

"I didn't 'come out.' I was just being me."

"So why not be you now? Why want to kill yourself?"

Tom stretched his arms above his head and clicked his back from side to side. "I choose to be openly gay as a designer. I didn't choose this disease."

I couldn't argue with that.

"What would you do in my position?"

"Tom, this isn't about me."

"Not an answer."

I had to think here. You don't reveal yourself to your patient, it's all about them, but to push that point home to Tom felt way too insulting.

"Tom, I don't know."

"Thanks for being honest."

I continued to see Tom as an outpatient now that he had been discharged, but I had other patients and my list was varied.

I met a number of men, some heartbreakingly young, who were scared to death of death. A few of them had never come out to their families, so they needed support to prepare themselves to disclose two huge and shattering pieces of news: "So, Mum, Dad, I'm gay. And I'm HIV positive."

There were those who were firmly entrenched in their denial and were doing the rounds of HIV services looking for someone to tell them it was all a big mistake. And then mixed in were a few of my regulars from the DDU who had chosen to inject themselves with infected blood, were happy with their HIV diagnosis and eagerly looking forward to their benefit eligibility.

And then there were the "worried wells."

The "worried well" was someone with chronic AIDS phobia. Their health anxiety had become so acute that many had become agoraphobic, due to their morbid fear that any toilet seat, cup rim or stranger brushing past them on the street would give them AIDS. After my session with Tom, I really struggled to remain in a nonjudgmental space with the worried well.

Looking back, I realize how revoltingly politically

correct I became on that placement. I was so over-whelmed by those facing death that I forgot to remember that psychological distress, however it presented, was real to the person experiencing it and I was privileged to be asked to help them get through it.

Chris and I met in a coffee shop near the clinic. I hadn't seen her for a while—she'd been on vacation—and when I saw her walking toward the table I had been sitting at for about fifteen minutes, I realized that I had missed her.

"Hey, good to see you!"

She dumped her many heavy bags down. "You got a coffee."

"Yeah. And I got a double espresso for you."

Chris smiled. "Nicely done." She took a sip, winced, and then poured in a sachet of brown sugar. "So, I hear you are seeing Tom."

Does this woman know everything about me?

"Yeah. He's a great guy. I am looking forward to working with him."

After another sip, Chris added another sachet. "I'm glad. But I wish that you had run him as a possible case past me first, before you just took him on."

Here we go: placement screw-up number one.

"Well, you have been off on leave. But anyway, why?"

"Because I think he's going to be more of a challenge than you can handle, even at this stage of your training. On top of this final placement, you need to complete your dissertation—I'll want a time frame from you for drafts of each section, by the way. That's a lot to take on."

I was shocked. How could Tom be too much of a challenge? Lovely, dying Tom?

"What? More than Ray or Imogen? More than Mollie or Harold?"

"Different."

I spooned off my cappuccino foam and licked it off the teaspoon. I can do cut-off; I can play her at her own game.

"You're going to have to explain this one to me, Chris. This is my final placement. Shouldn't I be ready?"

"Just trust me."

"I do, but I also need to understand what your problem is here."

"Problem?"

Shit, Chris looked pissed off.

"All right, I'll tell you my reservations about you seeing Tom."

"OK. I'm listening, but I have to tell you that I have made a commitment to this man, and seeing as you were off when I started this placement, I really do struggle with you coming in now and taking me away from him."

Chris smiled to herself. "Don't get too cocky."

"I am not going to renege on my commitment."

"That's OK. I can see him instead of you."

"No, you can't. He's mine."

The smile froze on Chris's face. "Tom is end stage. How much do you understand about this virus?"

I took a deep breath. "Seroconversion happens between three and twelve weeks of infection. Early symptoms of the acute retroviral syndrome generally present as an influenza-type fever, some swollen lymph nodes, perhaps a rash on the trunk of the body and mouth and genital sores."

I paused. Chris had her head down, stirring her coffee, listening.

"Following seroconversion, there is a period of clinical latency—a symptom-free period. But as the CD4+ T cells decline as the immune system becomes more and more compromised, opportunistic infections start to kick in."

I paused again; Chris still said nothing.

"So these symptoms would be nausea, vomiting, diarrhea, fever, weight loss, usually lasting between three and six months. Also generalized lymphadenopathy."

Chris looked up at me. "And that means?"

God, she could be one smug bitch.

"It means that the patient shows unexplained and nonpainful enlargement of more than one group of lymph nodes and—"

"Patient?"

Chris's interruption was abrupt; I felt slightly rattled.

"Yes, patient. And the problem here is?"

Chris smiled to herself. "Nothing. Carry on."

"Do you want another coffee?"

"In a minute. Carry on."

God, what was there left to say?

"So, once the T-cell count dips below two hundred, a diagnosis of AIDS is made. Associated symptoms are PCP, cancers, cachexia, which is the term for body wasting"—I smiled to myself—"thrush in the throat, which is called esophageal candidiasis, and also respiratory infections."

Chris started clapping slowly.

What?!

"Well done. A great description. Shame you're not doing medicine."

That stung. What the hell was she saying?

"Look, you asked me . . ."

Chris looked up and she looked pissed off. "Yes, I did. I asked you for an explanation as a psychologist."

"No, you asked me what I knew about the virus."

"And I expected you to answer me as a clinical psychologist."

What did this woman want from me?

"Do you know, I've just had a flashback to your first presentation to me of Imogen. Do you remember?"

I stood up and went to order another cappuccino and double espresso; I needed time to collect myself.

Why did I get so quickly irritated with this woman?

"OK, I'll start again." I slid Chris's drink over to her. "Tom is end stage. He has recurrent bouts of PCP and KS on his face. He is angry and has left it this long into his disease progression to ask for support to manage what he's facing. He has gone past the denial phase. He is no longer in shock; he's just bloody angry."

Chris nodded for me to go on.

"Yes, I am flattered that he asked me to be his support. Yes, I am pretty bloody impressed by who he is. But for God's sake, Chris, don't flake on me now. I know I can do this."

Chris looked straight at me. "Flake on you? A little too much familiarity here, I think. I do not *flake* on you or anyone else I give my time to support. Maybe you want to rephrase that?"

I was stunned. I took a deep breath. "Chris, that term

is a colloquialism, right? I didn't mean any offense. I think that is a bit of an overreaction."

I took a sip of my coffee and avoided her gaze; my heart was beating fast.

She continued, "I think there are some boundaries in this relationship. I think you need to consider your language at times. I think you need to remember my role in your training and that I am ultimately the person who will get you through to qualification. Don't forget that."

I felt a flame in my stomach, and despite feeling a need to placate my supervisor, I couldn't stop the clearly repressed and still unresolved resentment from bubbling up.

"I do remember all that. I also remember the moment you left me high and dry at a bloody difficult time on my second placement."

It was Chris's turn to sip her coffee and avoid my eye.

"In fact," I continued, "I don't recall any explanation of your sudden disappearance. No call from the uni to arrange coverage while you were away. Nothing."

Chris looked up slowly. Her face was taut and her eyes fixed. "So I have *flaked* on you." She smiled tightly to herself and shook her head.

What was I doing? This woman held my qualification in her hands. I needed to backpedal fast.

"No. Well, listen, Chris—"

"Point taken and will be considered. Let's move on, shall we?"

Her tone was chilling. Now I really understood how I'd overstepped the mark.

There was an uncomfortable silence as Chris drained her coffee.

"OK, then," she said. "Back to Tom. So, what are you going to do? This man has no intention of accepting his death. There are many others you could help."

"I'm going to do the best I can to do what he has asked me to do."

Chris smiled to herself and shook her head. "You are so bloody stubborn."

I attempted a smile back, although she wasn't looking at me. "Takes one to know one."

Chris made to leave. "Fine. Honor your commitment, but make sure you keep me in the loop, because this one will not be easy."

Thanks for telling me, lady, because after Ray, Imogen, Harold and Mollie, I expected this placement to be a walk in the park.

But my victory felt hollow. That was one holy screw-up of a conversation.

Despite being a place where people went to die, the ward often had a real party atmosphere, and never more so than when some of the big names in entertainment—singers, actors, comedians—some themselves infected with the virus, would give an impromptu performance. It was so surreal to be in a place of immense sadness and loss yet enjoy the company of the most enthusiastically vibrant people.

Some of the best live gigs of my life happened on that ward.

During one especially great afternoon performance by a singer whose concert tickets I couldn't afford, Pete asked me to come into a room where a young man was about to die.

"You're the only female available. Do you mind coming in? His mother is distressed."

I nodded but didn't move from my seat. I couldn't believe my luck as I sat only feet away from one of the most iconic musicians of the time, a man who, at least twice during his set, made eye contact with me as I sang along. I knew that I wasn't moving fast enough—the thought of being with a dying man seemed worlds away from the exclusive party I was attending and I didn't want to leave.

I jumped as Pete tapped me on the shoulder.

"Come on, sweetheart. I really need you here."

Guiltily, I leaped up and pushed myself through the throng, and as I turned back to take a last look at the singer, he blew me a kiss. I felt dizzy and couldn't stop smiling as I followed Pete through the double doors and down the long corridor, the music fading fast behind me.

The room was quiet and full of people all focused on the skeletally thin young man in the bed. Lying next to him and holding him was another young man whom I presumed was his partner. His mouth was up close to the dying man's ear; he was whispering to him.

On the other side of the bed was the only woman in the room. She sat ramrod straight in her chair, and her eyes were intently focused on the young man's face; she held his hand and stroked it with her thumb. I walked toward her and she, catching my eye, nodded before returning her gaze to her son. I tried to stand discreetly some distance behind her.

At the base of the bed were three other young men, all with their arms around each other, one sobbing silently into the chest of another. The dying man had his three boys there like one day I hoped my three girls would be there for me. The room was almost silent, but the anguish was palpable.

The patient was struggling to breathe. His breath was erratic, sometimes deep and slow, and at other times shallow and fast. On occasion he would struggle to take a deep inhale followed by an excruciating pause.

Pete leaned over the young man and gently moistened his dry lips. His partner looked up questioningly and Pete nodded. The partner looked to the young man's mother, who also nodded to him.

What were they doing?

The three friends at the end of the bed came forward and in turn leaned down to kiss their friend. One sobbed; another rubbed his friend's head while kissing him on his half-open mouth; the last put his arms around the dying young man's fragile body and laid his head on his chest.

It was then the turn of the young man's mother, who stood and leaned over her son while his partner slid off the bed and stood respectfully away. As she cupped her hands around his face, her voice was the first I'd heard in this still, calm room.

"My darling boy, I don't want you to fight anymore. I think it's time for you to go." Her voice cracked, but she carried on. "My darling Richard, I have always been so proud to be your mother. You have given me so many years of pleasure and I shall always cherish our Devon holidays and crabbing together and watching you graduate, the wonderful plays you took me to and the many brilliant articles you have written. You are the most wonderful boy, and I promise I shall always look after Joel."

The dignified woman leaned forward and kissed her son on his forehead, both his eyes and his mouth. "Off you go now, my darling. Time to rest. Mummy loves you."

The young man's mother stood away from the bed and sat back down, weeping silently. I took a few steps forward and placed my hand on her shoulder, and to my surprise she reached up and held it.

The boyfriend, whom I presumed was Joel, slid back next to his lover and cradled him gently while whispering against his ear.

Over time the breathing sounds became more and more labored, the rhythm erratic; the room was completely still. And then all the sounds stopped.

Pete moved gently toward the still body and, with a nod, closed the young man's eyes. The sound of sobbing broke through the silence.

The mother stood up and, after hugging each of the crying young men, walked out of the room. I followed her.

"Would you like me to take you to another room for a moment?" I asked.

"No, thank you."

"Would you like some water?"

"No, thank you. Nothing at all. Just if you could be so kind—would you order me a taxi?"

"Are you going home alone? Would you like me to travel with you?"

"No, that won't be necessary, thank you. My husband is waiting for me at home."

It felt so bizarre having a "normal" conversation with this woman who had just watched her son die.

"Oh. I am so sorry your husband wasn't able to be here."

She looked up at me and smiled. "He hasn't spoken to Richard for three years."

I didn't know what to say, so instead, numbly, I handed her a leaflet. "Should you ever feel you would like support, we run sessions for the bereaved."

She took my hand. "Thank you, my dear, but that won't be necessary." She handed the leaflet back to me. "I shall wait for the taxi downstairs in reception. Thank you for your kindness."

And off she went as I stood still, clutching the bereavement support leaflet, unable to breathe.

The next session with Tom was back in the ward, where he had been admitted during the night after taking an overdose. Hearing the news, I was shocked.

When I arrived in his room and sat in the chair next to his bed, I was panting, having run from my office at the unit.

Tom slid a glass of water toward me. "I guess you aren't too happy with me?"

Tom seemed to have a slight smile on his lips, still stained black from the charcoal he'd been forced to ingest to wash the poisons out of his stomach.

"I'm curious, actually, Tom."

"As in, why the fuck did you do it?"

I nodded.

"Well, why the fuck wouldn't I? It's my fucking life, sweetheart."

He had no argument from me.

"You've no idea, no fucking idea, how this disease is literally doing my head in. I am fucking tired of it. I'm tired of the fucking pity and the compassion. I am tired of people telling me I look well when I know I look bloody hideous. Oh God, I am sick to bloody death of the mercy fucks and all those who now want to be my special friend."

He looked at the glass. "My lips are dry."

I moistened a flannel and handed to him; he held it to his mouth.

"I hate the bloody charity benefits and the fucking fund-raisers. The sodding visibility of this bastard bloody virus. And most of fucking all I *hate* being a poster boy for this illness."

He gestured for the flannel to be wet again.

"Do you want me to wipe the charcoal off your lips?"

"Have I lost my fucking arms, sweetheart? Am I now not able to wipe my own bloody lips?"

He snatched the flannel angrily and started scrubbing at his dry, blackened lips; they started to bleed. "Fuck that." Tom threw the flannel across the room and started to pull at the cannula in his hand. "I've got to get out of this fucking place."

I jumped up and put my hand over his. "Stop."

Tom tried to bat my hand away.

"Tom! Please stop this now."

With a grunt he sat back in the bed and closed his eyes. "Wanna swap places, sweetheart?"

"How would that help?"

He looked at me and smiled. "It wouldn't, darling. Anyway, I wouldn't wish this on you; I wouldn't wish it on my worst enemy." He paused and closed his eyes again. "Correction: There are a couple of arseholes I'd happily see in this position."

The room descended into silence and I wondered whether Tom had fallen asleep.

I moved my chair.

"I'm still here, darling. Not dead yet. Ready to listen."

This wasn't what I had expected: He asked me to help him get his head around the virus, yet now he was raging so much I felt totally out of my depth.

"I'm not sure I can help you, Tom."

"And why's that, pray?"

"Because I think that you don't want to be helped."

He opened his eyes. "OK, sweetheart. Thanks for dropping by. Leave like all the others."

"What others?"

"The others who were defeated, like you are."

"Defeated by what, Tom?"

He turned to look at me. "Defeated by this fucking virus defeating me."

I was not going to be defeated.

"Listen, Tom. I feel bad if I've let you down, but let me just say this. I really think that what's going on here is that you've . . . is that you've . . ." I hesitated. *Did I dare say it?*

"I've what, sweet cheeks?"

I swallowed hard. "That you've set me, and the others that came before me . . . you've set us up to fail."

Tom put his head back, closed his eyes again and chuckled. "And why would I do that?"

"So that we can enable you to reinforce your help-lessness in the face of this virus."

There was no reply. I knew that I had screwed up badly.

"I don't believe in a higher power, so there's nothing for me to bargain with. I can't ask some god or other to get rid of my virus and in return I'll devote my life to good works, because I am not a believer. Also, there's no other place after this life that I believe exists. And even if it did, I wouldn't want to go there, because I have been so happy here nothing could be better."

I sat still. I didn't want to make any sound.

"I was never out and proud. I have always just been me in my world, accepted for who I am. I have never wanted to be defined by my sexuality, and I have been lucky that generally it hasn't been a major issue for me in my life. Maybe people expect men in fashion to be gay, who knows? But the point is, now I've got this virus, I am defined as a homosexual, and I am expected to be loud and proud and fight the discrimination, and . . ." Tom started crying.

I moved my chair closer to his bed.

"And I just want to go back to being me." Tom looked around for tissues and I passed him a handful.

"So tell me who you are, Tom."

He blew his nose loudly. "Sorry?"

"Who are you? What's your legacy?"

"As in what will be engraved on my gravestone?"

"No, as in what you leave behind."

"Some bloody nice clothes."

"What else?"

"Employment for young, talented people."

"And?"

"And wonderful parents, a sweet brother and many, many wonderful people that I am lucky enough to call my friends."

"And what do they like about you?"

Tom smiled. "You'll have to ask them."

"I'm asking you."

"Oh stop, you're making me blush."

I sat back in my seat.

"Well, people tell me that I am generous," he said finally. "They tell me that I care."

"And do you?"

Again Tom started to weep. "Yes, I do. Sorry—do you mind grabbing that flannel for me again."

I found a fresh one and soaked it and then wrung it out.

"Can you promise me one thing?"

"Not sure, Tom. Try me."

"Can you promise me that however I die, I won't lose my mind?"

Tom was asking about AIDS-related dementia, a cruel and nasty end to one's life.

"Why do you think that will happen to you?"

"My boyfriend died two years ago. I nursed him up until the end. He was completely gaga, in nappies and just reduced to nothing. He didn't even know who I was and at the very end became really aggressive."

I thought of Harold.

"You nursed him to the end."

Tom suppressed a sob. "Yes, I did."

"Your friends are right. You really are a good and kind man."

"I just can't lose my mind. Is there any way you can tell me that won't happen?"

I couldn't.

Tom closed his eyes again.

"Tom, tell me why you think you might be losing your mind."

Now he was upright, looking straight at me. "I forget so many things. I can't get myself going. I just don't have any interest in getting on with my day. My brain is sluggish." Tom punched himself in the forehead. "I fucking hate it."

"Tell me about your sleep."

"It's shit. I wake up early, I'm bloody knackered, but I can't get back to sleep and so I lie there thinking about how my brain is fucked."

Although I'd been training for more than two and a half years, I still wasn't qualified, so could I go with my instinct? Should I run this past Chris?

"Tom, what you are describing sounds like clinical depression to me."

His eyes were still closed, but I could tell that he was listening.

"I think that you are so overwhelmed by what you are dealing with and feel so hopeless in the face of it all that you have become depressed."

After having attended only a few lectures on clinical depression and written three essays, I arrogantly carried on.

"Your sleep is disturbed, you have early-morning waking, and you have no motivation and find no pleasure in your day. Your memory is poor. You feel confused."

Tom nodded.

"On top of this, I think that there may be an overlay of anxiety."

Tom smiled. "Really, sweetheart, you noticed?"

"Just a tad. Why wouldn't you be anxious? But the thing about anxiety is that it further erodes normal brain function and can cause memory loss."

Oh God, I hope I got that last bit right.

"So not dementia? Just anxiety and depression?"

"Well, not 'just,' Tom, but I think it's something we should explore."

"And can we sort the anxiety and depression out? Freshen my brain up again?"

"Tom, that's up to you. But if you want, we can try."

Pete was waiting for me anxiously on the other side of the door.

"So is Tom still a risk to himself? Should I get the duty psychiatrist back down?"

A million possible answers went through my mind.

"No, I don't think he is."

Pete looked relieved. "That's good."

"But call the duty psych anyway because I think Tom might be ready for some help with his anxiety and depression."

Pete shook his head. "He won't. We've been here before with him."

"Try again. This time he might be more ready."

"OK. If you're sure."

In truth, I wasn't and I was shit scared.

I sat opposite Chris, hugging myself.

"I can't do any more death."

"Why not?"

"I just can't. I can't disconnect myself from watching these men die, the raw grief of their loved ones, seeing their last breath. Chris, this is fucking up my head."

"Why?"

I couldn't speak; I was too busy trying not to cry.

"What's happening with Tom?"

I tried, as best I could, to summarize my recent sessions with Tom and talk through my hunch that he was anxious and depressed.

"Well, if you've enabled him to acknowledge that, then that might be a step in the right direction."

"But isn't that a psychology cop-out? Get the psychs in and pump in the drugs."

"Depleted serotonin is depleted serotonin. Give the psychs a break."

I felt relieved.

"And by the way. Good paradoxical intervention."

Paradoxical what?

Chris spared me from having to reveal my ignorance. "OK, so remember your lectures on Ericksonian family therapy? Well, by suggesting to Tom that he was setting you up to fail him, you strategically enabled him to prove you wrong and do the opposite."

I looked confused.

"That's when he engaged with you."

Paradoxical intervention. Whatever. I was done, worn out; I couldn't think about death anymore.

Chris changed gears. "So, about not being able to do any more death, what's all that about? Too much 'stuff' getting in the way?"

Stuff? Stuff! Is that what you call it?

"You could say that."

"OK, then let's talk about it."

I looked up at Chris. Her expression was soft, her eyes focused on me. As I wiped my face on my sleeve, she fumbled in her bag and handed me a packet of tissues.

"Look, Chris. Thanks for the offer. I appreciate your kindness." I paused to swallow hard. "Thing is, I don't think it's your job to give me therapy."

Chris smiled. "Yes, you're right. Mustn't overstep the boundaries of the role."

That wasn't the answer I expected.

"But maybe you don't need therapy right now. Perhaps all you need at this present time is a chat, some help to get you through this placement."

Oh, if only it could be that easy, but I knew that it wasn't. I dreamed funerals. I had flashbacks to my grandmother's blood on the carpet, a huge red stain. I kept hearing my father howl. This wasn't going to be dealt with via a chat.

Chris leaned forward. "Look, you are not ready for therapy. Maybe one day you will be, but at this moment I think you've got enough on your plate without also having to dismantle and then reassemble yourself. Not the right time."

"Then transfer me to another placement."

"No, that's not going to happen."

I didn't know what to say, so instead I put my face in my hands and started to breathe heavily.

"Talk to me. Come on, let's have it."

Did I trust this woman? Should I tell her about the worst moments of my life and let her hold them, interpret them for me? She continually surprised me with her intuition and kindness, but she also totally discombobulated me and, at times, either really irritated me or scared me.

"Harold told me that I hadn't really processed my grandmother's murder. He said that I was too angry still about her murder and hadn't grieved for her loss."

"Harold is a wise man. And?"

"And now all I am doing is a pathetic stumble through my sessions with men and their partners and friends trying to navigate their way through the hell of impending death without any kind of emotional compass of my own."

Chris lit a cigarette and offered me one.

"No, thanks. I'm trying to cut down."

She exhaled. It smelled lovely.

"OK," she said. "So did you have to be sexually abused to help Imogen?"

"No, of course not!"

"And did you have to go through the camps and survive the Holocaust for Harold to trust you with his life story?"

"Oh come on. Give me a break."

"Listen to me. Here's the break. If you think you can only do this job by having a perfectly rounded acceptance of all the shit in your life and also a complete understanding of the pain of your patients before you can help them with theirs, then dream on."

That statement shocked me by its informality and how it hit home.

"When I was fifteen, my grandmother was beaten to death with an iron poker by a heroin-using pregnant drug addict."

"I know."

How the fuck she knew bothered me but didn't stop me from talking.

"My grandmother was difficult. She was incredibly hostile toward my dad. They were like each other: creative, expansive, emotional. But she was really unpredictable. Sunday lunches were a nightmare. She'd come and after a while they'd argue loudly and aggressively and then she would go home. That defined my childhood."

"OK. People have lived through worse. And?"

"Can I have a cigarette?"

Chris lit one and handed it to me. "Go on."

"Dad is well known in TV. My grandmother would try to emotionally blackmail him into casting her in his shows. He did it because he felt he couldn't not, but it was a disaster because their relationship was so visibly hostile."

"Why?"

"I'm not entirely sure, but I know she never made him feel wanted. From when he was a small boy, he could never call her 'Mother,' only by her name—that's what she insisted on. They lived in chaos. She had her own life, with lots of lovers, while he was put into endless boarding schools. And then when she was murdered, my poor dad was a suspect."

Chris sat forward in her chair. "Not good. What happened?"

Oh, so much happened. What should I tell her?

"The press was camped outside our house, but Mum told them to fuck off."

Chris smiled. "I see where you get your chutzpah from."

"My sister and I were sent to stay with family friends, who were very kind but left the TV on and we saw the news reports."

"Not great. And?"

"There were these two detectives who knew it wasn't Dad. They found the murderer's fingerprints in blood on my grandmother's laminated medical cards and caught her, a pregnant drug addict, within three weeks."

"And?"

"And she was arrested and tried and got a shit nothing sentence, had her baby in prison and got out within eighteen months."

"So what did you do?"

"I read lots about the mind of the killer. I discovered psychology. I wrote to the bloody home secretary about my grandmother's murderer's pathetic sentence."

"And?"

"And I got a trite bullshit letter back explaining the justice system and commiserating on my family's loss."

I stood up and began to walk around the room; sitting down compressed my lungs and by this stage I was finding it hard to breathe.

Chris stayed in her chair; she didn't turn around to look at me pushing my back up against the wall at the far end of the room.

"So, just to be clear about all this," she began, "your grandmother was bludgeoned to death."

Nice choice of words, lady.

"Your father was implicated, but after a short while her killer was apprehended."

I nodded, but I don't think Chris saw and so she continued.

"The sentence was paltry and the response to your question about this less than satisfactory. But you found a place that intellectually stimulated you."

Nice summary.

"You became interested in why people do what they do, even if what they do sits on the darker side of life." Chris turned to me. "So, you saw the nastier side of death. You are angry. Well, think about this. These men have a starring role in a horribly nasty side of death and they are all bloody angry and they don't need some trite practitioner with no sense of the guts of death to lead them through it. They need someone like you."

Was that a criticism or a compliment?

"So here's my advice. Take that experience and put it in a box somewhere in the attic of your mind. It's not gone, but it is stored until you are ready to open it and look at the contents fully. For what it's worth, I don't think that time is now.

"Next, focus hard on what the experience of your grandmother's death has given you—an experience of the darkest side of life, and death, and an appreciation of the horror that such an experience can bring.

"Either you harness this, and objectively make it work for you and your patients, or you give up now in a way you didn't let yourself when your grandmother was murdered. You choose.

"OK," she concluded. "I think that's all for now. You OK?"

I nodded and Chris left.

Put it in a box, place it in the attic and one day, when you are ready to do so, open it and really look at it. But not now; use the experience to do the best job you can by your patients.

Once again Chris said it short and sharp and got it totally right.

I was twenty-five years old, and I was a funeral veteran. Working in palliative care, with the dying, I experienced a part of life I'd never thought about much before.

The funerals were exhausting. All the usual pressures were there, plus a real worry about what to wear. These guys wanted their psychologist to be stylish to the last; a couple even gave me outfit suggestions a few days before they died.

I had to go to about three funerals a month and I was emotionally drained. The pressure to be part of the inner circle of people you had known briefly at the most intensely focused time of their life—some you had had deeply personal conversations with as they tried to sort out how they felt about dying; others you had witnessed behaving strangely because disease was eating away at their frontal lobes—that pressure was intense.

At the funerals I often didn't know what face to wear, how to look, what to say when I was pressed for intimate confidences by grieving relatives wanting to know more about a loved one's final weeks—confidentiality existed even after death. There were times when I knew the deceased had hated the family member in question: "Watch out for her. She'll be the bitch with the crocodile tears."

Bloody hard.

It was my Sunday to have the girls around for a meal, and after something rather unspectacular (cooking was and has never been my thing), Megan, Ali and Rosie all sat on my bed to help me decide the next day's funeral attire.

This was going to be a big one. The well-known singer who had entertained us all on so many occasions on the ward had finally succumbed to this cruel virus; to be asked to his funeral was the invite of the year and I was going as Pete's plus one.

Megan wasn't impressed. "Plus one? Is this a funeral or a bloody party?"

"Both," I said as I pulled the contents of my wardrobe onto the end of my bed.

Megan still seemed unimpressed. "Sorry, girls, call me old-fashioned, but when I die, I want somber and misery. I want you all in black and sobbing. This is just too weird."

Megan, the girl from the Welsh Valleys, had moved to London but never lost that traditional sense of how things should be because that's how they always had been.

"Well, I'm bloody jealous!" said Ali. "Can't Pete wangle a plus two?"

Megan threw a shoe at Ali. "Pagan!"

The two girls started wrestling on the bed and Ali pinned down Megan.

"Listen here, boyo, when you die, I will be there in pink spandex!"

"You do that, sweetheart, and I'll haunt you forever!"

Some time later, while sipping a rather nasty, dismally warm Chardonnay, we applied ourselves to creating the funeral garb. Each of my girls selected an outfit, then took me solemnly to the bathroom, dressed me and made the big reveal to the others.

Ali went first and took the longest.

"Ouch! Bloody hell, Als, why the gripper knickers?"

"Because. Just shut up and breathe in." She pulled them firmly up and into place.

"I can't breathe in or out. I'll bloody expire at this funeral."

"Shut up and put your arms up."

Ali poured me into a short, tight, sequined dress with my hair fully back-combed, false eyelashes and a shiny glossed porn-actress mouth.

"OK," said Rosie slowly. "I see where you are going with this, Als, but I think too much party, not enough funeral."

"You've made her look like a drag queen," said Megan.

Next it was Megan's turn. She went for gothic widow in a black puffball skirt and DM biker boots.

Rosie again commented first. "OK, Megan, I can see you are trying to dilute the formal while keeping traditional, but—"

Ali interrupted. "But she looks fucking hideous."

This wasn't going well.

Rosie locked us in the bathroom.

"OK, so what do you *want* to wear?" she asked.

"Rosie, I have no bloody idea."

Rosie sat on the loo and, while peeing, looked pensive.

"OK, so here's the thing. You got to look the part, but also you got to look professional. Tomorrow it's the funeral; the next day you're back on the ward doing your stuff." She yanked at the loo roll and pulled her knickers up assertively. "Wait here, I've got it."

Ten minutes later the reveal was met with a round of applause; as always Rosie was on the button: black halter-neck pencil dress to just below the knee, short black cardigan, black sheer stockings, red lips, matching red clutch, black stilettos.

Outfit done.

The evening finished with a better bottle of wine and a lazy, simple chat.

"So, how would you want your funeral to be?"

The girls looked at me in horror.

"What the hell is that question?"

"Als, this is a serious question. Have you worked out your funeral? Who would be there? What do you want said? What about the music?"

Megan refilled the glasses. "That is just too weird!" she said.

"No, it isn't! Think about it. One of the only advantages of knowing that you are going to die is that you can plan your funeral. Loads of the guys I'm working with do it. It's awesome. They plan their final party and make it exactly how they would want it to be if they were there as a guest."

So then we had a long debate about our culturally inhibited way of sucking the life out of a funeral.

After a while Rosie got us all a piece of paper and a pencil. Megan opened another bottle of wine and Ali put some chips in a bowl. We then all munched, sipped and wrote our ideal funeral plan.

For me, there had to be "Perhaps, Perhaps, Perhaps" by Doris Day. I also wanted "That's Life" by Ol' Blue

Eyes and various other anthems. The rest is a secret until I die, but it will be one bloody good party.

And as for what the girls wrote down, well, that's a secret that only we know, and we all keep copies of one another's because we don't know which one of us will go first.

The placement raced to its end. I had never been so busy, living on a lot of coffee and very little sleep. I divided my clinical days between the two units and my university days and every night at home writing up case reports and slogging on with the dissertation. Even though I was tired all the time, I loved my clinical days and felt completely part of both services, especially the DDU. I began to wonder whether this was where I wanted to work once I qualified—if I qualified. The very thought of it made my heart leap with fear.

Mo had disappeared off the DDU radar and I was worried about her. Jessica was beginning to realize that she was better than results and was able to dump charlie. A few of my worried wells were now able to leave their homes and put their AIDS fear in a box in their attics.

Pete and I hugged and hugged and exchanged contact numbers. Sadly the last time I was with him was at his funeral, several years later.

And then it was time for me to say good-bye to Tom, and because it was another cold, sunny, spectacular day, we met in Soho Square.

"So where you off to?"

"I don't know, Tom. I have to graduate first. Then we'll see, but I'm hoping to work at a DDU."

"Ooh! That'll be a laugh a minute."

"I'll let you know when I've got there."

"You can't let me know."

What was he talking about?

"Why not, Tom?"

Tom took my hand. "Because we are not friends."

I felt assaulted.

"No, listen to me, sweet cheeks. I have been your patient. You are now moving on. We no longer have contact—I believe that is how it works."

He was right and I felt like an idiot.

We spent a while chatting, and while Tom was no less angry about the virus, he had decided not to kill himself.

"Are you happy with that decision?"

"What, to engage back into life?"

I nodded.

"Yes. And for what it's worth, you were right about what depression and anxiety were doing to my mind, and actually just knowing it helped: I didn't take any medication in the end. I guess you could say I have shifted my focus from dying to living."

I smiled and suppressed the urge to hug this beautiful man.

"Yes. I am happy to be doing life again and designing like a lunatic."

We laughed.

Tom reached into a bag. "For you."

I opened the package slowly, wondering how I could tell him that receiving gifts from patients was frowned upon.

It was a small leather-bound Moleskine sketchbook. I held it in my hand.

"Look inside, for God's sake!"

Tom had given me a book of the most exquisite sketches that I had ever seen, each one a work of art. On every page there was a woman in an outfit that fitted her body perfectly.

"Do you know who that woman is, sweet cheeks?"

I shook my head.

"Look at her—she has curves and one fucking attitude."

This was my style makeover. Protocol aside, I hugged my soon-to-be ex-patient.

"You are one fucking tough bird! Where'd that come from?"

The thin, still extremely beautiful man's face broke into a dazzling smile.

EPILOGUE

I qualified in 1992. The day of my graduation I cele-
brated with my girls in Central London. That evening,
walking from the pub to the Tube station, I passed a heavily pregnant young woman who was begging, and mind-
ful of how she might use any money I put into her cup, I
went and bought her a sandwich and a hot drink.

As she looked up at me, her pupils constricted, and I
instantly recognized this emaciated, drawn young
woman—it was Mo.

She didn't recognize me and wasn't impressed with
my offerings: "Fuck off and go look after someone who
wants you to."

So I did. I got a position in drug-dependency services
and for a few years worked with a dedicated team while
also completing my doctorate on the treatment of stimulant misusers.

One of my first jobs as a newly qualified clinical psychologist was to set up support groups, and I ended up

working with pregnant users like Mo, whom I thought about often. Indeed, it wasn't until some years later, talking to Chris—who became a dear friend and to this day has remained my professional mentor—that I realized I had started my professional life back at the beginning of my own journey, age fifteen in my grandmother's living room, when she had been killed by a pregnant drug user. By the time I had qualified and was treating addicts, I had come full circle.

I have now been a practitioner for nearly twenty-five years, and I have spent twelve of them thinking about this book.

I have read many books written by people working in the field of mental health in which they've described cases they've worked. One thing that has always struck me is that the spotlight tends to be on the people being treated, never also on those of us doing the treating.

For me, this approach appears to collude with the prevailing and dangerous belief that there are people who are "mad" and people who aren't. It also elevates the role of the mental health practitioner unduly—we appear to observe, assess, formulate and treat from some distant vantage point. I don't believe that it works like that.

In these pages, I have tried to capture my own journey, to show how the differences between patient and clinician are often slight, merely a matter of degrees. In the cases I have written about here, I have tried to convey the journey from chaos to clarity that psychological therapies can offer. And as I thought back to my younger self, someone I'm not always proud of, I realized that I too was managing my own journey from chaos to clarity as my training progressed.

I could be anxious, arrogant and naive. I often had no more depth of insight than the people I was meant to be treating. I now realize that the understanding, perception and certainty I was seeking at that time come only through practice, through immersion in the experience and through people letting you into their lives. I owe a huge debt to the people I worked with in my early years for providing me an opportunity to become a skilled practitioner and, perhaps, a better person.

Some of those who generously read drafts of this book were surprised by my willingness to disclose my own, at times massive, ineptitude. Some, especially my mother, were worried I would come out looking like someone who should never be allowed near any person with mental health difficulties: "Aren't you revealing too much of yourself, darling?" she asked me.

Ever since I understood that my grandmother's murderer was a woman struggling with her own psychological troubles, I've wanted to challenge the way we stereotype those with mental health difficulties. I am passionate about destigmatizing vulnerable people grappling with the weight of their own distress, the fear that they are unable to cope with life and the terror that perhaps they are losing their minds. Revealing my own doubts and inadequacies when trying to help anyone with a mental health problem feels like an important part of breaking down the false barriers we've constructed between the "well" and the "sick."

After all, where does sanity end and insanity begin? Some of us are lucky to be able to manage the challenges of our lives or within our support networks and make them work for us. We define ourselves as "successful" as a result. Yet, others of us manage to cope by living in denial or by finding people who will let us project our "shit"—our baggage and our insecurities—onto them.

Nurture is fundamental. Some of us are born into lives and families where the protective factors outweigh the risk factors, so we develop a stronger sense of self-awareness and self-belief; we have a strengthened base of resilience and an ability to weather life's storms. But others who endure early lives of abuse and neglect are often set up to fail from the minute they arrive.

Nature also has a key role in the narrative of our lives. Some of us may inherit an underlying predisposition to mental health vulnerability. When the stresses and pressures of life become overwhelming, we can be tipped into really debilitating mental health difficulties, repeating a family history familiar in terms of stories about previous generations.

We understand these difficulties using narrative. Often the key part of the journey from chaos to clarity is telling the *story*. Stories give us a handle on how we feel and an ability to tolerate and accept those feelings.

I guess it's fair to say that the characters in this book are the most challenging in terms of their stories and journeys—journeys I felt, and still do to this day working in my field, enormously privileged to be part of. They imprinted themselves onto my heart and my mind.

However, please don't think the people I've described represent all those with mental health difficulties. Such difficulties exist on a spectrum of severity, a spectrum we all sit on.

I suppose I should now give this book a neat and tidy epilogue: What did I learn? What happened to those I worked with? I should let you know that they all got "better" and lived on in greater happiness. But the reality is that I can't. Unlike in physical health, where fundamentally there is a diagnosis and hopefully a cure, in mental health things are just not that clear-cut. In mental health we see patients getting better as being able to function with an improved quality of life—often this is a process that continues and completes long after treatment has ended.

We tend to say that, in general, a third of those we treat will get "better," a third will stay the same and a third will get worse. We can't "cure" everyone, and this is not only because some cannot be "cured"—sometimes we just don't know how to. In fact, the term "cure" can be detrimental in our understanding of the best way to support those with mental health difficulties.

And of course there are people who just aren't ready or willing to be helped. There are those for whom their mental health difficulties are part of who they are and how they will continue to live. And sometimes there isn't an end to their stories because, however much we want to, as practitioners, we may not hear about them as they move on in their lives and we move on in ours.

Sometimes we meet patients we can see will have to fall—to deteriorate brutally—for us to be able to get in and help them; waiting and watching for that to happen is really tough.

What this means is that as practitioners we can become pretty hardened. The personal-professional boundary becomes nailed down, and we learn to cut off from the despair of not being able to help everybody. We learn to soldier on. This is one of the most crucial lessons I was forced to learn in my training years. With patients like Harold, even Ray and Mo, I had to acknowledge that there was little I could do to "fix" them and that my fantasies of rescuing them were just that—fantasies.

But acknowledging our limitations as therapists can also be dangerous. Many of us resort to gallows humor to brush away the horror of what we see or hear in our work—like the joke told after Imogen was released from her noose. Cynicism can become a useful defense mechanism.

Sometimes we struggle to engage with those we treat because we've been verbally or physically abused by them. Patients often lash out when they feel threatened and in distress, which leaves the therapist feeling the same anxiety. It is not rare for us therapists to identify the parts of ourselves that frighten or challenge us in our patients. It's difficult when we're forced to confront aspects of ourselves we'd prefer to ignore. So we make it the patients' issue, not ours, and hide behind the patient label, relishing the notion that it's them, not us.

In telling these stories, I didn't want to cause distress, but I do feel strongly that to get past a diagnosis, a label, we have to see the real human being who sits underneath and acknowledge how bloody sad that person's story can be. Edith and her sweet vulnerability; Imogen, the child with a secret so dark it is almost unbearable to contemplate; Tom, the wonderful man who was angry and dying. Real people, real lives.

I have also included the stories of people for whom it can be more difficult to summon immediate compassion. Martin and Elise, struggling with intimacy; the frustrated and controlling mother Daisy; Jess, the top-earning city girl shoving coke up her nose. These individuals came from privileged backgrounds, so it's easy to question their struggles. But a comfortable lifestyle often provides a mask of sanity for some very vulnerable people . . . It's something I see often.

Then there is Mo and her DDU cohort, and young Paul, the former dweller of the stained sleeping bag— what do we do with our feelings about them? In my experience, as a society we tend to discard these people. Angry, aggressive kids; marauding, thieving drug users— why do they deserve our understanding and compassion? Surely all that does is condone and justify their antisocial behavior and stop them from getting on with "sorting themselves out"?

But I don't like being part of a society that feels comfortable with discarding people who do not express their vulnerability in a way that we can accept, understand and tolerate. We will reach out with compassionate arms to Imogen and Mollie as they withdraw and cower in the corners of their lives, but not to angry Mo and physically aggressive Paul. They challenge us, frighten us, take from us and, yes, sometimes harm us.

And then there is Ray. What do we do about people like him—those perhaps considered to have a "personality disorder," occasionally considered by default as untreatable? Do we lock them up in case they do something antisocial because they have no empathy or understanding for the needs of others? Or do we respect their civil liberties and let them live their lives?

Listen, just to be clear, if I had ever met the woman who smashed my grandmother's head open, I can't say for sure that I wouldn't have had a strong urge to take a poker to her. But my grandmother's murderer was a damaged, vulnerable woman, something I try hard to remember.

In the twenty-five years since I began my training, I've learned that there are no easy answers to these questions. I often find myself conflicted, split between my cool professional head and my more visceral emotional response based on my experiences as a mother and granddaughter. It is all extremely complex; there are no neat answers.

What I do know is that the mental health profession— even society at large—has made great strides in the way we view and treat those we consider mentally ill. But we have not reached the place of destigmatization and compassion I long for. Marion's, June's and Frank's stories show how our segregation and marginalization of people considered mentally or morally deficient at an earlier time in history hasn't really changed. We no longer take a day-trip to the asylum as an entertaining outing, but we still enjoy the voyeurism of staring at people in crisis, whether on callous TV programs where we can shout at them and tell them to "sort their lives out" or in our insatiable desire to read about people who are breaking down. And we rejoice most when the breakdown happens to someone who "had it all."

Did June and Frank want to remain institutionalized because they would then continue to live in a place where they were accepted and appreciated for who they were, where they had an identity? For them, that was perhaps a better solution than moving into the community, a community that does not care.

Nothing has changed. We don't like mental illness. We don't want it in ourselves because it frightens us. We have no time or desire to engage with it in others except as something to gawp at and to define ourselves against. We expect people to be mentally ill in ways that are comfortable for us, or we discard and disown them. We buy into a model of health that requires mental illness to be cured within prescribed time frames and narrow parameters.

But as we saw with Mollie, the young woman I met in my final year of training, when I was beginning to get more of an understanding of my professional identity and approach, people in crisis are manifesting much more than the sum of their own illness. Their problems are symbolic of an overall system—usually a family—in crisis.

And we, as a society, are in crisis. I am now a consultant in child and adolescent mental health. Rocketing numbers of children and young people with significant mental health difficulties come through my clinic and clinics like mine across the developed world. And these children are struggling at younger and younger ages.

Our young people show us the uncomfortable truth that as a functioning system, our society is failing. They represent our lack of compassion and understanding, our preoccupation with the survival of the fittest. We struggle to "hear" what they are saying and so we prescribe them drugs.

As I write this epilogue, it strikes me that it may appear that I have written this book as a vehicle to address some of the many complexities and injustices that sit around the care and treatment of those with mental health difficulties. Actually, I didn't. Quite simply I wrote this book to tell some incredible stories about people who, each in their own way, were struggling to live challenging lives. People I feel enormously privileged to have met and from whom I have learned a lot.

I will end now by reiterating that none of these people I have written about in *The Skeleton Cupboard* exists; I have betrayed no confidence by telling their stories.

But then again, I would suggest, and forgive me for leaving you with this, that actually they *do* exist—bits of them exist in us all.

ACKNOWLEDGMENTS

Throughout my career in mental health services, I have worked with many teams of talented and dedicated people, and in the writing of this book, I have met and worked alongside a new and fantastic team.

Thank you to my agent, Sophie Laurimore, for putting me together with literary agent Will Francis (and his team at Janklow & Nesbit), who has been an incredible support, encouraging me to write what had been in my head for so many years, working with me on the book proposal, and then on so very many drafts.

My thanks to all at Pan Macmillan and the team led by Jon Butler, especially my editor, the brilliant and talented Cindy Chan. My thanks also to P. J. Mark and to Bob Miller, Whitney Frick and the team at Flatiron Books and to Kate Cassady and her colleagues at Harper-Collins Canada for taking *The Skeleton Cupboard* to North America and for editing it so brilliantly so it would make sense to my American readers while still retaining my British voice.

I am particularly indebted to my fellow trainees from over twenty-five years ago: the clinical psychologist Jeanette McLoughlin for her extremely helpful comments on the whole book, and to the clinical neuropsychologist Judy Wall for her detailed notes on my assessment of Harold. My friends Dr. Ruth Whitby—the best GP I know—and the brilliant psychiatrist Professor Dr. Michael Craig have given essential feedback.

My greatest thanks go to my career mentor, Dr. Wendy Casey—a woman of compassion, skill and dedication to all those she has treated. Thanks also go to valued colleagues from years past—Dr. Ron Alcorn, Dr. Dylan Griffiths and Professor Tony Roth—who taught me so much, and to Dr. Elza Eapen and Maggie Cohen.

I owe a huge debt to Mrs. Kay Moore, my favorite teacher, who taught me English at school and inspired me to love reading and to write.

My deepest gratitude to the brave and wonderful Avram Schaufield for generously sharing his experiences of the concentration camps during the Holocaust, and to his wife, Vera, for telling me about her experiences on the Kindertransport.

To "my girls": Kate, Jen, Ruth, Jeanette, Janaki, Jayne— you are brilliant and supportive friends. Also to Bettina, Emma, Lesley and Victoria, and to Lynn, Steph and all my friends at our weekly Zumba and kettlebell classes!

Also, my thanks to my friend and brother-in-law Mathieu, and to Michael and Eric.

Most of all, my deepest love and thanks to my most special girls: my amazing mother, Elfie; my sister and best friend, Katrina; my beautiful niece Clara; and most especially my daughter, Lily—you are an awesome young woman, and I love our laughs.

My wonderful, inspirational father, John, died in 2005: Dad, I miss you every day and wish you could have read this.

To my husband, Bruce—I couldn't have written this or pretty much done anything else in the last twenty-four years without you by my side. And to my gorgeous son, Jack—you make me very proud, and thanks for the endless cups of tea.

Finally, to all those mental health professionals who work tirelessly in often very underresourced conditions to support those who are vulnerable and afraid—I salute you. And to the many children, young people and adults that I have worked with throughout my clinical career: Thank you for the privilege of spending time with you on your journey—I'll never forget you.